THE ARCTIC
IN QUESTION

THE ARCTIC IN QUESTION

Edited by

E. J. DOSMAN

Contributors

P. A. BRENNAN

R. B. BYERS

P. C. DOBELL

J. GELLNER

J. L. GRANATSTEIN

F. J. C. GRIFFITHS

T. A. HOCKIN

J. W. LANGFORD

Toronto
OXFORD UNIVERSITY PRESS
1976

Cover design by FRED HUFFMAN
Maps by GEOFFREY MATTHEWS

ISBN-0-19-540267-7

1234-9876

Printed in Canada by
WEB OFFSET PUBLICATIONS LIMITED

PREFACE

Scholarly works on Canada's Arctic concentrate on the social and economic aspects of development north of 60. The progressive integration of the Arctic into the North American economy is viewed as a domestic issue; the implications for northern sovereignty, and therefore for Canadian foreign policy, tend to be ignored. Nevertheless the question of Arctic sovereignty has not been settled.

The present volume, the result of discussions among Canadian academics from various backgrounds and disciplines, is an attempt to outline and explore northern sovereignty as an issue in Canadian foreign policy, for this apparently straightforward matter contains difficult questions. Why is the Arctic still not undisputedly Canadian, a century after Ottawa decision-makers perceived northern sovereignty as a matter of grave importance for Canada? What precisely are the stakes involved? To what extent did the famous voyage of the S. S. *Manhattan* bear on northern sovereignty? Does Ottawa possess the imagination, the will, and the technological capabilities to enforce a distinctive Canadian approach to northern development? It is hoped that this volume will present new material and contribute to an improved understanding of a long neglected subject.

I am indebted to many individuals and agencies for their assistance in preparing this volume. Not only colleagues in Canadian universities but also senior officials, particularly in the Departments of External Affairs, National Defence, and Transport Canada gave generously of their time in raising useful questions and clarifying technical and legal considerations involved in northern sovereignty. Specifically I wish to thank Professor John Gellner of York University for his assistance, as well as Ms T. Crawley of Oxford University Press for her efficient editing of the manuscript. Finally I wish to express appreciation to Mrs F. Griffin for her tireless secretarial work throughout its preparation. I am responsible for all errors.

EDGAR J. DOSMAN

TO MY PARENTS

Contents

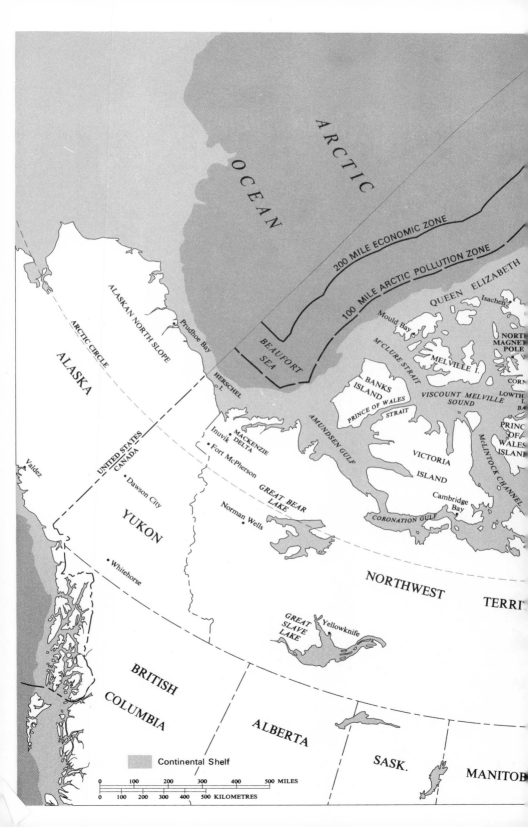

1 NORTHERN SOVEREIGNTY AND CANADIAN FOREIGN POLICY

by E. J. Dosman

Canadians are both fascinated by and worried about their Arctic. Already immense natural resources have been uncovered north of 60; increasingly they will be in demand by a resource-hungry world. And as the North is opened, as new and stronger ships and icebreakers clear Arctic waters, its commercial and strategic importance will rapidly grow. But Canada's hold over its Arctic domain is uncertain. It is the last major region where the territorial integrity of Canada could be challenged.

What exactly is the current legal status of Arctic lands and waters? How likely is a challenge to Canadian sovereignty in the North? Which state or states are likely to defy Ottawa in Arctic territories? Is Canada equipped to deal vigorously with rivals? Above all, what are the stakes in maintaining a Canadian (rather than a North American) Arctic? The purpose of this volume — essays by scholars from a variety of backgrounds — is to explore these questions in a systematic fashion, and within a foreign-policy framework broad enough to place the issue of northern sovereignty in clear perspective.

THE CANADIAN POSITION

The general position of the Canadian government regarding northern sovereignty is still most accurately set out in the oft-quoted ambiguous statement of the Honourable A. Hamilton, Minister of Northern Affairs, delivered on 10 June 1958 before the House of Commons Standing Committee on Mines, Forests and Waters: 'The area to the north of Canada, including the islands and waters between the islands and areas beyond are looked upon as our own, and there is no doubt in the minds of this government, nor do I think in the minds of former governments of Canada, that this is national terrain.'

More recent government action and statements have been somewhat more specific. On 15 May 1969 Prime Minister Pierre Elliott Trudeau declared that the mainland north of 60 as well as the islands of the Canadian Arctic archipelago were sovereign parts of Canada.[1] He also reiterated Canadian sovereign rights over the resources of the continental shelf in the Arctic region. Neither claim was likely to be challenged by any foreign government. As Professor Granatstein points out in assessing the historical background to the U.S. challenge to northern sovereignty in 1968-70, Ottawa had met previous U.S. and Danish threats to Canadian sovereignty in Arctic lands with enough conviction to support the claim to sovereignty, and the 1958 Geneva Convention on the continental shelf to which Canada was a signatory provided a solid foundation for the assertion of rights to the resources of the Arctic continental shelf. Moreover the continental shelf included most of the submerged areas, and therefore the mineral wealth, of Arctic waters.

The same clarity was not at all apparent regarding the legal status of the waters within the Canadian Arctic archipelago. Both Professor Granatstein and Mr Dobell agree that prior to 1968 Ottawa had not followed a consistent policy of establishing a claim to sovereignty over Arctic waters in general and the Northwest Passage in particular. When confronted by the U.S. in 1968-70, Ottawa was thrown on the defensive and had to be content with an extension of limited jurisdiction over pollution control with the Arctic Waters Pollution Prevention Act of April 1970, as well as the simultaneous extension of the territorial sea from three to twelve miles by amending the Territorial Sea and Fishing Zones Act. Professors Byers and Gellner discuss the significance of both pieces of legislation, particularly the effect of a twelve-mile territorial sea in closing the eastern and western gateways of the Northwest Passage: Barrow and Prince of Wales Straits respectively. The U.S. vigorously opposed the legality of the Arctic Waters Pollution Prevention Act as well as Canada's contention that the extension of the territorial sea affected the status of the Northwest Passage as an international strait.

Nevertheless, although Ottawa has not formally declared Arctic waters to be sovereign parts of Canada, and therefore has not gone beyond the more limited approach to northern jurisdiction as embodied in pollution legislation since 1968, the government has repeatedly asserted that it considers Arctic waters as Canadian. In a statement outside the House in 1970 Mitchell Sharp indicated that 'we have regarded the Arctic waters as Canadian waters. This has always been the position of the Canadian government . . . other people may not always agree with us, but that's our position ... there has never been any doubt about this.'[2] Similarly five years later, in a statement by the Secretary of State for External Affairs before the House of Commons Standing Committee on External Affairs and National Defence on 22 May 1975, it was flatly asserted that 'Arctic waters are considered by Canada as being internal waters.'[3]

It would appear therefore that the overall objective of Canada in the North is not in doubt: eventually to obtain the international recognition of full Canadian sovereignty in the North by enclosing Arctic waters as internal Canadian waters.

THE LAW OF THE SEA IN THE ARCTIC

The law of the sea in the Arctic operates at two levels – *regional* and *national*. The former involves co-operation among the five nations with Arctic responsibility – Canada, the Soviet Union, Norway, Denmark, and the United States – to ensure the orderly and optimal development of the region as a whole. None of these states acting independently can implement an effective management system: Arctic eco-systems operate without regard for national boundaries and rivalries. As the pace of activity in the North increases, multilateral action becomes ever more important to prevent damage to a shared Arctic environment. In any approach to many of the law-of-the-sea issues relating to the Arctic, such as the control of marine pollution; the exploitation of the mineral resources of the continental shelf; scientific research; exploitation of the living resources of the sea; and issues relating to navigation, there is no effective alternative to multilateral action. At the same time there is considerable opinion that apportioning the whole of the Arctic seabed among the bordering states would be contrary to the United Nations declaration of principles of 1970 on the law of the sea.[4] Should the UN contention be accepted there would be an area in the centre of the Arctic basin where an international regime must operate.

The scholars in this volume therefore agree on the importance of the multilateral interests in the Arctic. Interdependence among the Arctic states is a fact of life; Canada, as little as the Soviet Union or Denmark, can presume to legislate for this immense region. In short, co-operation is essential between the countries in the region as well as within the broader community covered by the United Nations Law-of-the-Sea Conference. Professor Griffiths discusses various possibilities for multilateral action among the Arctic powers, and Mr Dobell also indicates the importance of these negotiations. Indeed as the Third Law-of-the-Sea Conference, initiated in Caracas in the summer of 1974, enters its third session in New York in March 1976, it appears increasingly likely that further regional agreements will be essential in any case to supplement the broadly worded compromises that are likely to emerge.

The second or *national* aspect of the law-of-the-sea problem relating to the Arctic is very different. It refers to the status of the 'Canadian' Arctic; the 'national terrain' mentioned in the 1958 statement; or the 'internal waters' described by the Secretary of State in 1975. It is here that the

northern-sovereignty debate in Canada has flourished. The status of
Canadian Arctic waters remains very confusing. Some key concepts in
international law must be clarified to sort out relevant issues and questions.

(a) INTERNAL WATERS

International law divides the world's oceans into zones; national authority
diminishes over these zones as the distance from shore increases. Internal
waters are those within a nation's boundary or those that are so defined —
normally they include tidal areas, river mouths, harbours, legal bays, and
historic waters. Legal bays refer to those bays that, by international
consent, are closed as internal waters by straight baselines drawn from the
seaward land points across the mouth of the bay. Historic waters similarly
refer to an international consensus that certain bodies of water, such as
Hudson Bay, constitute internal waters by virtue of effective occupation
and control, geographic proximity, economic activity, or other recognized
criteria of historic rights.

Apart from tidal areas, the other categories of internal waters would be
separated from territorial waters by closing lines. Closing lines can be
defined as a technique for establishing internal waters by drawing straight
baselines between land or island extremities rather than following the
precise curvature of the coast. The increasing use of closing lines by
coastal states as a device for augmenting their internal waters has pro-

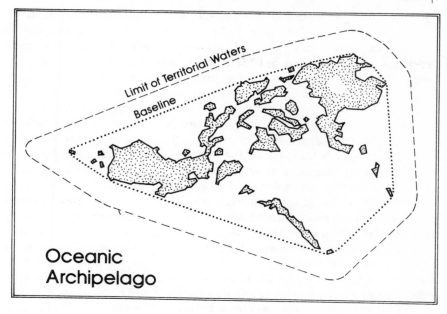

duced new categories of internal waters of direct relevance to Canada's North. Unlike river mouths, harbours, and legal bays, where baselines originate from land points, the practice of imposing closing lines spread to islands and archipelagos after 1945.

In 1951 the World Court decision in the so-called Anglo-Norwegian Fisheries case, in favour of Norway's drawing an extensive series of straight baselines off its deeply indented and fjorded coast fringed with islands, produced a contentious principle for establishing internal waters: the coastal archipelagic principle. The World Court argued that the islands could be joined by straight baselines from which the territorial sea could be measured (Figure 1), since the waters between these islands and the mainland were so closely linked to the land mass that they could be subjected to the same legal regime.[5] Following Norway's success in 1951, other states throughout the world with similar island structures introduced baseline legislation.

Whether the archipelagic principle applies to oceanic archipelagos, or to such enormous coastal archipelagos as Canada's Arctic islands, remains in doubt before the law of the sea. Oceanic archipelagos are groups of islands such as Indonesia or the Philippines that form a geographic unit unrelated to any mainland. While these states claim the right to join the outermost points of the outermost islands with straight baselines (Figure 2), the maritime states fear the inhibiting effects on world navigation of such far-reaching claims, because the archipelagic principle would permit a widely scattered group of islands to claim large areas of the ocean.[6]

In the Arctic the waters of a coastal rather than an oceanic archipelago are in dispute. The Norwegian Fisheries case involved relatively short baselines (some fifty miles) even at the largest distance, so its value as a precedent is diluted when considering the vast expanse of the Canadian Arctic archipelago. The issue in the Arctic is that a claim to sovereignty based on the coastal archipelagic principle would cover such an enormous area.

The coastal state exercises complete sovereignty over internal waters. While in general usage sovereignty is often defined as supreme authority or jurisdiction, it is useful to clarify the concept with greater precision when discussing maritime law. If sovereignty is defined as comprising every right over which jurisdiction is exercised, the distinction between the *sovereignty* Canada enjoys in such internal waters as Hudson Bay and Canada's *limited jurisdiction* in Arctic waters is immediately clear. In Hudson Bay Canada possesses the entire bundle of rights — navigation, pollution protection, overflight, mineral and economic regulations, and so on — that constitute sovereignty. In Arctic waters, on the other hand, only the right of pollution protection and the exercise of that jurisdiction is claimed. Thus when Canadian officials speak of a *functional* approach to the law of the sea, they are referring to an approach that aims at certain *specific* rights and jurisdiction to guard against specific and *imminent* dangers, in contrast to a formal assertion of sovereignty.

In short, complete sovereignty over internal waters means that the national will can be imposed. Canadian sovereignty has not been recognized in Arctic waters, nor has it been claimed by Ottawa in an Act of Parliament. Although the waters of Hudson Bay are considered historic and internal waters, those of the Canadian Arctic archipelago retain the traditional maritime zones in international law: the territorial sea, and the high seas.

(b) THE TERRITORIAL SEA

The territorial sea is a strip of water lying seaward of internal waters over which coastal states assert most rights associated with sovereignty, except that foreign ships have a right of innocent passage. The current law-of-the-sea conference has demonstrated that a majority of states now favour a twelve-mile territorial sea, Canada among them. The Geneva Convention entitles coastal islands to a territorial sea as well, so the islands of the Canadian Arctic archipelago would each be enclosed by a twelve-mile territorial sea. In international law at the moment, therefore, the territorial sea in Canada's northern waters is recognized as following the coastline of the mainland and the individual Arctic islands.[7]

(c) INNOCENT PASSAGE

Nations not only disagree about the breadth of the territorial sea, but the doctrine of innocent passage provides an equally rich opportunity for controversy. The concept of innocent passage provides the chief legal base for navigation in territorial waters, granting maritime powers a high degree of security against interference by the coastal state. According to the Geneva Convention, passage is considered innocent 'so long as it is not prejudicial to peace, good order or security of the coastal state'.

If the coastal state decides that passage is prejudicial on these grounds, it may take action to stop it. But the provocation must be grave, and the coastal state bears the burden of proof. Moreover, although a coastal state under the most serious circumstances may suspend the right of innocent passage on grounds of national security, there can be no discrimination between the ships of foreign countries. Further the Geneva Convention implies that the right of innocent passage exists for warships as well as commercial vessels, except that submarines must surface.

Canada has argued that the doctrine of innocent passage would not provide Canada with sufficient authority to safeguard the Arctic environment against navigational hazards. Lightly constructed vessels entering Arctic waters, for example, might well constitute an environmental hazard in the unusually rigorous northern climate, but innocent passage as currently defined would not condone interference with, or the boarding of, such ships. Ottawa has asserted that environmental integrity is as valid as territorial integrity and therefore that coastal states threatened with pollution can suspend the movement of foreign ships through the territorial sea and appropriate waters. Maritime powers such as the United States disagree, arguing that restricting the applicability of the doctrine of innocent passage would unduly interfere with the movement of merchant ships and naval vessels.[8]

In international straits however, innocent passage is further strengthened in the Geneva Convention. It cannot for example be suspended, even temporarily, by a coastal state on grounds of national security.* International straits form the lynchpin of maritime mobility; maritime powers both for defence and commercial reasons can be expected to press for as extensive a right of transit as possible. The United States therefore will not easily acquiesce in restrictions imposed on the right of innocent passage in either Arctic waters in general or the Northwest Passage in particular.

(d) HIGH SEAS

The high seas are defined as those parts of the ocean not included in

---

*As codified in the 1958 convention on the territorial sea, the unconditional right to deny innocent passage in internal waters would not apply to waters that had the status of high seas or territorial waters before the delimitation of straight baselines according to the Anglo-Norwegian World Court decision of 1951.

internal or territorial waters. All countries have the freedoms of navigation, fishing, flying over the high seas, and laying submarine cables and pipelines in these waters. All ships have complete immunity from the jurisdiction of states other than the flag state. Canada's view is that 'the Arctic waters and ice do not constitute high seas to which the traditional freedoms apply.'

> [So] far as Canada is concerned, the special characteristics of the Arctic waters and ice combine to give them a special status — however defined — which implies special rights and responsibilities for the coastal state.[9]

Canada alone among the Arctic powers has made this claim. For that reason, and in view of rapid advances in Arctic transportation technology that have increasingly opened ice-infested waters for commercial navigation, the Canadian position is extremely weak.

(e) CONTIGUOUS ZONE, POLLUTION-PREVENTION ZONE

Despite the legal status of the high seas, many nations including Canada have sought jurisdiction beyond the territorial sea for special purposes. These areas, called contiguous zones, have been ill-defined prior to the current Law-of-the-Sea Conference, where efforts are being made to introduce a common formula acceptable to all coastal states. Although the Geneva Convention specifies that contiguous zones must not reach further than twelve miles from the baseline used to measure the territorial sea, many countries have claimed jurisdiction over contiguous zones that are wider than twelve miles. As one author has suggested, 'The number of multiple jurisdictions being asserted in contiguous zones has increased dramatically since the end of World War II, often to the point where the high seas status of such waters is thrown into serious doubt.'[10] The Arctic Waters Pollution Prevention Act of 1970 set out a zone, extending 100 miles seaward from the Canadian coastline, for which Canada claimed a specific right to exercise jurisdiction for the purpose of preventing pollution. The Third Law-of-the-Sea Conference, in order to obtain a consensus among coastal states on the extension of jurisdiction for specific purposes in the contiguous zone, will almost certainly adopt the concept of a 200-mile economic zone.

The 'economic zone' would establish an internationally accepted offshore limit inside which the coastal state would exercise specific rights over marine resources and the environment, while accepting the existence of and obligation to protect community interests within the zone regarding navigation, overflight, and pollution prevention in particular.[11] However the claims to jurisdiction in the economic zone, discussed extensively by Professor Byers and Mr Dobell in this volume, do not amount to a claim of sovereignty over the waters in question.

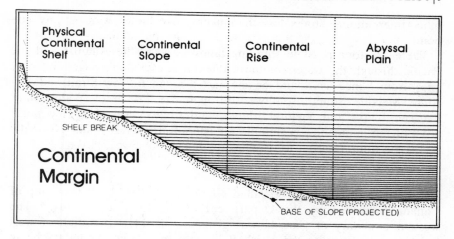

| Physical Continental Shelf | Continental Slope | Continental Rise | Abyssal Plain |

SHELF BREAK

Continental Margin

BASE OF SLOPE (PROJECTED)

(f) THE CONTINENTAL SHELF AND MARGIN

The 1958 Geneva Convention on the continental shelf recognized that coastal states exercised sovereign control over the continental shelf 'for the purpose of exploring them and their natural resources', including not only mineral resources but also sedentary fisheries such as crabs and oysters. The Geneva definition of the outer limit of the shelf — *either* a depth of 200 metres, *or* the depth to which seabed resources can be exploited — has proved to be inadequate as the technology for exploiting the mineral resources of the seabed has improved. Countries such as Canada with long continental margins, extending in some cases beyond a 200-mile economic zone, have not hesitated to claim the entire margin.

In the law of the sea, therefore, the continental shelf is a subject of considerable debate. The Canadian position can be given as follows: Ottawa claims the exclusive right to the seabed resources of the entire continental margin, comprising the physical continental shelf, the continental slope, and the continental rise (Figure 3).[12]

(g) THE NORTHWEST PASSAGE

Article 16 of the 1958 Geneva Convention on the territorial sea defined international straits as those 'used for international navigation between one part of the high seas and another part of the high seas or the historical sea or territorial sea of a foreign state.'[13] Was then the Northwest Passage an international strait or not? Canada held that it was not since it had not been used for international navigation. The U.S., given technological developments in ship construction that increasingly permit Arctic navigation, has argued that the Northwest Passage is an international strait and therefore subject to the appropriate legal regime of transit. Washington has also rejected the contention that an extension of the territorial sea to twelve miles could close the Northwest Passage or other international straits less than twenty-four miles wide at any one point.

There are four possible shipping lanes between the Atlantic and the Pacific through the waters of the Canadian Arctic archipelago. But only one — from Lancaster Sound on the east through Barrow Strait and Viscount Melville Sound, southwest through the Prince of Wales Strait between Banks and Victoria islands, and finally west along the north coast of the mainland — is suitable for deep-draft surface ships. Normally this is the route referred to in speaking of the Northwest Passage.

(h) THE SECTOR THEORY

The murky origins of the so-called sector theory date back to a map of Canada published by the Department of the Interior in 1904.[14] The western boundary of Canada was given as the 141st meridian of west longitude extending to the North Pole, with the eastern boundary being the 60th meridian of west longitude extending also to the Pole and beginning at a point north of the 78th parallel between Ellesmere Island and Greenland. Within this area — Canada's slice, so to speak, of the entire Arctic basin, sovereign control could be exercised by Ottawa.

In the most general sense, this concept generated the sector theory. However the precise motivation and intent of the sector principle remain unclear. Although it surfaced in 1904, it received public attention only some years later. According to Professor Maxwell Cohen,

> The sector theory is an accident of speech, as it were, a speech by Senator Poirier who gave an address in the Senate in 1909 in which he suggested, based upon a remark by a Captain Bernier [the Arctic explorer] that, after all, the proper attitude Canada should take to the Arctic system is to say that the whole of our Arctic basin represents a great circular basin system with a series of coastal states — Denmark, the Soviet Union, the United States — and that in a way the very geography and geology of the area makes it logical that one treat all of the land extensions and island systems as part of the coastal community, and therefore it should be shared accordingly by the coastal communities that are in the whole basin.[15]

The sector theory has not gained any particular international acceptance. Just as Norway rejected the application of the principle in recognizing Canadian sovereignty over the Sverdrup Islands in 1930, so also the United States has rejected it in recent years as a basis for a Canadian claim to sovereignty over the waters of the Canadian Arctic archipelago.

THE CHALLENGE

For Canada the 'northern problem' lies not merely in ensuring the orderly development of the Arctic in light of the accelerating pace of activity there, but also, and in the first instance, in consolidating sovereign control of the region.

The discovery of oil and gas on the Alaskan North Slope catapulted the issue of northern sovereignty into the forefront of Canadian-American relations and Canadian foreign policy in general. It ended the isolation of the North and the possibility that Ottawa could indefinitely postpone clarifying its position on northern sovereignty. With the Bering Straits unsuitable for large-scale traffic, the Northwest Passage emerged as a major transportation route to northern Alaska for commercial shipping as well as for the movement of strategic raw materials, so important in light of Soviet-American relations. Washington's interest in preventing the assertion of Canadian sovereignty over Arctic waters was thus increased. A head-on collision loomed.

It came in 1969. The U.S. chose the voyages of the S.S. *Manhattan* in that year and in 1970 as the occasion for challenging Canadian sovereignty in the North. Ottawa faced a major crisis with a new and untried Prime Minister. How have we fared?

NOTES

[1] House of Commons *Debates*, 15 May 1969, pp. 8720-1.

[2] Mitchell Sharp, *Interviews*, 19 February 1970.

[3] House of Commons, Standing Committee on External Affairs and National Defence, 22 May 1975, 24:6.

[4] Donat Pharand, *The Law of the Sea of the Arctic* (Ottawa, 1973), p. 320.

[5] *Ibid.*, pp. 108-12. See also Department of External Affairs, *The Future of the Oceans* (Ottawa, 1975), pp. 17-20.

[6] *The Future of the Oceans*, p. 20.

[7] The U.S. repeatedly asserted this position (regarding a three-mile territorial sea) in bilateral communications at the height of the sovereignty crisis, 1968-70.

[8] *The Future of the Oceans*, p. 17.

[9] J. A. Beesley, 'Rights and Responsibilities of Arctic Coastal States: The Canadian View', *The Arctic Circular*, 22, (1972), 98-110.

[10] R. M. Logan, *Canada, the United States and the Third Law of the Sea Conference* (C. D. Howe Institute, July 1974), p. 10.

[11] *The Future of the Oceans*, p. 8.

[12] *Ibid.*, pp. 6-7.

[13] Pharand, *op. cit.*, pp. 54-64.

[14] *Ibid.*, p. 134.

[15] House of Commons, Standing Committee on Indian Affairs and Northern Development, 18 April 1969, p. 620.

Captain Bernier's ship the 'Arctic' at Pond Inlet.
Courtesy Ministry of Transport

A FIT OF ABSENCE OF MIND: CANADA'S NATIONAL INTEREST IN THE NORTH TO 1968

by J. L. Granatstein

'What we have we hold.' Those ringing words of the Rt Hon. W. S. Fielding, the Minister of Finance in 1922, express the idealized image that Canadians have of their rights to the Arctic. It is ours alone, ours to exploit, ours to develop. But ironically, when Fielding issued his pronouncement, he was responding to questioning in the House of Commons about Canada's dubious right to Wrangel Island, a small territory north of Siberia claimed by the Soviet Union. Canada did not then hold the island and never had, and the Dominion formally abandoned any claims two years later, much to the relief of a Canadian government chary of international complications.[1]

A small issue, hingeing on a patch of frozen and probably worthless land, of course. But Wrangel Island holds a certain symbolic significance. The Minister of Finance probably did not even know where it was; his ignorance was shared not only by his colleagues on the government and opposition benches but by the public too. The North was ours to hold, but where was it? what was it? who wanted to go there? Few knew, few cared. Except for occasional explorers, prospectors, or missionaries, the North was *terra incognita*. The rapidity with which Canada abandoned its claim to an Arctic island that it did not occupy and had never administered could have been duplicated over much of the Canadian-claimed archipelago. Nowhere in 1922 was effective administration carried on, nowhere was there white settlement, nowhere was there anything more than claims. And claims can be dubious things at best. The Canadian casualness about the Arctic was a danger, and if the Canadian claims were never seriously challenged that was only because other, more powerful nations had little sustained interest in such seemingly unproductive parts of the earth. The North *was* ours, but only because no stronger power actively sought it.

I

Canada's claims to the North are based on a series of explorations undertaken by British seamen and explorers over a period of some 400 years—Frobisher, Hudson, Franklin, and the others who sought the Northwest Passage in vain and fruitless voyages that often ended in death and despair on the ice. The British explorations formed the basis of British claims, claims that were transferred to Canada in part in 1870, along with all the lands of the Hudson's Bay Company. By the cession in that year, Canada acquired the North Western Terrritory, essentially all the British land between Hudson Bay and British Columbia, and Rupert's Land, all the territories draining into Hudson Bay and Hudson Strait. This gave Canada its prairie frontier, its empire to be exploited, its own West to settle. It also conveyed rights to the problems that Louis Riel's Métis rebellion had created at Red River. None doubted that the bargain was a good one, but Canadian eyes were fixed mainly on the accessible West, not on the far North.

Ten years later Britain transferred sovereignty over its remaining claims in the North to Canada. The lands in question consisted of the Arctic archipelago, and Britain moved primarily to counter American commercial pressures in Baffin Island. In 1874 requests had been received for permission to establish a whaling station and a mining operation on the island, and Britain feared further American penetration would follow. The British claims to Baffin Island and to much of the remainder of the archipelago were uncertain, the Colonial Office believed, and the solution that commended itself to Whitehall was to turn all rights, however vague and nebulous they might be, over to Canada. This would forestall any American attempt to establish jurisdiction in the area. 'The object in annexing these territories to Canada', a Colonial Office memorandum noted, 'is, I apprehend, to prevent the United States from claiming them, and not from the likelihood of their proving of any value to Canada.' Gordon Smith, a Canadian historian of the Arctic, suggests that the British motive was based on London's belief that Canada, being nearer, could look after the lands better and that the Americans, standing on their Monroe Doctrine, would be less likely to resent Canadian sovereignty than British.[2] Another possibility is that Britain was simply dropping the problem and its potential difficulties into Canadian hands.

The Canadian government of Alexander Mackenzie, facing depression in industry and all the difficulties of running a government with a Liberal Party that was united only in a desire to trample on the Macdonald Tories, was interested in the archipelago, but not very much. In 1874 the Cabinet approved an order in council expressing the Dominion's interest in taking control of the territory, but matters lagged thereafter. What were the boundaries of the land in question? How should the territory be transferred — by Imperial order in council or by Act of Parliament? Finally in 1878, just a week before the dissolution of Parliament, the Minister of the Interior introduced a resolution in the House of Commons recommending that the British offer be accepted, a proposal that one Conservative immediately attacked as being wasteful of public monies. Sir John A. Macdonald and many others on both sides of the House, however, differed. The territory would cost nothing to administer until such time as Canada was ready to settle and exploit it, Macdonald argued, and as the alternative seemed to be control by the United States, Canada's course was clear. On this inglorious but practical note the resolutions carried. Two years later the order in council approving the transfer of sovereignty passed the British Cabinet. Canada was now the proprietor of 'all British Territories and Possessions in North America, not already included within the Dominion of Canada, and all Islands adjacent to any of such Territories or Possessions. . . . '[3] The deliberate vagueness of the wording (it could have been construed to include the British West Indies, for example) was matched only by the snail's pace of action since 1874.

Nor did Canada rush to assert its newly acquired sovereignty. An order in council of 1882 recommended that 'no steps be taken with the view of legislating for the good government of the country until some influx of population or other circumstances shall occur to make such provision more imperative than it would at the present seem to be.'[4] Fortunately for the Dominion, no other power challenged the Canadian claim by establishing effective occupation on any part of the archipelago. If any country had, Canada might easily have forfeited its patrimony. But as Morris Zaslow noted, 'What need was there to challenge [the Canadian claims] so long as the region was completely open to all comers, and Canada did nothing to obstruct activities there?' Not until 1895 and 1897 did the Canadian government even draw boundaries on the map to subdivide the Canadian North into administrative districts, 'the first formal acceptance by Canada of the territories and islands transferred in 1880'.[5]

The precise reasons for this new-found interest are unclear, but by 1897 there was no doubt that pressures were mounting for Canada to secure effective control of its North. American whalers moved freely (or, at least, as freely as ice conditions permitted) through the territory, and horror stories of rape and the destruction of Eskimos and their villages filtered slowly to the South. The government of Sir Wilfrid Laurier, nationalistic and determined to make the twentieth century belong to Canada, gradually began to make its presence felt. Official missions were sent into the Arctic where they encountered similar American and Norwegian parties, but there was at first scant financial support for the efforts of such northern veterans as Captain J. E. Bernier to explore and effectively bind the North to the Dominion. In such circumstances, nationalism and morality were the most effective devices to employ against tight purse-strings. 'The cost of carrying law and order into the Arctic regions may cause hesitation,' the Commissioner of the North West Mounted Police reported in 1901, 'but when our territory is being violated and our people oppressed, cost should be the last consideration.' That argument worked, and in 1903 the government despatched a police detachment of six men to Hudson Bay; included in its instructions was the following:

> The Government of Canada having decided that the time has arrived when some system of supervision and control should be established over the coast and islands in the northern part of the Dominion, a vessel has been selected . . . for the purpose of patrolling, exploring and establishing the authority of the Government of Canada . . . .[6]

A beginning had been made, and just in time. The Alaska Boundary Dispute with the United States and its unsatisfactory resolution by an 'impartial' tribunal demonstrated clearly that the American appetite for territory and belief in manifest destiny were by no means satisfied. Indeed in 1909 the American explorer Robert Peary reached the North Pole, planted the Stars and Stripes, and claimed 'the entire region and adjacent' for the United States. Peary's claim was given little credence, primarily because Laurier's government had put flesh to the Canadian presence in the Arctic. Six government expeditions in all explored and patrolled the area between 1897 and 1911 and, acting under instructions, they collected customs duties and licensing fees from whalers and advised all inhabitants, white and native, that they lived under Canadian law.

The culmination of this new activity came in 1907 and 1909. In 1907 Senator Pascal Poirier enunciated the sector theory in a speech in Parliament; this theory claimed for Canada all the territory between the Canadian north coast and the North Pole enclosed by longitudinal lines drawn from the east and west extremities of the coast line. Two years later Captain Bernier claimed for the Dominion everything between the degrees 141 and 60 west longitude, in effect a restatement of the sector theory. An official government statement along these lines was not made until 1925 when Charles Stewart, Minister of the Interior in the first Mackenzie King government, claimed the territory specified by Bernier. Dominion sovereignty, he told the House of Commons, ran to the Pole. Less than a year later the Soviet Union announced its own sector theory, claiming 'all lands and islands already discovered, as well as those which are to be discovered in the future' between its coast and the Pole from approximately 32 degrees east to 168 degrees west.[7]

The sector theory notwithstanding, Canada's sovereignty was not yet clear and free of challenges. Just after the Great War the Danish explorer Knud Rasmussen, supported by his government, claimed Ellesmere Island. In consequence of this and other challenges Loring Christie, the

Dominion Day, 1909. Captain Bernier claimed for Canada all the islands and territory within the degrees 141 and 60 W longitude.
Courtesy Ministry of Transport

Captain Bernier's expedition leaving for Salmon River, 1 August 1910.
Courtesy Public Archives of Canada

legal adviser to the Prime Minister, appraised the Canadian position and frankly noted that 'we have at times asserted a claim of sovereignty broad enough to cover these islands; that in respect of some of them our case on grounds of discovery and exploration seems better than that of other nations, but that in respect of a number of them other nations could probably make a better case on these grounds than we could. But the important point', Christie added, 'is that mere discovery and exploration, even accompanied by a formal assertion of sovereignty, are not enough without more, to create a permanent perfect title.' What had to be done now, the legal adviser said, was to establish effective occupation on Ellesmere Island, something that could be accomplished by putting police onto the Island and enforcing Canadian customs and game laws.[8] This the government did, and the Danes tacitly let the matter drop. In 1930 the Norwegians recognized Canadian jurisdiction over the Sverdrup Islands, a concession smoothed along, after some extraordinary negotiations, by an *ex gratia* payment of $67,000 to Captain Otto Sverdrup, the Norwegian who had explored the islands.[9]

Canada had rather more difficulty in dealing with the United States. In 1925 an American scientific expedition led by Dr D. B. MacMillan entered the Canadian Arctic without first seeking permission from Ottawa, a factor of some significance because of the assistance the expedition was receiving from the United States Navy. To its credit, the government reacted courteously but firmly. The Canadian government ship in the area, the *Arctic*, encountered the MacMillan expedition and offered to issue it a permit to carry out air exploration over Ellesmere Island. The American rejoinder, delivered by Commander Robert Byrd 'in full uniform' was that the expedition already had a permit, a straight untruth. The Canadian commander told the American that 'so far as he knew no such permission had been granted but that there was a possibility that his Government had omitted to inform him. . . .' In fact, as the Governor General advised the British Ambassador in Washington, Canada 'has never received an application by the MacMillan Expedition. . . . I would request your excellency to have the goodness to draw the attention of the United States Secretary of State to the apparent failure on the part of the Expedition to observe the requirements of the Canadian laws.'[10] This protest apparently had its effect, and subsequent MacMillan expeditions in 1926, 1927, and 1928 all punctiliously observed Canadian regulations and laws.

By the end of the 1920s, therefore, Canada's claims in the North were well established. In 1933 the historian V. K. Johnston could write with some confidence that Canada's sovereignty was clear.[11] Effective occupation had been established — or at least an occupation whose effectiveness could be argued. Similarly, foreign powers recognized these claims: the Danes had conceded; the Norwegians had sold out; and the MacMillan expeditions of 1926-8 implied acceptance by the United States of the Canadian claims.

Still, there had been no major effort to develop the Canadian North — not even the discovery of oil at Norman Wells, N.W.T. after the Great War and the successful establishment of an operating well in 1920 changed this — and the government's efforts in aid of the Eskimos and the northern Indians were minimal. Vilhjalmur Stefansson, the Canadian-born American Arctic explorer, summed up the position in an article in *Foreign Affairs* in April 1939: 'Canada is less interested in her Arctic domain than most people suppose ... [and] has no immediate need for her Arctic regions ...'[12] The United States government was fully aware of this undeniable statement, and it was concerned by what it perceived as a Canadian reluctance to arm to defend Canadian soil. And as American policy after 1938 focused very deliberately on the need to protect the western hemisphere,[13] naturally interest in Canada increased. One sign of this was Roosevelt's pledge to protect Canada, delivered at Queen's University in Kingston in the fall of 1938, in effect placing Canada under the Monroe Doctrine. Another was increased concern in Washington for the Pacific coast, a topic that formed an important part of pre-war Canadian-American military discussions.

II

The coming of the Second World War would soon awaken Ottawa and create the need for action to protect Canadian sovereignty in the North. The British-French débâcle in France and Flanders in May and June 1940 forced Canadians to think of their own safety in a changed world, and the Ogdensburg Agreement, signed by Mackenzie King and Franklin Roosevelt in August 1940, was the first tangible sign of this new awareness. Ogdensburg established a Permanent Joint Board on Defence with the power to recommend action to the two governments. Japan's entry into the war on 7 December 1941 increased the pressures for defence integration, particularly in the exposed Northwest. Concerned for their Alaskan territory, the Americans pressed for and quickly won Canadian concurrence in the construction of the Alaska Highway; the Canol Project, an oil-distribution system based on the small oil field at Norman Wells, N.W.T.; the Northwest Staging Route to Alaska and on to the Soviet Union with its airfields; and a host of weather stations throughout the Arctic. The North's development was speeded, but the new American presence created problems.

Mackenzie King, a man who had spent most of his public life fighting the centralizing pretensions of Downing Street and being accused as a consequence of pro-Americanism, greatly feared the effects of the increased American influence in Canada. The Alaska Highway, he told Malcolm MacDonald, the British High Commissioner in Ottawa, 'was less intended for protection against the Japanese than as one of the fingers of the hand which America is placing more or less over the whole of the Western hemisphere.'[14] To another visitor he said much the same thing, adding that it was clear 'to my mind that America has had as her policy, a western hemisphere control which would mean hemispheric immunity ...from future wars but increasing political control by U.S.'[15] King had grounds for his fears, for the lavish American projects in the North implied plans for permanent occupation. One example will suffice: at Fort Chimo in far northern Quebec, the United States built a small air field and a 'winterized base' that Canadians expected would consist of a few buildings. The construction, however, was so extensive that Canada had to pay $7 million to take it over after the war — and the refrigeration plant alone cost $600,000.[16]

With nearly 15,000 Americans in the Canadian North by the end of 1942, Canadian measures to protect and enhance sovereignty had become essential, and this was forcibly impressed on the Prime Minister by the British High Commissioner. After a visit to the North in 1942, Mac-Donald told King that the absence of a Canadian presence simply appalled him. He told the Under Secretary of State for External Affairs, Norman Robertson, that 'for most practical purposes the Canadian Government's representative in local contacts with the American forces in the Northwest is the Secretary of the Alberta Chamber of Commerce and Mines whose offices are in Edmonton and who acts as an unofficial representative of the Department of Mines and Resources.' The American presence had grown in a Canadian fit of absence of mind, Robertson told the Prime Minister, and a good and competent staff would have to be sent to the area 'capable of collaborating with and controlling the American developmental activities. . . . '[17]

In May 1943 the King government finally appointed a Special Commissioner for Defence Projects in the North-West, Brigadier W. W. Foster, and instructed him secretly that his duties were to ensure

that the natural resources of the area shall be utilized to provide the maximum benefit for the Canadian people and to ensure that no commitments are to be made and no situation allowed to develop as a result of which the full Canadian control of the area would be in any way prejudiced or endangered.[18]

Foster's appointment and his effective performance of his duties assuaged some of Ottawa's worries about the 'army of occupation', but Mackenzie King still fretted about the American plans for the future. In February 1944, when the Cabinet War Committee was considering the future of the Canol Project, the Prime Minister 'held strongly with one or two others to the view that we ought to get the Americans out of the further develop-ment' at Norman Wells 'and keep complete control in our hands.'[19] His concerns lay behind the government's decision, announced in the House of Commons on 1 August 1944, to purchase all United States installations on Canadian soil,[20] a process completed by 31 March 1946 at a cost of some $111 million all told. The next year the Cabinet War Committee decided that Canada would accept full responsibility for all defence measures on Canadian soil.[21]

But looming on the horizon was the problem of the Soviet Union. The implications of a possible Soviet-American confrontation were studied from 1944 onward by the government's planners for the post-war period, and they quickly realized that the United States would have to take a greater interest in Canadian defences after the war than it had before, primarily because 'Canada lies astride the overland route between the United States and the USSR. . . . '[22]

Certainly the Americans expressed concern over what Dean Acheson described for President Truman as the 'gap between Alaska and Green-land'.[23] The American worries led to pressures on a broad front. In the Permanent Joint Board on Defence, for example, discussions early in 1946 led to the conclusion that air bases in the North should be main-tained and that in particular the long runways at Goose Bay, Labrador were vital. The Labrador air base was one of the subjects discussed at a high-level meeting in Ottawa in December 1946. James Eayrs' account is succinct:

> The Americans minced no words. 'The most probable route of approach to North America,' a U.S. Army Air Force spokesman told the meeting, 'included Iceland, Greenland and the line Newfoundland-Labrador-Eastern Canada, the latter portion of which was only about 1200 miles from the main continental industrial centers. Goose Bay was considered to be the only suitable base for very heavy bombardment groups and in fact could be said to be the most impor-tant all-round strategic air base in the western hemisphere'.
>
> Clearly it would be hard . . . for the Canadians to reject [this] request. . . . Sensing an impending capitulation, L. B. Pearson and A. D. P. Heeney cast about for some protective colouration. Might it be possible, they inquired, to emphasize, for political reasons, the training side of the Goose Bay project? The United States representatives responded by reminding the Canadians of the facts of life. 'Mr. Parsons [the first secretary at the U.S. Embassy in Ottawa] pointed out that Goose Bay was intended for offensive purposes. He added that it was a "facility in being" and there were evident advantages to be derived from this fact.' An enemy was not deterred by concealment of the mechanism of massive retaliation. Here was the Canadians' first lesson

in the school for strategy. . . . By the end of 1947, US B-47 bombers were parked at the end of the Goose Bay runways.[24]

In addition, American requests to operate in the North included a naval exercise (called, to Canadian horror, Operation Nanook) and impatient demands, Mackenzie King was advised, to open new weather stations in the Arctic. The United States also sought the maintenance of existing base facilities, and widely expanded research on cold-weather warfare.[25]

How justified was this American concern for the (admittedly) defence-less condition of the Canadian Arctic? Not very justified at all. There was no actual threat to North America in 1946, and no one envisaged one until 1950 at the earliest. In April 1947, for example, the Americans' Joint Strategic Survey Committee placed Canada bottom on a list of sixteen countries requiring American aid, hardly an indication of extreme urgency. Everyone recognized, of course, that airborne troops could be emplaced at points in the North, but few took this threat seriously and the Americans expected 'ideological' warfare, not airborne invasions.[26] As one senior military officer put it, in Canada's northern regions there was no place to go from a military point of view and nothing to do when you got there.[27] And Lester Pearson archly called Canada's defence scheme for the North a policy of 'scorched ice'.[28]

But if there was no threat from the Soviet Union, there was a potential American threat to Canadian sovereignty. The United States' pressure demanded a Canadian response, and Canada had to be seen to be defending its territory or else the United States might insist on doing it. The first stage had to be the development of an Arctic military force — incredibly, the Canadian armed forces had never been geared to operate in Canadian conditions, a reflection of this country's long subservience to British policy and British wars. Exercise Musk-Ox, a joint army-airforce-scientific exercise in the winter and spring of 1946, was a first attempt to test equipment, transportation methods, and supply tech-niques, and the United States Army, of course, had observers present.[29] In addition, when Canada took over the Alaska Highway from the United States Army, the government voluntarily agreed to maintain the road and assigned the task to the Canadian Army with headquarters at White-horse.[30] And in September 1946 a winter warfare centre, largely of an experimental nature, was opened at Fort Churchill, Manitoba. The Royal Canadian Air Force also undertook to speed up the aerial mapping of the North, a first step of great importance to future planning, and in March 1947 the Minister of Reconstruction and Supply, C. D. Howe, announced the establishment of nine new weather stations in the North. 'The United States', Howe told the Members of Parliament, 'has . . . undertaken to assist Canada in the establishment and operation of these northern stations which will, of course, be under the control of the Canadian government, which will supply the officers in charge. United States technical personnel will be included in the staffs required.' In addition, in 1948 the Royal Canadian Navy launched its first northern exercise and announced the construction of a large icebreaker.[31]

Most important was the joint statement made in Washington and Ottawa on 12 February 1947. The two governments announced their intention to continue defence collaboration in the future, to exchange personnel, and to work and plan closely together. The Prime Minister read the statement in Parliament, and then added his own gloss. 'There is a persistent rumour', Mackenzie King said, 'that the United States Government has asked for bases in the Canadian North. This is a rumour which I should like to deny emphatically. There has been talk of Maginot Lines, of large-scale defence projects, all of which is unwarranted and much of which is fantastic.' The Prime Minister went on to outline the areas in which Canada was acting in the North: improved flying and communications facilities; greater knowledge of the topography; and general economic development. 'Canada's northern programme', he maintained with a straight face, 'is thus primarily a civilian one to which contributions are made by the armed forces. This has been the pattern for many years.'[32] The next day, to still fears of massive military preparations, the Minister of National Defence invited military attachés stationed in Ottawa to visit Fort Churchill. Many did, including the Soviet Union's attaché.

But there was criticism nonetheless. The Soviet Union was not reassured by its attaché's visit to the tattered, ramshackle base on Hudson Bay, and its press viewed the February 1947 statement as tantamount to a Canadian-American defence pact. Many members of the Cooperative Commonwealth Federation worried about this, too, and the matter came under discussion in Parliament in June 1947. In the course of the debate Louis St Laurent, the Secretary of State for External Affairs, said that Canada had no intention of permitting the United States to establish bases in this country, but 'no man can undertake to say that there may not unfortunately be some time when all Canadians will be glad to see posts established here.' Those remarks were passed to Washington by the American Embassy.[33]

In the next few months Canada experienced its worst financial crisis since the early war years, and the nation's economy came perilously close to collapsing because of a shortage of American dollar exchange. Mission after mission went south to seek aid, aid that was ultimately granted when the United States permitted recipients of Marshall Plan help to make purchases in Canada. By early 1949, $706 million in Marshall Plan credits had found their way to Canada. Thus in April 1948, when St Laurent again spoke about the North, there was a fervent note: 'It would be criminal folly on our part if we did not co-operate with the United States in self-defence.' St Laurent, just a few months away from succeeding Mackenzie King as Prime Minister, also added that American activities 'must be within the limit of a programme previously approved by the Canadian government'. This was not very restrictive, but after January 1948 the government at last had an Advisory Committee for Northern Development, a senior body of civil servants from every department concerned with the North, which could suggest policy to the Cabinet.[34] The potential mechanism for a co-ordinated response to American pressures now existed, but the Advisory Committee for Northern Development would not often be used.

III

As we have seen, the activity in the North in the first years after the Second World War was designed to counter a potential threat. But with the coming of the Cold War in earnest after 1948, with the Soviet development of the atom bomb, and with the Korean War in 1950, the potential threat to North America began to look more real. The increased Russian bomber capability added to these worries, and the nature and needs of defence began to alter. The Arctic had always been a barrier, but now for the first time its strategic significance became recognized. R. J. Sutherland, an operational research analyst for the government, outlined the potential benefits afforded by the North:

> The first was additional warning against Soviet bombers approaching targets in the central portions of North America along the shortest and most direct route. The second was defence in depth. By extending the air defence system northwards such bombers could be engaged before reaching their intended targets. Almost equally important, by extending the area of radar coverage the risk of saturation of the defences could be reduced. Finally, by locating strike aircraft or refuelling aircraft on the northern bases, the range and speed of response of the strike forces could be improved.[35]

Out of this kind of analysis came the North American Air Defence Command and the equipment of Canadian forces with nuclear weapons; out of it, too, came the three great radar lines constructed in Canada in the 1950s. And as a by-product of these developments the United States became more interested than ever before in the Canadian North.

Ideally perhaps Canada would have preferred to construct the northern radar lines entirely by itself. But the costs were very high — the first Canadian studies of radar defences in 1947 had identified cost as the major deterrent to action[36] — and the technological problems, in addition, were such that the government decided independent action would be impractical. Arrangements would have to be made with the United States, even though Canada's share of the cost of constructing radar warning lines would be expensive enough. The results were pronounced. In 1951 Canada and the United States agreed to build the Pinetree Line, a radar belt located in southern Canada and in the northern United States for which the Americans picked up two-thirds of the cost. Discussions continued in 1952 and 1953, and were accelerated by the Soviet Union's successful explosion of a hydrogen bomb in August 1953.[37] The result was a Canadian decision to finance the Mid-Canada Line, roughly along the 55th parallel, in 1954, and a joint Canadian-American agreement in the same year to construct the Distant Early Warning (DEW) line along the 70th parallel.

The DEW line demanded new technology, a challenge that was met; it also tested sovereignty more vigorously than before, and this challenge was not so successfully handled. The official announcement of the project on 19 November 1954 noted that 'Experience has shown that projects of this nature can be carried out most effectively by vesting responsibility for all phases of the work of construction and installation in a single authority... it has been agreed that although both Canada and the United States will participate in the project, responsibility for the work of construction and installation should be vested in the United States.'[38] The costs of the DEW line eventually reached $600 million.

The DEW line was a mixed bag of blessings and disasters for Canada. At the peak of construction 4,140 people were employed with a payroll of almost $33 million,[39] a significant infusion of money into an area still operating with a barter economy. And, according to Dr R. J. Sutherland, in the agreement 'Canada secured what the United States had up to that time assiduously endeavoured to avoid, namely, an explicit recognition of Canada's claims to the exercise of sovereignty in the Far North.'[40]

Canada did not want to become 'the world's most northerly banana republic', and the DEW line agreement went well beyond the arrangements made in the easier and more anxious days of 1942. Ottawa did indeed try to safeguard its rights in the Arctic, and the result was a detailed agreement that sought to protect Canada's sovereignty. The location of sites had to be the subject of mutual agreement, and plans had to be submitted for the Canadian government's approval. Electronic equipment 'as far as practicable' should be of Canadian manufacture, and Canadian labour had to receive preference. Canadian law was to be applied. And Canada reserved the right to determine its share of participation in the manning of the stations, adding that 'It is understood that... Canada reserves the right, on reasonable notice, to take over the operation and manning of any or all of the installations.'[41] In 1959 the Diefenbaker government did just that.

On the other hand, as construction and operation of the stations began, it became increasingly clear that Canadian sovereignty was nominal, not real. Ralph Allen of *Maclean's* visited the DEW line sites in 1956 and came back appalled by what he had seen. To save money, he charged, Ottawa had surrendered 'our independence. . . . In law we still own this northern frontier. In fact we do not.' Reporters had to submit their material to American censors, he said, and Canadian military officers had to get clearance from American security officers before they could reply to questions.[42] Other reporters saw American flags flying alone or above the Canadian ensign at DEW line stations, and there were suggestions that the United States was enforcing segregation of Eskimos and whites.[43] There were even reports that the Minister of Northern Affairs, Jean Lesage, had to secure American clearance before he could visit the DEW line area.[44]

Ironically, the DEW line was on the verge of obsolescence from the time it went into operation. The ICBM (intercontinental ballistic missile) era opened in 1957, and the manned bomber, although still in operation in the mid-1970s, lost its pre-eminence. One result of this new strategic situation was a downgrading of northern defence from the end of the 1950s onward. The Navy's single large icebreaker was transferred to the Department of Transport, and the Army passed responsibility for the Alaska Highway and northern communications to civilian agencies. The test station at Churchill similarly reverted to civilian control, and the last Navy exercise until the 1970s in the North took place in 1961. The only RCAF aircraft in the area on a regular basis were transport craft supplying radar stations, and there were no regular surveillance flights in the Arctic until 1967 – and even then such flights were infrequent. In 1969 Canada had reduced its military strength in the area north of the 60th parallel to 397 officers and men. This would not change until Prime Minister Trudeau's new-look defence policy of 1969 and 1970.[45]

IV

The DEW line controversies raised the question of sovereignty in the North yet again, and did so at a time of some confusion in Canadian thinking on the subject. In 1946 Lester Pearson had written that Canada's territory 'includes not only Canada's northland, but the islands and frozen seas north of the mainland between the meridians of its east and west boundaries extended to the North Pole.'[46] That had been the Canadian view since 1925, at least. But in 1956, to confuse matters, the Hon. Jean Lesage told Parliament,

We have never subscribed to the sector theory in application to the ice. We are content that our sovereignty exists over all the Arctic Islands.

...To our mind the sea, be it frozen or in its natural liquid state, is the sea; and our sovereignty exists over the lands and over our territorial waters.[47]

A few months later, however, Prime Minister St Laurent replied to a question in Parliament and almost offhandedly took back the Arctic waters: 'Oh, yes, the Canadian government considers that these are Canadian territorial waters.'[48] A more explicit statement was offered on 10 June 1958 by Alvin Hamilton, the Minister of Northern Affairs in the Diefenbaker government. As Hamilton told the House of Commons Standing Committee on Mines, Forests and Waters,

The area to the north of Canada, including the islands and waters between the islands and areas beyond, are looked upon as our own, and there is no doubt in the minds of this government, nor do I think in the minds of former governments of Canada, that this is national terrain.

But by this date the question of sovereignty had again become a live issue, primarily because the United States had launched icebreaker-construction programs and because in 1958 the U.S.S. *Nautilus*, one of the first atomic-powered submarines, travelled under the polar ice cap en route from Pearl Harbor to Iceland. The *Nautilus*' voyage seemed an explicit challenge to the sovereignty of both Canada and the Soviet Union and an indication of a tougher American posture. Shortly thereafter American international lawyers began arguing that Arctic ice 'constituted international territory'.[49]

The confusion in the Canadian position seemingly showed in the arguments of Canadian international law specialists as well. Professor Maxwell Cohen, for example, wrote early in 1958 and before the *Nautilus*' adventure that 'while we may claim the lands within our Arctic triangle up to the Pole, the open water is something else again.' Later Cohen seemed to change position, now arguing that the waters of the archipelago had to be considered Canadian. If they were not wholly inland waters, Cohen said, they should be treated 'as an extension of the idea of "territorial waters", in some modified form'.[50] The best statement of the Canadian case was made in 1962 by Ivan Head, then a member of the Department of External Affairs. Canada, he said, 'regards the water between the islands as Canadian territorial waters and this claim has been recognized by the United States. Prime Minister St Laurent reported to the House of Commons in 1957 that United States vessels servicing DEW line stations are required to apply to Canada for waivers of the provisions of the Canada Shipping Act before proceeding.' Head then convincingly argued that the location of the waters supported Canada's claim to consider them 'as internal waters. Surrounded on all sides by Canadian territory, they possess the *character* of Canadian waters.'[51]

Still the doubt remained. In 1963-4 the government of Lester Pearson, pushed by the 'unilateralists' in the Department of External Affairs, apparently made tentative moves to enclose the Arctic channels of Canadian internal waters, but when the United States reacted sharply, the Canadian government retreated and abandoned its plans, at least for a time. This was unfortunate for, as Maxwell Cohen noted, Canada was henceforth limited 'by a three-mile territorial waters concept with, perhaps, historic bays, a three-plus nine-mile fisheries zone (introduced in 1964), and a tentative claim for treating old semi-permanent ice between some islands as if it were a land bridge.'[52] Nonetheless in April 1970 the Secretary of State for External Affairs, Mitchell Sharp, said flatly that 'Canada has always regarded the waters between the islands of the Arctic archipelago as being Canadian waters. The present Government maintains that position. . . . '[53] A day after his speech, the government extended Canada's territorial waters to twelve miles,[54] thereby securing control over the normal entrances and exits of the Northwest Passage.

Even if Canada's territorial waters extended to all the waters in the Canadian sector rather than just to twelve miles, Canada's rights were not absolute. Canada could not bar the innocent passage of foreign vessels, not even of foreign warships. This was the authoritative conclusion of one student of international law in 1968.[55] But in one area at least Canada's claims seemed more or less secure. The continental shelf in the Arctic (as elsewhere on Canada's coasts) belonged to the Dominion. The Conference on the Law of the Sea in 1958 had defined the outer edges of the shelf in terms of the limits of 'exploitability', and later International Court of Justice decisions had affirmed that the continental shelf was the actual physical extension seaward of the submerged land mass. Canadian government research, begun in 1958, effectively demonstrated that most of the Arctic seabed was in fact a continental shelf.[56]

This Canadian control soon became vital, for advances in the technology of transportation and resource extraction began to make the North more accessible. Iron was present in abundance, as were copper, gold, silver, asbestos, tungsten, and lead-zinc on Little Cornwallis Island. Oil was discovered after a long search (the first drilling in Alaska had started in 1944) at Prudhoe Bay. And where there was oil there was gas. Where there was oil, there were also American commercial interests desirous of exploiting the nation's resources. In 1961 the Diefenbaker government had promulgated its Oil and Gas Land Regulations in an attempt to open the North to oil exploration and, secondarily, to assure some degree of Canadian financial participation. The effectiveness of the regulations was limited. Alvin Hamilton told a press conference that 'any lawyer could tear holes in them',[57] something that became readily apparent when in the late 1960s the oil exploration boom finally hit the Canadian Arctic. American-controlled oil companies secured most of the permits and most of the oil.

The oil discoveries on the Alaska North Slope led to new challenges to Canadian sovereignty. During the construction of the DEW line shipping had been proven feasible in Arctic waters, and 324 ships in all had carried 1.25 million tons of cargo into some places where no ships had ever been before. By late 1968 plans were afoot to send the large tanker S.S. *Manhattan* through Canada's waters on a test run, a voyage that would run headlong into and clash with burgeoning Canadian nationalism, would pose a danger to the ecology, and would arouse concern that Canada's manifest destiny might be lost in the North to American multinational corporations.[58]

By 1968, then, the Canadian position in the North was not as clear as one might have wished. There was no doubt about Canadian sovereignty over the Arctic archipelago, and the continental shelf seemed indisputably Canadian. On the debit side, however, Canada's rights to the Arctic waters surrounded by the archipelago were very unclear, and contrary claims could be supported by quoting the words of Canadian politicians and experts. Most important, perhaps, Canada's *de facto* sovereignty throughout the entire North had been weakened by government actions — and lack of action — since the Second World War and the construction of the DEW line. Regrettably, the lack of concern for the North and the regular and almost automatic acquiescence in American requests since 1942 had eaten away some of Canada's rights. As Canada began to face new and severe challenges in the 1970s, the result seemed to be that the nation had handed away part of its sovereignty. To get it back might be difficult indeed.

NOTES

[1]R. J. Diubaldo, 'Wrangling over Wrangel Island', *Canadian Historical Review*, XLVII (September 1967), 201ff.

[2]Gordon Smith, 'Sovereignty in the North: The Canadian Aspect of an International Problem', in R. St J. Macdonald, ed., *The Arctic Frontier* (Toronto, 1966), p. 203.

[3]Morris Zaslow, *The Opening of the Canadian North 1870-1914* (Toronto, 1971), pp. 253-4.

[4]Smith, *op. cit.*, p. 204.

[5]Zaslow, *op. cit.*, p. 255.

[6]*Ibid.*, p. 263.

[7]House of Commons *Debates*, 1 June 1925, p. 3758; 10 June 1925, p. 4056. See Maxwell Cohen, 'The Arctic and the National Interest', *International Journal*, XXVI (Winter 1970-1), 58-9; Smith, *op. cit.*, p. 217.

[8]L. C. Clark, ed., *Documents on Canadian External Relations*, vol. III: *1919-1925* (Ottawa, 1970), 566-7.

[9]A. I. Inglis, ed., *Documents on Canadian External Relations*, vol. IV: *1926-1930* (Ottawa, 1971), 947ff., provides occasionally humorous detail on the Sverdrup affair.

[10]Clark, *op. cit.*, vol. III, 582-3; D. H. Dinwoodie, 'Arctic Controversy: the 1925 Byrd-MacMillan Expedition Example', *Canadian Historical Review*, LIII (March 1972), 51ff.

[11]V. K. Johnston, 'Canada's Title to the Arctic Islands', *Canadian Historical Review*, XIV (March 1933), 24-41.

[12]'The American Far North', *Foreign Affairs*, XVII (April 1939), 517.

[13]S. Conn and B. Fairchild, *The Framework of Hemisphere Defence* (Washington, 1960), p. 410.

[14]Public Archives of Canada, W. L. M. King Papers, Diary, 21 March 1942.

[15]*Ibid.*, 18 March 1942.

[16]Trevor Lloyd, 'Frontier of Destiny—The Canadian Arctic', *Behind the Headlines*, VI (1946), 10.

[17]Department of External Affairs, External Affairs Records, file 52-B(s), Memo, 30 March 1943 and MacDonald's note 'on Developments in North-Western Canada', 6 April 1943; King Diary, 29 March 1943; C. P. Stacey, *Arms, Men and Governments: The War Policies of Canada, 1939-1945* (Ottawa, 1970), pp. 384ff.

[18]External Affairs Records, file 5221-40C, letter to Foster, 29 May 1943.

[19]Cited in James Eayrs, *In Defence of Canada*, vol. III: *Peacemaking and Deterrence* (Toronto, 1972), 350.

[20]House of Commons *Debates*, 1 August 1944, pp. 5837-9; S. W. Dziuban, *Military Relations Between the United States and Canada, 1939-1945* (Washington, 1959), chapter XII.

[21]See Eayrs, *op. cit.*, vol. III. 375ff.

[22]*Ibid.*

[23]*Foreign Relations of the United States, 1946* (Washington, 1970), v. 56.

[24]Eayrs, *op. cit.*, vol. III. 354-5.

[25]*Ibid.*, 352; *Foreign Relations of the United States 1946*, v. 60; Lloyd, *op. cit.*, 14; F. H. Soward, *Canada in World Affairs 1944-1946* (Toronto, 1950), pp. 272ff.

[26]See John Swettenham, *McNaughton*, vol. III: *1944-1966* (Toronto, 1969), p. 177; *Foreign Relations of the United States, 1947* (Washington, 1972), I. 749.

[27]R. J. Sutherland, 'The Strategic Significance of the Canadian Arctic', in Macdonald,ed., *The Arctic Frontier*, p. 256.

[28]Toronto *Globe and Mail*, 27 November 1948.

[29]For later U.S. military research in the Arctic, see 'And the Arctic Trails have their own Secret Tales', *Last Post*, I (Summer 1971), 59ff.

[30]See 'Transportation Problems on the North-West Highway System', *Canadian Army Journal*, VIII (October 1954), 128ff.

[31]C. D. Howe in House of Commons *Debates*, 4 March 1947, pp. 989-90; Claxton in Department of External Affairs, *Statements and Speeches* 48/36; D. J. Goodspeed, *A History of the Defence Research Board of Canada* (Ottawa, 1958), pp. 177ff.

32Printed in *Canadian Army Journal*, I (July 1947), 10ff. Cf. King's comments in J. W. Pickersgill and D. Forster, *The Mackenzie King Record*, vol. IV: *1947-1948* (Toronto, 1970), 24-5 and Trevor Lloyd, 'Canada's Strategic North', *International Journal*, XXVI (Winter 1970-1), 66.

33*Foreign Relations of the United States, 1947*, V. 112; Toronto *Globe and Mail*, 6 June 1947.

34Quoted in Robert Spencer, *Canada in World Affairs 1946-1949* (Toronto, 1959), p. 313; R. D. Cuff and J. L. Granatstein, 'Canada and the Perils of "Exemptionalism"', *Queen's Quarterly*, LXXIX (Winter 1972), 478-9; E. J. Dosman, 'Transport Policy in the North: Organizational Goals and Policy Environment', in K. W. Studnicki-Gizbert, ed., *Issues in Canadian Transport Policy* (Toronto, 1974), p. 456.

35Sutherland, *op. cit.*, p. 267. Cf. J. E. G. de Domenico, 'The Strategic Importance of Canada's North', *Canadian Army Journal*, XIV (Fall 1960), 5ff; John Gellner, 'Problems of Canadian Defence', *Behind the Headlines*, XVIII (1958), 3-5.

36Sutherland, *op. cit.*, p. 268.

37See esp. Eayrs, *op. cit.*, vol. III. 358ff.

38Press release, printed in R. A. Mackay, *Canadian Foreign Policy 1945-1954: Selected Speeches and Documents* (Toronto, 1971), pp. 246-7.

39K. J. Rea, *The Political Economy of the Canadian North* (Toronto, 1968), pp. 308ff.

40Sutherland, *op. cit.*, pp. 270-1.

41James Eayrs, *Canada in World Affairs 1955-1957* (Toronto, 1959), pp. 148ff.

42Ralph Allen, 'Will Dewline Cost Canada its Northland?', *Maclean's*, 26 May 1956, 68-70.

43E.g., Ottawa *Journal*, 12 April 1956; Vancouver *Province*, 16 January 1960.

44*North American Defence: How Much Say Should Canada Have?* (Toronto, 1959), p. 12; Toronto *Globe and Mail*, 13 February 1959.

45See articles in the National Defence publication, *Sentinel*, November-December 1970; Sutherland, *op. cit.*, p. 275.

46L. B. Pearson, 'Canada Looks Down North', *Foreign Affairs*, XXIV (July 1946), 638-9.

47House of Commons *Debates*, 3 August 1956, p. 6955.

48*Ibid.*, 6 April 1957, p. 3186.

49E.g., Halifax *Chronicle-Herald*, 21 October 1958. An earlier example can be found in the usually anodyne volumes in the *Foreign Relations of the United States* series. In *FRUS 1947*, III. 135 there are references to American memoranda 'Concerning existing and potential territorial claims in the Arctic' and on policy towards 'the so-called "sector" claims'.

50'Partnership Problems for Canada and U.S.', *Saturday Night*, 4 January 1958; 'Polar Ice and Arctic Sovereignty,' *Ibid.*, 30 August 1958.

51Ivan Head, 'Canadian Claims to Territorial Sovereignty in the Arctic Regions', *McGill Law School Journal* (1962-3), 218.

52Cohen, 'Arctic and National Interest', 65-6.

53*Statements and Speeches* 70/5, statement in Parliament, 16 April 1970.

54*Ibid.*, 70/6, statement, 17 April 1970.

55A. D. Pharand, 'Innocent Passage in the Arctic', *Canadian Yearbook of International Law* (1968), 60.

56Cohen, 'Arctic and National Interest', 66; J. A. Beesley, 'The Law of the Sea Conference: Factors Behind Canada's Stance', *International Perspectives* (July-August 1972), 28-9, 31-2.

[57] J. G. Wasteneys, 'The Place of the Military Engineer in Meeting the Challenge of the Canadian North', *Canadian Defence Quarterly*, II (Summer 1972), 20-1; Peter Newman, *Renegade in Power* (Toronto, 1963), pp. 140, 262.

[58] See on Arctic shipping, T. C. Pullen, 'Canada and Future Shipping Operations in the Arctic', *Canadian Defence Quarterly*, III (Autumn 1973), 10 and Pullen's 'Expanded Arctic Shipping: Canadian Challenge', *Sentinel* (February-March 1971), 30ff.

THE NORTHERN SOVEREIGNTY CRISIS 1968-70

by E. J. Dosman

The U.S. challenge to Canadian sovereignty in the Arctic 1968-70 produced a severe crisis in Canadian-American relations. It caught the new
Prime Minister, Pierre Elliott Trudeau, unawares and forced his government to take a position on the extent of Canadian control over northern
lands and waters including the Northwest Passage. By 1968, after a
century of muddling through, Ottawa had not yet clarified Canadian
jurisdiction in the North, nor had it elaborated consistent principles and
approaches to support its claims. It was precisely this confusion that gave
Washington an opening to probe and if possible to roll back a generalized
commitment to a 'Canadian' rather than a 'North American' Arctic.

The commitment to a Canadian Arctic is accepted by Ottawa policy-
makers as a touchstone of Canadian external policy. One of the few
shared and deeply felt beliefs in Ottawa is that Canadian sovereignty in
the North is non-negotiable. The political cost of retreating publicly from
a position of Canadian control over the Arctic is unthinkably high for a
Canadian government. Accepting the loss of Canadian control in the high
Arctic, whether over the territorial land mass, the islands, or the waters
between the Arctic islands, is perceived by both senior officials and the
leaders of all political parties as intolerable and a certain defeat for any
government in office.

I

It appears that northern sovereignty is now a 'core' objective of Canadian
foreign policy. But there would seem to be a contradiction here: government policy, and the statements of Canadian leaders give the impression
of being confused and ambiguous about that objective, both now and in
the past.

During the golden tranquil years of the 1960s the North had low
priority, and Ottawa failed to deal decisively with the issue of northern
sovereignty. Despite fifty years of explicit and implicit challenges to

Canadian control in the Arctic by Norway, Denmark, and the United States, no lessons were learned: jurisdictional claims were not nailed down when international opposition would have been least vocal—when the North appeared most remote, economically unimportant, and impenetrable. Diefenbaker's vision of the North had failed to materialize by the mid-1960s. There was no sudden burst of economic activity following the Oil and Gas Land Regulations of 1961, and test drilling for oil and gas was proceeding slowly. By 1965 oil and gas exploration in the Mackenzie Delta and the Arctic islands in the Sverdrup Basin was only beginning. And without a crisis in the North, the attention of the interested departments, particularly External Affairs, congealed elsewhere.

Moreover the strategic interests of the United States in the Canadian North appeared to be diminishing as the manned bomber threat from the U.S.S.R. declined. Indeed by 1965 agreement in principle was reached to turn over DEW airfields to Canadian control.[1] At home it was hard enough to justify the already significant outlays for expenditures on transportation, communications, and social services in the North. With the North seemingly secure, the sovereignty question could wait. Time seemed to be on Canada's side. As the years went by *de facto* occupation would result in an even more irrefutable claim to the Arctic, along with diminishing U.S. resistance to a Canadian initiative enclosing the waters of the Arctic archipelago as *internal* waters.

For ultimately that was the issue: either the Arctic mainland, islands, and waters, including the Northwest Passage were or were not sovereign parts of Canada. Enclosing the Arctic waters as internal waters would place no restriction on Canadian regulatory power in these areas; it would mark off the area as a Canadian security zone. While Ottawa would not likely unnecessarily restrict commercial navigation as such traffic increased, the status of internal waters would clarify the jurisdictional issue. Drawing baselines at the edges of the Arctic island system, with or without the sector theory, would enclose the waters of the Canadian Arctic archipelago as internal waters.

Indeed Prime Minister Pearson attempted to do precisely this in 1963-64. But he was sharply reproached by Washington when he communicated his intention to enclose northern waters. Washington argued that any such unilateral action by Canada would be taken as a precedent for similar claims by Indonesia and the Philippines. U.S. interests, it was claimed, would be negatively affected. Confronted by this opposition, Pearson had backed down.

Pearson's reasons for retreating in 1964 were tactical. Neither he nor Diefenbaker doubted that the United States would *eventually* come around to the Canadian position, i.e., sovereignty over the Arctic islands with baselines enclosing the waters between the islands, with or without the sector theory.

The Pearson government saw the possibility of using the northern-sovereignty question as a lever to resolve outstanding issues elsewhere in the law of the sea, both on the Atlantic and Pacific coasts. Canadian fishermen in both areas were clammering for action. Ottawa therefore agreed in 1964 to defer action on northern sovereignty if agreement could be reached between Canada and the United States on the other contentious matters. In fact Pearson would have been better advised to have done nothing at all, for despite much bilateral discussion the proposed compromise failed. The Pearson government, unable to achieve U.S. agreement, unilaterally created a twelve-mile fishing zone under the terms of the Territorial Seas and Fishing Zones of Canada Act in 1964. The northern issue, however, was allowed to slide.

At the same time departments other than External Affairs must share the responsibility for being caught off guard by the American challenge in 1968-70. Statutory responsibilities for surveillance and control of Canadian territory were shared by six major departments and agencies: the Department of Transport, the Department of National Defence, the Department of Energy, Mines and Resources, the Department of Indian Affairs and Northern Development, the Department of National Revenue, and the RCMP. Jurisdictional responsibilities for resource development and national defence were rarely clear and always interrelated. The Advisory Committee on Northern Development chaired by the Deputy Minister, Department of Indian Affairs and Northern Development, and including deputy ministers from other interested departments, among them the Department of External Affairs, was an appropriate forum for interdepartmental co-operation. Only in an advisory committee to Cabinet such as the Advisory Committee on Northern Development could monitoring of foreign economic interests and activities take place. But the Committee did nothing to initiate action when Alaskan and Canadian oil and gas exploration got under way. Unfortunately it had fallen into disarray itself during the 1960s, held few meetings, had poor attendance, and had no secretariat to retain continuity from one meeting to the next. The Transportation Sub-Committee fell into abeyance altogether.[2]

The technological revolution in the Arctic during the 1960s therefore went unnoticed. Commercial navigation through Arctic waters was now entirely feasible. In an increasingly resource-hungry world, with tremendous advances in mineral extraction and transportation technology, the North would become an integral part of the North American economy. In short, the Canadian North might well become an economic area of very considerable importance. Increased economic activity would raise the stakes and alter subtly Canadian defence interests in the area. Not Russia but our allies and particularly the United States would challenge Canadian control north of 60.

Discussions during the infrequent meetings of the Advisory Committee on Northern Development provide an excellent indication of the misperceptions of senior officials concerning the link between sovereignty and northern economic activity. At the seventy-first meeting in December 1967, just a month prior to the Prudhoe Bay discoveries, the Committee received a report that an intensive hunt for oil could be expected in northern waters. It underlined the fact that Ottawa had no controls regarding the use of Canadian Arctic waters by ships of foreign registry, and that the Committee might well wish to have an Interdepartmental Committee including the Department of External Affairs and the Department of National Defence review the situation. The Advisory Committee on Northern Development agreed to form a group, but it never met. This must be counted as one of the great lost opportunities for a coherent Canadian foreign and defence policy in the North. However without the atmosphere of crisis occasioned by a direct challenge there was insufficient stimulus for action. Meanwhile the country was heading into a new election under an untried Liberal leader.

Significantly the implications of the Atlantic Richfield discoveries at Prudhoe Bay in January and June 1968 were not at all clear at the seventy-second meeting of the Advisory Committee on Northern Development in June 1968. Quite the opposite. The finds were considered good news for the Mackenzie Delta and for Panarctic Oils Limited (45 per cent owned by the Canadian government). The Department of Indian Affairs and Northern Development was particularly enthusiastic. Nobody foresaw a U.S. challenge to Canadian sovereignty in the North. The Committee noted with approval the interest of the Arctic Institute of America in a comprehensive study of northern transportation as well as an indication of interest by the U.S. Coast Guard in such research. That the Alaskan breakthrough opened a period of great dangers as well as opportunities went unnoticed in the Committee. Not until November 1968 is there evidence that senior officials appreciated Washington's interest in exploiting the North Slope discoveries. Concern, such as there was, remained centred on the Russian icebreaker fleet. A resolution had been approved a year earlier to be sent forward to Cabinet 'that this committee sees no advantage in permitting Russian icebreakers to move through Canadian Arctic territorial waters to Coronation Gulf.'

Officials were haunted by the realization that their departments had failed to develop national capabilities to meet national responsibilities in Arctic navigation and traffic control. The Department of External Affairs was in the throes of a major reorganization; the Prime Minister was new and untried; public opinion was certain to be vocal; Canadian-American energy relations were on the boil. With the election of Richard M. Nixon as U.S. President, a man who would appreciate American security interests in northern waters, the sovereignty issue seemed likely to get relations between Trudeau and Nixon off to a very bad start. It did.

THE CHALLENGE

By late November the Department of External Affairs and the Advisory Committee on Northern Development realized that Washington rather than Moscow was concerned about the pretensions of Canada to sovereignty over Arctic waters. Official Ottawa was astonished.

The Advisory Committee on Northern Development had not been able to anticipate the possible use of northern waters as a major transportation route for liquid hydrocarbons (or other resources) from either the Alaskan North Slope or the Canadian Arctic. The Prudhoe Bay discoveries rendered a tanker route through the Northwest Passage to the U.S. east coast a serious enough possibility to warrant a trial with a reinforced super tanker; the decision to refit the S.S. *Manhattan* to test the feasibility of the Northwest Passage was announced in October 1968. Canadian officials had to admit among themselves that they had little worthwhile information on ice and marine questions. The situation was awkward. Atlantic Richfield, British Petroleum, and Humble Oil were demanding scientific information on northern ice conditions in the Northwest Passage that Ottawa simply did not possess. An oil official indicated that the oil companies might seek their own answers if Canada wouldn't or couldn't provide them. The U.S. Coast Guard similarly volunteered to assist Canada. Transport officials sensed an impending U.S. demand for a joint Canadian-American development agency in the North.

In itself the proposed trial of the S.S. *Manhattan* was only an implicit challenge to Canadian sovereignty. It raised the possibility of commercial navigation through the Northwest Passage; it confronted Canada with the proposition that Arctic waters beyond the three-mile territorial sea were 'high seas' like any other ocean. According to the 1958 Geneva Convention, innocent passage within the territorial sea must be accorded to commercial shipping. Canada had not signed this particular Convention, but legal opinion in Canada upheld the view that commercial vessels might notify authorities that they were passing through the territorial sea as a courtesy but doubted that they would have to notify as a matter of law.[3] In the wording of the Geneva Convention the right of innocent passage favoured maritime powers: it would be very difficult to interfere with a ship. Given the extremely hazardous navigation conditions in Arctic waters, Canada would almost certainly wish to impose far-reaching navigational safeguards. But the challenge of the S.S. *Manhattan* remained implicit – the oil companies were prepared to notify Ottawa. Nevertheless it was serious enough, given Ottawa's lack of preparedness in navigational, research, and surveillance capabilities.

What transformed the S.S. *Manhattan* trial of 1969 into a Canadian-American crisis was the position of Washington, particularly in regard to icebreaker support. Unlike Canadian Coast Guard icebreakers, their

American counterparts were considered military vessels. As such, under Canadian practice they would have to notify the Canadian government of their use of Canadian waters as a matter of law rather than of courtesy.[4] In Arctic waters, where jurisdictional questions were particularly important, failure of the State Department to notify Ottawa would be a particularly obvious red flag.

In November 1968 the U.S. Coast Guard indicated that it would send a vessel to accompany the S.S. *Manhattan*, but no official request for permission from the Canadian government had been received. It was this development that sparked an awareness in External Affairs that the U.S. Navy was continuing the strategic probing of Arctic waters that had prompted the U.S. Coast Guard icebreakers *Edisto* and *Eastwind* to attempt the Soviet Vilkiskiy Straits without Soviet permission. The Soviet Union perceived the voyage as an attempt to challenge its jurisdiction in its northern waters beyond the territorial sea. If successful, the test would have been a wedge in Soviet control of its northern sea route. The Soviet Union confronted the U.S. vessels and turned them back.

In essence the U.S.C.G. *Northwind* had the same mission in the Northwest Passage in 1969; accompanying the S.S. *Manhattan* offered a splendid opportunity to test the resolve of Trudeau and his government. The general effrontery of the U.S. Coast Guard, magnanimously assisting the *Manhattan* although Canadian icebreakers were just as good, the secrecy surrounding the data collected by the S.S. *Manhattan* (Ottawa, despite repeated requests, and after spending millions of dollars accompanying the S.S. *Manhattan*, was consistently refused access to the data; data on the ice was extremely important for polar-icebreaker construction and would probably be used in the construction of the new generation of U.S. Coast Guard icebreakers, the *Star* class) added credence to a belief in Ottawa that the U.S. Navy was funding the S.S. *Manhattan* operation.

In any case the U.S. was doing no more than behaving as a Great Power. As a maritime nation it had an interest in maximum freedom of movement of vessels in all waters, including the Canadian North; as well it had an interest both for economic and security reasons in maintaining unrestricted passage through the Northwest Passage to Alaskan oil and mineral supplies. The S.S. *Manhattan* offered an excellent opportunity to accomplish the latter by challenging Canadian jurisdiction beyond the three-mile territorial sea.

Ottawa immediately suggested informally to the State Department that the U.S. apply for permission for a U.S. Coast Guard escort. But Washington's silence was eloquent. From its point of view any U.S. application for permission from Canada would be taken as a recognition of Canadian sovereignty beyond the three-mile limit in Arctic waters.

It was agreed at the seventy-third meeting of the Advisory Committee on Northern Development in December 1968 (a very well-attended meeting) that the Canadian Department of Transport should co-operate to the fullest extent to ensure *de facto* Canadian sovereignty, including the provision of the icebreaker *John A. Macdonald*. Similarly it was considered appropriate for the Canadian government to take the initiative in suggesting that Coast Guard vessels of both countries accompany the S.S. *Manhattan* in northern waters, both in Canada and in Alaska. Such joint arrangements involving the oil companies and the two governments would make it difficult for the U.S. to refuse co-operation and might avoid a confrontation. It could be taken as a recognition of Canadian jurisdiction and just possibly prepare a basis for future co-operation with Washington. When Mitchell Sharp, Secretary of State for External Affairs, later indicated that Canada had 'concurred and co-operated throughout', he was referring only to the above measures taken unilaterally in Ottawa in response to U.S. unwillingness to co-operate with Canada.

Perhaps a more experienced Trudeau would have adopted a more forthright position: thanking the U.S. Coast Guard for its interest, but indicating that Canada had sufficient capabilities to regulate and assist commercial vessels in its waters. Quite possibly a public acknowledgement that the U.S. was challenging Canadian jurisdiction would have created a public protest so severe as to make a formal declaration of sovereignty over Arctic waters and the Northwest Passage inevitable, that is, to change their status to internal waters. Such a step, however, would have required considerable courage. By acquainting Canadians with the facts of the situation Trudeau would have risked focusing public opinion squarely on an exposed nerve.

On the other hand, by deceiving Parliament and public opinion with a legal fiction, the Trudeau government similarly took a tremendous risk. Moreover it was unstatesmanlike, unworthy, according to some circles, of elected politicians. The following factors help to explain Trudeau's selection of this strategy to soothe public opinion.

HOPE

If at all possible External Affairs wanted to avoid northern sovereignty becoming a subject of direct bilateral talks, as it would almost certainly involve all the political risks of a major confrontation. External hoped that by achieving a 'correct' level of Canadian participation in the voyage of the S.S. *Manhattan* it could protect the Canadian position while avoiding the necessity of direct diplomatic exchanges altogether. In effect it would be saying to the U.S. State Department, 'We know you are challenging Canadian sovereignty in the North, but we have decided that you are not challenging northern sovereignty. You may not have asked our permission for sending the U.S.C.G. *Northwind*, indeed you have explicitly refused to notify us, but we are granting permission anyway.'

So startlingly abject a strategy might confuse Washington enough to shame it back into the special relationship. The voyage might slip through without a Canadian-American incident and without a public outcry. In this case the status of Arctic waters would remain unchanged.

FEAR

Senior officials were acutely aware of the strength of U.S. feeling on Canadian legislation restricting or threatening to restrict the movement of naval and commercial vessels in the North. They feared U.S. retaliation, particularly in restricting oil exports from Alberta to the mid-west states. This was the other disconcerting side of the Alaskan North Slope discoveries that deeply disturbed Ottawa by the fall of 1968. Alaskan oil, it was believed, would increase U.S. oil self-sufficiency and therefore threaten Alberta oil markets. Indeed this possibility was taken so seriously that a high-level interdepartmental Task Force, the Task Force on Northern Oil Development, was created in December 1968 to devise mechanisms to protect Canadian oil exports.

Canada was of course vulnerable in other ways to U.S. retaliation. Therefore the sovereignty debate carried on within the federal government in 1968 and 1970 was not limited to narrow jurisdictional questions. The intense internal discussions culminating in April 1970 in the Arctic Waters Pollution Prevention Act and the extension of the territorial sea to twelve miles revealed the intimate association of the sovereignty, economic, trade, and energy aspects of Canadian-U.S. relations. In 1968-70 the chief issues were taken up not merely by the Department of External Affairs but also by the key interdepartmental committees dealing with northern economic development: the Task Force on Northern Oil Development; the Advisory Committee for Northern Development; and the Interdepartmental Committee on Oil.

It was the most serious crisis in Canadian-American relations since the nuclear-arms débâcle under Diefenbaker.

ADMINISTRATIVE CONFUSION

The strategy chosen in winter 1968-9 is easier to understand against the background of dismay, chaos, and lack of preparation in the Department of External Affairs. Its Legal Affairs Bureau was ably staffed, but in the midst of a major reorganization the Department lacked the necessary stature to undertake dynamic leadership in the crisis. The reflex therefore was to buy time, to avoid going public until External had a grip on the issue.

For its part the Advisory Committee on Northern Development similarly failed to command sufficient prestige to co-ordinate Canadian activities to protect Canadian jurisdiction during the S.S. *Manhattan* trials. At its seventy-third meeting in December 1968 it had recommended the creation of a special task force of the Inter-departmental Committee on

Territorial Waters to set out a detailed program of the Canadian position. The special task force never met. Northern sovereignty was far too important to leave to the Advisory Committee on Northern Development.

Instead its role was allocated to the new Task Force on Northern Oil Development: its Transportation Committee would recommend what actions to take to protect Canadian sovereignty during the crisis. Indeed the first two *Memoranda* of the Task Force on Northern Oil Development to Cabinet in March 1969 and April 1970 dealt far more with sovereignty than with energy matters. The first stressed the urgency of increased activities of the relevant departments to ensure 'effective occupation' of the high Arctic; the second underlined the importance of an icebreaker program to ensure a Canadian capability exceeding or at least matching that of the United States.

Eventually some order returned. The new Under-Secretary of State, Ritchie, restored morale to External Affairs. A new Inter-departmental Committee on the Law of the Sea supplanted the Inter-departmental Committee on Territorial Waters. Operational and policy roles could now be identified more clearly. Above all a small group of capable individuals in the Legal Affairs Bureau of External Affairs and the central agencies developed clear policy alternatives.

But this took time. Again the culprit was lack of preparation in the absence of a crisis. It further reinforced the temptation to turn the other cheek and to allay Canadian public opinion.

LEGAL COMPLEXITIES

Contingency planning for the kind of U.S. challenge represented by the S.S. *Manhattan* trials had been neglected. Past U.S. threats were associated primarily with air-defence matters such as the DEW line; in this area Ottawa had some experience. The U.S.S.R. had been considered the chief enemy in Arctic waters and Canada had developed a simple but effective strategy to deal with Soviet warships in Canadian waters—to order them out. The support of the U.S. could be relied upon. Indeed the irony of the December 1967 resolution of the Advisory Committee on Northern Development, 'that this committee sees no advantage in permitting Russian icebreakers to move through Canadian Arctic territorial waters to Coronation Gulf', could not have been lost on senior colleagues within the federal bureaucracy—the trouble with this strategy was the difficulty of applying it against Canada's closest ally and protector.

Once the threat came from the south rather than from the Soviet Union, Ottawa realized that its political position for dealing with Arctic claims was far more difficult. There was far greater potential for retaliation from the U.S. It was a situation that magnified, perhaps too much, the knowledge that Canada's legal position was not airtight. Sovereignty over the mainland, the islands, and the continental shelf was pretty much nailed down, but not, it appeared, over Arctic waters. Historical claims; the sector theory; precedents for the drawing of baselines; the 'sea-is-land' theory; the archipelagic principle; and the lack of consistent government policy—all singly or together didn't add up to an unchallengeable claim. The government was not yet willing to reject the jurisdiction of the International Court of Justice. If Canada drew baselines and was challenged by the U.S. in the International Court, it might lose. This was another reason for delaying tactics.

In the best of all worlds Trudeau could hope to ride out the storm without committing himself in Parliament to any position. All options would remain open. However this posture could not be maintained. An influential *Globe and Mail* article on 26 February 1969 underlined public concern and indicated that the northern-sovereignty question could not lightly be skidded over without incident. The article was bound to raise questions in the House of Commons and therefore necessitated the preparation by senior officials of a tentative policy position for the use of the Secretary of State for External Affairs. However from the point of view of External, the *Globe and Mail* article was not without value. It had asserted that Canadian sovereignty was not likely to be challenged by the United States and gave positive indications that the U.S. accepted the *de facto* recognition of Canadian jurisdiction in the area.

Answers to the questions expected in the House were therefore prepared immediately. The Secretary of State was to indicate that 'there is no foundation for the suggestion that the U.S. Government is challenging Canadian sovereignty in connection with these trials. I should also point out that the American oil companies involved have requested the co-operation of Canadian authorities in the project.'

The die was cast. The government never retreated from this interpretation. In September 1969, again in the Toronto *Globe and Mail*, Secretary of State Mitchell Sharp once more insisted that the Canadian government had long been preparing for an experiment such as the voyage of the S.S. *Manhattan*, that it had concurred in the commercial decision to attempt the Northwest Passage, and that it both welcomed and was participating in the trials. According to Sharp the voyage of the S.S. *Manhattan* did not involve a challenge to Canadian sovereignty. Such an association would be 'wholly misleading'.[5]

1969

Until May External Affairs still hoped that the voyage of the S.S. *Manhattan* might pass without incident. A diplomatic exchange with the U.S. State Department had not yet taken place. It hoped that Washington would come around to recognizing Canadian jurisdiction in Arctic waters and that the working relationships between the two Coast Guards and between the oil companies and Washington would protect Canada's position in the North. But by the end of April the implications for northern sovereignty of oil developments in Alaska and the voyage of the S.S. *Manhattan* were increasingly grave.

The U.S. State Department steadfastly refused to recognize Canadian jurisdiction beyond the three-mile territorial sea. Public concern mounted both in the press and in the House of Commons. Sooner or later a statement from the Prime Minister had to be made and on 15 May 1969 Trudeau outlined the Canadian position. His statement has provided a touchstone for Canadian policy on sovereignty in the North ever since.

First the speech attempted to clarify for the House the term 'Arctic sovereignty', as if to provide background information on the subject for Members of Parliament. In fact Trudeau's speech was a closely studied document that was meant for Washington's as well as the public's consumption. It asserted that Canadian sovereignty over the mainland as well as the islands of the Canadian Arctic was well established and that there was 'no dispute concerning this matter'. Publicly the U.S. had not accepted this position, and U.S. negotiators are rumoured to have raised it at the Ditchely Draft Conference on the Law of the Sea in 1971, preparatory to the Caracas meeting in 1974. Trudeau now nailed down this claim in Parliament. Second Trudeau unequivocally asserted Canada's exclusive sovereign rights to explore and exploit the resources of the Arctic continental shelf. As he pointed out:

Canada's sovereign rights over the Continental Shelf in the Arctic follow from Canada's sovereignty over the adjacent lands, and again there is no dispute on this matter. No country has asserted a competing claim to the resources in question; no country has challenged Canada's claim on any other basis and none can do so under international law. Foreign companies carrying out exploration activities on the Continental Shelf in Canada's Arctic areas operate under Canadian permit and licence and in so doing expressly recognize Canada's sovereign rights.[6]

The next section of Trudeau's speech, however, was ambiguous and did not deal directly with the real issue of the voyage of the S.S. *Manhattan*. This concerned the Canadian position on the waters between the islands of Canada's Arctic archipelago. The Prime Minister was indeed unclear and in effect repeated the statement of the Minister of Northern Affairs before the House Standing Committee on Mines, Forests and Waters on 10 June 1958:

The area to the north of Canada, including the islands and waters between the islands and areas beyond, are looked upon as our own, and there is no doubt in the minds of this government, nor do I think in the minds of former governments of Canada, that this is national terrain.

But then, crucially, he detracted from the force of that position by adding that 'not all countries would accept the view that the waters between the Islands of the archipelago are internal waters over which Canada has full sovereignty'. Indeed by going on to indicate the nature of the disagreement the Prime Minister appeared to retreat from the 1958 position and the speech did not include an official reaffirmation of Diefenbaker's stand. The wording of his speech appeared to provide an opening for a challenge:

> The contrary view is indeed that Canada's sovereignty extends only to the territorial sea around each island. The Law of the Sea is a complex subject, which it can be understood, may give rise to differences of opinion. Such differences, of course, would have to be settled not on an arbitrary basis but with due regard for established principles of international law.[7]

Trudeau's extended elaboration of the northern-sovereignty issue and his apparent determination to clarify it puzzled both the leader of the Opposition, Robert Stanfield, and T. C. Douglas of the New Democratic Party, not least since the remainder of the speech went on to indicate Canada's concurrence with and interest in the S.S. *Manhattan* project as well as the importance for Canada of the development of Arctic navigation. Indeed the speech gave every indication that the United States and Canada were at one in the planning of the project.

> ...For these reasons the Canadian government has welcomed the *Manhattan* exercise, has concurred in it and will participate in it. The oil companies concerned and the United States Coast Guard have consulted with appropriate Canadian authorities in the planning of the operation...the government has also selected and appointed an official Canadian government representative on board the S.S. *Manhattan* who will act as technical advisor and as a coordinator of Canadian support for the operation.[8]

Stanfield and Douglas sensed correctly that Trudeau was protesting too much about the benefits to Canada arising out of the projected S.S. *Manhattan* trials. They were concerned about the effects on Canadian sovereignty of Trudeau's statement, which did not clearly assert the position taken by previous Canadian governments. Stanfield urged the Prime Minister to be more forthright. He was disturbed by 'the manner in which the Prime Minister seems to have abandoned the position taken by previous governments with regard to the assertion of our sovereignty.'[9] And Douglas commented in a perceptive statement:

It seems to me that if the Canadian government leaves this matter in an indefinite state we are almost inviting someone else to suggest that we do not have jurisdiction, and that this is a question upon which we are prepared to compromise. I think the Canadian government ought to make its position clear beyond any shadow of doubt.[10]

Having presented a formal statement to the House of Commons, it was now incumbent on the Department of External Affairs to communicate directly with the U.S. Embassy. In June 1969 it set out the official Canadian position on the question of northern sovereignty, substantially repeating the line of argument adopted in the Prime Minister's comments.[11] It explicitly underlined the Canadian view that the status of Canadian jurisdiction over the waters of the Arctic archipelago was not affected by the S.S. *Manhattan* project. And in repeating Trudeau's sentiments about the mutually beneficial effects of the project, it looked forward to a happy future of U.S.-Canadian co-operation. The thrust of the Note was to avoid any indication that Canada had perceived any U.S. State Department actions that could be construed as questioning Canadian sovereignty. Rather the complementarity of Canadian and international responsibility and the Canadian determination to support scientific research and oil and gas exploration was elaborated. However on the important issue, namely the jurisdiction of the Northwest Passage and the waters between the islands, the Canadian Note merely repeated the 1958 position, implying Canadian sovereignty but not stating it. The Note apparently went further than the Prime Minister's statement to Parliament in including a statement to the effect that Canada had inevitably the greatest interest in Arctic waters in the Northwest Passage given historic, geographic, climatic, and economic factors. Nevertheless, by only implying rather than stating Canada's determination to uphold the 1958 statement, the Note provided the U.S. State Department with a lever to pry open the Canadian position.

Above all it did not support Pearson's 1963-4 initiative. Implicitly, therefore, the government had withdrawn from the option of enclosing the waters of the Canadian Arctic Archipelago as internal waters.

The first round had gone to Washington. It had been successful in frightening Ottawa out of the most straightforward and best response to the American challenge. The Canadian government simply did not feel strong enough to stand firm. A clear and unambiguous declaration of sovereignty carried with it the risks of U.S. retaliation. It also could be challenged if brought before the International Court. Nor would such a declaration necessarily guarantee acceptance by the world community; the enforcement with appropriate capabilities of a claim to internal waters would be required.

But the great advantage of enclosing the waters of the Canadian Arctic archipelago with baselines at this stage in the Canadian-American confrontation was the exposed *American* position. They were rudely challenging a Canadian position that if not perfect was certainly very strong. Their argument that the Arctic archipelago was similar to the Malaysian or Indonesian archipelago was extremely weak. Moreover Washington would resent *any* initiative and would probably retaliate whatever was done. Except for the extension of the territorial sea to twelve miles, Canada would have to reserve a position before the International Court for measures (such as pollution control) that fell far short of drawing baselines around the island system. Formally claiming the waters of the Arctic archipelago including the Northwest Passage as internal waters would certainly have been accepted by the Canadian public, long since accustomed in any case to the belief that the high Arctic was 'Canadian'.

The significance of formal declaration of internal waters in the Arctic would go well beyond gratifying the national ego. A single regime of law applicable to the North as a whole would vastly simplify the regulatory structure required to guide Arctic economic development and transportation. Perhaps more important, enclosing the waters would split off the northern-sovereignty issue from other issues of the law of the sea. It would have greatly simplified Canadian law-of-the-sea diplomacy, since a chief Canadian objective in ensuing negotiations at Caracas and Vienna has aimed at strengthening northern claims. It would indicate to the world community that Canada considered the North a security zone that required undisputed national attention. The potential economic importance to the Canadian economy of northern resources and the Arctic's unique climate and history supported this contention. While Canada had no interest whatsoever in discouraging legitimate commercial traffic in Arctic waters, it required sovereign control to define innocent passage, enforce an appropriate liability code, and the like. There were excellent reasons in 1969 to doubt the virtue of a special relationship between Canada and the United States as it related to the North. In a perfect world it might not matter who controlled northern waters; in an imperfect world there was too much at stake not to enclose the area as internal waters.

The unwillingness to draw baselines permitted the North to remain the last area in Canada where its territorial integrity could be challenged. But timidity won the day; Washington had manoeuvred Ottawa into doubting the strength of its position. It was now Washington's turn to reply.

Unhappily for the Department of External Affairs, the U.S. response was both clear and uncompromising. The State Department, while recognizing the Canadian claim to sovereignty over the Arctic islands and mainland, and the sovereign rights of coastal states over the continental shelf for purposes of exploration and exploitation of natural resources, refused to recognize Canadian jurisdiction beyond the three-mile limit.

Thus it took precisely the position that Trudeau had invited in his May 15 speech. To Washington, the general principles of the international law of the sea, including the right of innocent passage and freedom of the high seas, applied to the Arctic waters. Washington could not accept Canadian pretensions that the waters between the islands were internal waters or territorial waters. The latter applied only within the three-mile limit, and the U.S. would insist on the right of innocent passage through channels in the Northwest Passage even within such territorial waters. The Northwest Passage was an international strait with total freedom of navigation, and the U.S. would consider any unilateral extension of maritime jurisdiction as prejudicial to its interests.[12] It refused to recognize the sector theory as a valid principle for claiming Canadian jurisdiction over Arctic waters.

The American reply indicated beyond a shadow of doubt that the U.S. was prepared for a confrontation over the status of Arctic waters. The ball was now clearly in Ottawa's court. Canada was confronted by the worst of both worlds: having thrown away a strong bargaining position, it would face retaliation anyway. It was politically impossible for the government to do nothing: it had to find a formula that would go some distance to extend Canadian jurisdiction in northern waters without producing a lasting strain on relations with Washington.

A long period of indecision followed the Canadian-American diplomatic exchange after Trudeau's May speech on the subject in the House of Commons. While a host of initiatives were taken to strengthen the Canadian 'presence' in the Arctic, such as official visits, and maintaining equity control in Panarctic Oils, senior officials sought a formula for extending Canadian jurisdiction over Arctic waters.[13]

One difficulty, however, was the considerable interest, in Canada and elsewhere, in the outcome of the sovereignty debate. In May 1969 *Pravda* reported that 'the U.S. military has been rapidly encroaching on the Sovereignty of that state [Canada].' The Canadian Embassy in Yugoslavia reported that the U.S. cultural attaché was giving attention to an interesting definition of the Northwest Passage:

...the name given to the water route from the Atlantic to the Pacific Ocean that penetrates the Arctic region from East to West above the Canadian land mass.

In August 1969 External Affairs sent a kit of questions and answers to Canadian Embassies around the world to ensure that Canadian diplomats were holding the same line. First it maintained the official line that the S.S. *Manhattan* trials raised no difficult problems for Canada or that Canada was being defensive. If approached on the subject diplomats were to concentrate on the positive implications of the venture for the future economic development of the North. Second it was considered essential to say, if asked, that Canadian authorities had been consulted and welcomed and concurred in the voyage. Legal questions regarding the Arctic archipelago or the status of the waters between the islands were not at issue in the voyage of the S.S. *Manhattan*.

Third the Department of External Affairs pointed to the Canadian hope that Arctic navigation would encourage trading fleets from many countries, as had the building of the St Lawrence Seaway. The interests of foreign nations were not in any way jeopardized by jurisdictional questions arising out of the S.S. *Manhattan* experiment.

Fourth officials, while not advancing comment on the sovereignty issue, should provide answers to questions relating to it, but with great care. Particular sensitivity was shown to the status of the waters of the Arctic archipelago. They were to emphasize that the Prime Minister had not deviated from the 1958 position, but not to elaborate except to say that historic and geographic factors gave Canada the greatest direct interest in Arctic waters and the Northwest Passage. References to the Prime Minister's statement concerning possible differences of opinion 'regarding the Canadian view that waters between the Arctic Archipelago are internal Canadian waters over which Canada has full sovereignty' were to be played down.

For official purposes Ottawa would continue to recognize service-to-service agreements between the U.S. and Canadian Coast Guards as the equivalent of official State Department notification. But External was candid with its overseas diplomats about the awkward situation occasioned by the S.S. *Manhattan* trials:

> While the oil companies have sought the cooperation of the Canadian government in the project, the appropriate U.S. authorities have failed to formally request consent for, or to provide requisite notification of U.S. Coast Guard participation in the project.

References to the Prime Minister's statement concerning a possible difference of opinion with the United States regarding the Canadian view of the status of waters between the Arctic islands were to be played down. In fact any suggestion that Canada's position was in any way affected was avoided.

Officials were not to comment on possible countries that might dispute the 1958 statement that the waters between the Arctic islands were internal Canadian waters over which Canada exercised full sovereignty. Rather, if asked, they should limit themselves to a statement that the Prime Minister's speech was not intended to refer to actual differences of opinion and certainly not differences of opinion with the United States, but instead to indicate that such a complex subject as the law of the sea could give rise to such differences. To questions concerning the Prime Minister's statement that differences would have to be settled with due regard for principles of international law, officials were to avoid any impression that there was any doubt in international law as to the legitimacy of the Canadian position. The Prime Minister's statement merely reflected the traditional Canadian position that international differences could, and should, be settled peacefully. Finally, all references to the sector theory or to straight baselines joining the outermost islands of the Arctic archipelago were to be avoided.

Gradually alternative strategies emerged for the consideration of the small team assembled around Trudeau to finalize a position: Mr Ivan Head of the Prime Minister's Office; Mr J. A. Beesley, legal adviser to External Affairs; Mr A. A. Gotlieb, former legal adviser; and Gordon Robertson, Secretary to the Cabinet and Clerk of the Privy Council. Three strategies emerged.

1. The Bureau of Legal Affairs in the Department of External Affairs had proposed from the first a simple interim response to the U.S. challenge: the extension of the territorial sea from three to twelve miles by amending the Territorial Sea and Fishing Zones Act. It argued that this step would obtain widespread international acceptance. Fifty-seven states already had proclaimed a twelve-mile (or wider) territorial sea. Second, it would constitute a first step in enclosing the waters of the Arctic archipelago by controlling the eastern and western gateways to the Northwest Passage, between Young and Lowther Islands in the Barrow Strait and the Prince of Wales Strait respectively. The Bureau thought it too risky to go beyond this step, which the Americans already were certain to resent.

2. Against this gradualist approach, however, opinion in Parliament and the press called for stronger action. The House Standing Committee on Indian Affairs and Northern Development took an immediate interest in the issue of northern sovereignty. After extensive hearings in spring 1969, and a visit to the Arctic in September during which they welcomed the S.S. *Manhattan*'s 'daring voyage through the Canadian Arctic archipelago', the Committee reported a far-reaching recommendaation to the House on 19 December 1969.

Your Committee recommends that the Government of Canada indicate to the world, without delay, that vessels, surface and submarine, passing through Canada's Arctic archipelago are and shall be subject to the sovereign control and regulation of Canada . . . the waters lying between the islands of the Arctic archipelago have been, and are, subject to Canadian sovereignty historically, geographically and geologically.[14]

The Committee accepted the concept of innocent passage except 'that any passage which poses a danger to Canada whether this danger takes the form of a threat of pollution or otherwise, is not innocent.' In short, it would be innocent passage as defined by Canada.

As regards the Northwest Passage, 'Your Committee rejects the suggestion that an international waterway exists through the Canadian Arctic archipelago.'[15] The activist approach of the House Standing Committee was popular throughout the country and in the Liberal caucus.

3. The rationale for the Standing Committee's recommendations stemmed in part from its concern that the effective protection of 'the delicate balance of nature in the Arctic' required the full exercise of Canadian control. The environmental issue appealed to certain Trudeau advisers, although not in the context of a declaration of sovereignty. First, anti-pollution legislation would appeal to Canadian, American, and international opinion and therefore evoke some sympathy in Washington. Recent disasters such as the S.S. *Torrey Canyon* episode had alerted public opinion to the dangers of tanker traffic. Indeed Canada was about to face a smaller but nevertheless disastrous oil spill off Chedabucto Bay when the S.S. *Arrow* ran aground. The United Nations as well as bodies such as the Intergovernmental Marine Consultative Organization were discussing measures to combat pollution.

It was embarrassingly true that Ottawa had little actual evidence regarding the fragile character of the northern environment; it simply had not done research in this area. But environmental dangers in the North certainly offered a plausible hypothesis, sure to obtain a favourable response from the more enlightened segments of American public opinion. There would be no difficulty in obtaining support for anti-pollution legislation in Parliament.

Second, anti-pollution legislation would extend Canadian jurisdiction over northern waters on a functional basis, stopping short of formally enclosing the waters of the Arctic archipelago as internal waters with a declaration of sovereignty. The Americans would protest, but less, some thought, than they would to the extension of the territorial sea to twelve miles.

In any case the functional approach seemed less a break with traditional Canadian emphasis on multilateral agreement. Just as Mr Pearson was forced to take initiatives to protect Canadian fishing grounds, so now Ottawa would enact legislation giving Canada only that amount of jurisdiction required to achieve the specific purpose of environmental protection. At the same time the government was careful to stress that enacting specific but limited jurisdiction did not prejudice its claim to more extensive sovereignty over the whole sea area enclosed by the Canadian Arctic archipelago.[16] Canadian public opinion would be pacified; the international community would see Canada's approach to be defensive and responsible rather than monopolistic and acquisitive. The Arctic Waters Pollution Prevention Act was taking shape.

The government had ruled out enclosing the waters from the beginning, and they were not to be stampeded by the recommendations of the House Standing Committee on Indian Affairs and Northern Development. Essentially Trudeau's team debated the respective merits of the extension of the territorial sea and the functional approach embodied in anti-pollution legislation. For a time the territorial-sea extension was clearly ascendent, on the argument that the Americans could not challenge it in the International Court and that it would provide control over the vital waterways of the Northwest Passage. Opinion then swung behind the functional approach given the unlikelihood, some believed, of the U.S. contesting it.

But as the tension in the Liberal caucus, Cabinet, Parliament, and the country mounted, the team reluctantly agreed to introduce both measures and to place a reservation on the acceptance of the compulsory jurisdiction of the International Court. By March 1970 the Arctic Waters Pollution Prevention Bill and the amendments to the Territorial Sea and Fishing Zones Act extending the territorial sea to twelve miles were prepared.

THE APRIL LEGISLATION AND THE AMERICAN RESPONSE

As in his speech of 15 May 1969 concerning the voyage of the S.S. *Manhattan*, so also on 8 April 1970 Prime Minister Trudeau stated in the House of Commons that the proposed anti-pollution legislation was based on the right of coastal states such as Canada to protect themselves against 'grave threats to their environment', since existing international law did not adequately recognize the need of such states to protect themselves against irrevocable dangers posed by new developments in transportation technology. He recognized that the legislation represented a unilateral initiative by Canada in that commercially owned shipping would be subject to Canadian construction and navigation safety standards within zones extending up to 100 miles off shore. The protective measures were also to apply to the exploration and exploitation by submarine of the resources of Canada's northern continental shelf. However Canada's action though unilateral was not to be seen as contrary to international law; it was merely an attempt to assist in the development of new concepts in international law and he referred to the 1948 Truman Proclamation on the continental shelf, which had become established in international law a few years after being announced. According to Mr Beesley, speaking later to a group of international legal experts:

Thus, the Canadian government embarked upon the unilateral course of action which is both compatible with existing law and in advance of it; both based in the most fundamental principle of the law and pressing against its furthest frontier ... on the basis of these concepts and with its combined unilateral and multilateral approach to the Arctic waters problem, Canada is seeking to contribute to the progressive development of international environmental law. It was with the development of such a body of law in mind that Prime Minister Trudeau described the Arctic Waters Pollution Prevention Legislation as 'an assertion of the importance of the environment, of the sanctity of life on this planet, of the need for the recognition of the principle of clean seas, which is in all respects a principle of the world of today and tomorrow as with the principle of free seas for the world of tomorrow.'[17]

Washington's response to the April 1970 legislation was the primary concern of Ottawa's group, steering a precarious course between an aroused Canadian public opinion and a charged atmosphere in Canadian-American relations. The U.S. response, at least the first retaliatory measure, was already known in Ottawa. On 10 March President Nixon announced a new limit of 395,000 barrels a day on Canadian oil imports for the period 1 March to 31 December 1970. A week later Nixon telephoned Trudeau to indicate the likelihood of further retaliation should Canada go ahead with the anti-pollution legislation and the extension of the territorial sea to twelve miles. He was furious that Canadian public opinion was persuading Ottawa to adopt 'uncooperative' measures, and that Canada was trying to spring something on the U.S. without adequate consultation.

Was there 'adequate consultation'? The mounting pressure in Parliament and in the press for action was not lost on Washington. By the first week of March, the U.S. Embassy in Ottawa knew informally that Canada would go ahead with legislation to 'extend Canadian jurisdiction'. Still there was no diplomatic Note informing the State Department of this decision.

The Department of External Affairs was well aware of the likely target of U.S. retaliation – restrictions on U.S. imports of Canadian oil. Nixon's *Task Force on Oil Policy*, established in February 1969 to review the oil-import program, had recommended cutting back oil imports to 615,000 barrels a day effective 1 July 1970 pending State Department negotiations regarding 'measures looking toward a freer exchange of petroleum, natural gas and other energy resources between the two countries'. The sovereignty issue could only exacerbate Canadian-U.S. friction that had been developing around the energy issue for years, and that Nixon's *Task Force* had explicitly linked to a continental energy policy.[18]

In these circumstances External Affairs was torn between a desire to initiate discussions immediately to try to ease the crisis and a wish to *respond* to an American initiative and therefore to appear reactive and defensive rather than aggressive. By 10 March Nixon solved Ottawa's dilemma by cutting imports; the next day Ottawa delivered the formal communication to the U.S. Embassy in Ottawa outlining the steps it would take in the Arctic.

In his telephone conversation with Trudeau, Nixon had indicated his intention to dispatch a high-level U.S. team to Ottawa immediately to clarify respective positions in the light of the March developments. The Americans were firmly negative, indicating that such action by Canada would be taken as a precedent by other nations for a similar unilateral extension of territorial sovereignty and that it constituted a serious blow not only to U.S. but also to Canadian security because of the restrictive effect such measures had on the movement of U.S. naval vessels. For their part the Canadians outlined the nature and extent of political pressure in Canada together with commitments to Parliament and indicated that they had no option but to proceed under these circumstances. They pointed out the numerous occasions on which Washington had acted unilaterally in far more grave and legally precarious situations. However the Canadians underlined their country's commitment to co-operate with the U.S.

The U.S. delegation's reply remained negative. It shared the Canadian concern for domestic political pressure, but the Canadian actions were illegal and unacceptable and would result in serious economic and security problems for the United States around the world. Washington would not only refuse to acquiesce in an assertion of Canadian jurisdiction over Arctic waters, it would also take whatever lawful and 'appropriate' steps it considered necessary to protect its position in these matters. The American team urged Canada to delay any legislation preparatory to an International Conference regarding Arctic problems of common concern to both Canada and the United States. It recommended that the International Joint Commission draw up an interim bilateral agreement pending a multilateral convention dealing with Arctic pollution and navigation. Indeed it invited Canada to join with the United States and the U.S.S.R. in reaching a world-wide agreement on the breadth of the territorial sea, rights of passage in international straits, and the fishing rights of coastal powers. It reiterated its objection to the extension to twelve miles of the territorial sea. Any interference with the freedom of passage through the straits of the Northwest Passage, even those no wider than three miles, was considered intolerable. While the implementation of pollution control to a twelve-mile limit would be considered satisfactory, the enforcement of anti-pollution legislation to a limit of 100 miles was not. But even within such a twelve-mile zone of pollution control the U.S. demanded full freedom of shipping in the case of international straits.

After extensive discussions the Canadians proposed a compromise that would involve the legislation now in the hands of the Cabinet going forward, but with a series of agreements that would help avoid an impasse in the Arctic over anti-pollution legislation. But Ottawa was not successful in gaining U.S. acquiescence to Canadian jurisdictional claims. Official U.S. statements remained adamant in their opposition to the assertion of Canadian jurisdiction beyond the three-mile limit and in particular over the straits of the Northwest Passage.[19]

CONCLUSION

Although a sharp confrontation with the United States could not be avoided over the sovereignty issue 1968-70, some heat went out of the dispute when it became apparent that the oil companies preferred pipelines to tankers for the transportation of Alaskan oil to southern markets. While Arctic marine transportation would definitely increase in the future, the S.S. *Manhattan* trials had revealed serious problems confronting commercial traffic through the Northwest Passage. Therefore no further incident was expected immediately after the acceptance by Parliament of the sovereignty legislation in April 1970, with the accompanying bitter exchanges between the U.S. State Department and the Department of External Affairs.

This left Ottawa with an opportunity to catch its breath. It expected a further U.S. challenge in the North at some point but there appeared to be an agreeable interval in which Ottawa could enlarge and consolidate its claims over northern waters and develop policies to ensure a more effective Canadian presence in the Arctic. At the same time it hoped that the 1968-70 crisis would fade into the background of Canadian-American relations, and that bilateral discussions would help ease Washington into an acceptance of Canada's position — that the waters of the Arctic archipelago are internal waters. By 1972 northern sovereignty, although potentially explosive, was no longer the most divisive issue in Canadian-American relations.

Certainly Washington had won the first round in early 1969 when Ottawa backed off before the U.S. challenge. But it is equally the case that the April 1970 legislation was a blow in Canada's favour. With this step considerable ground was regained in the goal of achieving sovereign control over Arctic waters. Moreover the team of Canadian negotiators who would take up Canadian claims at the United Nations, in particular at the various sessions of the law-of-the-sea conference, was coherent and very ably led. Canada would present a strong hand.

But there was a cloud on the horizon as well. Northern sovereignty was only one of several issues to be taken up at the law-of-the-sea conference. Without a crisis atmosphere in the North, the issues south of 60 that attracted provincial interest, fisheries in particular, would gain primary attention. The security interest represented by northern sovereignty would receive less attention that it deserved. In fact after 1970 capabilities in surveillance and control over northern waters have been seriously neglected. In no other area is recent Canadian foreign and defence policy as weak as in developing appropriate national capabilities to support jurisdictional claims. The North is no exception – the issue of northern sovereignty remains far from settled.

NOTES

[1] Agreement Between Canada and the United States to Govern the Establishment of D.E.W. System on Canadian Territory, *Canadian Treaties Series*, 1955, No. 8.

[2] Only five meetings were held in the years 1965-9. J. Smith, Commissioner of the Yukon, repeatedly stressed the dangers of the prevailing chaos among the thirty departments and agencies with major responsibilities in the North. Treasury Board, in particular, was unimpressed and has proved to be a major stumbling block in attempts to revitalize the Advisory Committee on Northern Development.

[3] Maxwell Cohen, Dean of the Faculty of Law at McGill University, gave his opinion to the House of Commons Standing Committee on Indian Affairs and Northern Development, 18 April 1969, p. 638.

[4] *Ibid.*, pp. 637-8.

[5] Toronto *Globe and Mail*, 18 September 1969.

[6] House of Commons *Debates*, 15 May 1969, p. 8720-1.

[7] House of Commons *Debates*, 15 May 1969, p. 8721.

[8] *Ibid.*

[9] *Ibid.*

[10] *Ibid.*

[11] Note Bruce Thordarson, *Trudeau and Foreign Policy* (Toronto, 1972), pp. 140ff. concerning Trudeau's statements on Canadian defence policy in spring 1969, which outlined sovereignty as a first priority but which defined it very imprecisely.

[12] Trudeau's decision to reduce Canada's military contribution to NATO, announced on 3 April 1969, is certainly consistent with the realization that the national interest was threatened in the North. However the U.S. determination to achieve a 'North American' Arctic is entirely comprehensible given the strategic implications of unimpeded navigation in all possible waters. There is no evidence that Washington's intransigence on the issue of northern sovereignty after April 1969 is related to Canada's NATO decision.

[13] The decision to maintain control of Panarctic Oils was taken in January 1970.

[14] Standing Committee on Indian Affairs and Northern Development, *Report to the House*, 16 December 1969, pp. 1:6-1:7.

[15] *Ibid.*, p. 1:6.

[16] J. A. Beesley, interpreting the Secretary of State for External Affairs' position, described the Arctic Waters Pollution Prevention Legislation as 'a constructive and functional

approach whereby Canada will exercise only the jurisdiction required to achieve this specific and vital purpose of environmental protection', but added 'that Canada has always regarded the waters of the Arctic archipelago as Canadian waters. . . . ' J. A. Beesley, 'Address to the 9th Regional Meeting of the U.S. Society of International Law', Syracuse University, 8 April 1972, p. 9.

[17] *Ibid.*, p. 17. A growing number of articles is appearing on this subject, together with official presentations (particularly by J. A. Beesley). Beesley's preparatory Statement to the London Ditchely Draft Conference (mimeo) in July 1971 presents the tightest formulation of the Canadian position. For U.S. scholars' reactions see (among others) R. B. Bilder, 'The Canadian Arctic Waters Pollution Prevention Act: New Stresses on the Law of the Sea', *Michigan Law Review*, 69, 1970-1; L. Henkin, 'Arctic Anti-Pollution: Does Canada Make or Break International Law?', *American Journal of International Law*, 65, 1971. Note also two important special studies: Claude Forget, 'Pollution and Territorial Sovereignty in the Arctic', ed. Hugh Innis, *International Involvement* (Toronto, 1972). Beesley's Ditchley Conference paper was reprinted in the *Journal of Maritime Law and Commerce*, 3 October 1971.

[18] J. L. Granatstein, 'External Affairs and Defence', *CAR*, 1970, is worth noting in this regard.

[19] The determination to proceed with polar-icebreaker construction is clear evidence of this position.

SOVEREIGNTY AND CANADIAN FOREIGN POLICY: THE NEED FOR ENFORCEMENT CAPABILITY

by R. B. Byers

A sense of national identity slowly appears to be emerging within Canada, but like most things Canadian—in a country fragmented regionally, culturally, linguistically, economically, and socially—the process is painful and at times one step forward seems to require two steps backwards. Nevertheless since the early 1960s there has been a noticeable nationalistic trend within the country, and an articulate cross-section of the attentive public, the civil service, and politicians have advocated policy options that reflect an increased sense of Canadianization. Initially the debate largely revolved around symbolic objectives such as the Canadian flag, but by the end of the decade more substantive issues such as foreign control of the economy assumed greater prominence.

To some extent changes in Canadian foreign policy paralleled the changed domestic environment. It has been argued that Prime Minister Trudeau's perception of the international system, of Canada's role within the system, and of the need to link internal domestic interests with external interests have partially accounted for the increased 'domestication' of the country's foreign policy.[1] At least in terms of declared policy the signals have been clear and unambiguous during the Trudeau era. For example the Prime Minister announced on 3 April 1969, prior to the completion of the foreign-policy review, that 'surveillance of our territory and coast-lines—i.e., the protection of our sovereignty' would be the pre-eminent defence priority.[2] After completion of the review, the underlying basis of *Foreign Policy for Canadians* stated that 'Canada, like other states, must act according to how it perceives its aims and interests. External activities should be directly related to national policies pursued within Canada, and serve the same objectives.'[3] Similarly Mr Sharp's

October 1972 paper on Canadian-American relations recommended policy options to achieve greater Canadian independence: 'we can pursue a comprehensive, long-term strategy to develop and strengthen the Canadian economy and other aspects of our national life, and in the process reduce the present Canadian vulnerability.'[4] In each case the message is the same – Canada's foreign policy must reflect perceived national interests and in the process more emphasis should be placed on objectives to increase national identity and integrity.

While a number of issues could be singled out for analysis, the increased importance of 'sovereignty' since the 1960s serves as an excellent example. Government statements clearly indicate that protection and enhancement of Canadian sovereignty is a policy area that requires more attention than it received in the past. There are a number of interrelated aspects of the sovereignty question, as suggested by the statement in *Foreign Policy for Canadians* that 'safeguarding *Sovereignty and Independence* is largely a matter of protecting Canada's territorial integrity, its constitutional authority, its national identity and freedom of action.'[5] Even though the link between sovereignty and independence is important, this paper focuses specifically on the extent to which the Trudeau administration has taken action to ensure the protection and enhancement of Canadian sovereignty.

Implicit in upgrading the sovereignty theme in *Foreign Policy for Canadians* is the assumption that challenges are not only possible and probable, but also that their frequency will increase in the future. Is this a realistic viewpoint? If so, where, how, and by whom are challenges likely to arise? If there are no threats then a number of conclusions seem to follow: one, that the emphasis is primarily for domestic political purposes and to that extent the general public has been misled; secondly, that the need to allocate resources for the protection of sovereignty is minimal and government departments should not be asked to develop programs for this purpose; and thirdly, that the government should publicly indicate that the sovereignty theme will be downgraded to a more appropriate relationship vis-à-vis other foreign-policy themes.

Fortunately Canada has not been plagued by the fear of external intervention whereby other nation-states directly challenge the sovereignty of Canadian governments. Thus, despite a few minor examples such as de Gaulle's 1967 'vive le Québec libre' speech, external challenges to the constitutional authority of the federal government – in effect a sovereignty threat – are more myth than reality. Similarly internal challenges have been few, and in large measure the federal government over-reacted during the FLQ crisis. The reference in the 1971 Defence White Paper to 'times of confrontation when growing numbers of people appear to be prepared to resort to violence with a view to destroying the democratic process'[6] seemed out of place by 1976. Sovereignty challenges that attack the constitutional authority of the Canadian government will probably remain insignificant and by themselves should not require much attention.

In fact there are only two forms of challenge that need serious consideration. The first could be a direct or indirect challenge where Canadian claims to territory, water, or airspace are disputed; the second where Canadian jurisdiction in establishing regulations and exercising control over the environment, resources, or fisheries is questioned or ignored in areas that affect the country's territorial integrity. In both cases the main geographical areas involved are the Canadian Arctic and waters off the east and west coasts. From 1968 to 1972 Ottawa appeared to be primarily concerned with challenges in the Arctic. Since then the focus has shifted to issues concerning the law of the sea. The latter have greater immediate significance for Canadian jurisdiction over the waters off the east and west coasts than for the Arctic. Yet some of the law-of-the-sea issues also have important implications for the Canadian North, and while they may be settled within the multilateral forum of the Conference on the Law of the Sea, the major issues relating to the Arctic may have to be settled either by unilateral action or through bilateral negotiations. In effect protection of Canadian sovereignty in these two geographical areas has resulted in different approaches and warrants separate discussion.

THE CANADIAN ARCTIC AND UNILATERALISM

To a large degree the Arctic represents the last Canadian frontier. It is a vast hinterland not readily accessible, understood, or appreciated by the large majority of Canadians. Yet the Arctic will have an important bearing on the future development of Canada, and this has become most apparent since the late 1960s. The 1968 oil discoveries near Prudhoe Bay, Alaska, the 1969 and 1970 voyages of the S.S. *Manhattan*, the active exploration for oil and gas in the Mackenzie Delta, the potential development of pipelines, mineral exploration and extraction, as well as expanding air and sea transport all point to the Arctic as a region of immense importance to this country. Yet because of its geographical nature, its isolation, and its native people, significant social, environmental, and political problems may arise as the pace of economic development quickens. Thus the situation in the Arctic has changed considerably since John Diefenbaker's Northern Vision, and as the report of the 1971 Ditchley Foundation Conference, held in the United Kingdom, observed: 'The Arctic has therefore suddenly become one of the focal points for the resolution of problems of industrial development, conservation and pollution which are arousing national and international interest.'[7]

Needless to say, other countries and a number of large multinational enterprises have recognized the importance of the Arctic. As a result challenges to Canadian sovereignty could and have occurred. The countries most likely to be involved are those with geographical links to Canadian territory or waters: that is, the Arctic-rim states such as the Soviet Union, Norway, Denmark, and the United States. In addition states with commercial interests in the North including West Germany, France, and Japan cannot be ignored.

The most serious challenges from other countries have been, and are likely to be mounted by Canada's closest friend and ally — the United States. At the 1971 Ditchley Park conference the Canadian and American delegates disagreed on most major issues vis-à-vis the Arctic, and 1970 Canadian legislation on the Arctic Waters Pollution Prevention Act and amendments to the Territorial Sea and Fishing Zones Act brought immediate protests from the United States State Department and President Nixon. American scholars have discussed some of the areas of disagreement[8] and Professor Colin Gray has claimed that 'the only plausible challenger to the writ of Canadian law in the Arctic is Canada's principal ally, the United States.'[9] Thus Arctic sovereignty constitutes a source of friction in Canadian-American relations. U.S. concerns reflect a mixture of direct self-interest in terms of economic development, transportation, communication, and defence, and a broader apprehension that Canadian unilateral action might be followed by other states and in the process complicate American international interests elsewhere.

Multinational enterprises may or may not operate with the consent of their home governments. But as their role in the world reaches proportions that allow the largest of them to confront nation-states over a wide range of issues, the danger of these enterprises influencing international politics to suit their own ends increases. Certainly in the field of resource development — particularly petroleum and to a lesser extent minerals — the major corporations are in a sufficiently influential, and to some extent independent, position to be of concern to the Canadian government in the Arctic. While it seems remote, Colin Gray has suggested that 'one can well imagine a situation in the late 1970s in which multinational corporations would be the *de facto* sovereign of a portion of one of Canada's Arctic islands. No denial of the legal competence of the Canadian government would be issued, either by the corporation or by interested foreign governments. Canada's sovereign rights would be quite intact. The "joker" would be that the only law actually obeyed by the commercial enterprise would be its own.'[10] This is more likely to be the case if Canadian sovereignty claims are ambiguous.

Unfortunately there is confusion over the extent of Canadian claims, and this has complicated the government's position on the Arctic. For example the late General Charles Foulkes, former Chief of the General Staff, expressed the following opinion to the Standing Committee on

External Affairs and National Defence on 12 February 1969: 'The Canadian claim for ownership of the Arctic islands is still not beyond dispute. I was informed recently that even some of the U.S. maps show the Arctic islands within the Canadian sector as "disputed territory". . . . [T]here is some doubt that Canada can lay claim to all the islands on the grounds of discovery or occupation.'[11] In a statement on 15 May 1969 to the House of Commons the Prime Minister rejected this interpretation:

> Canada's sovereignty over its Arctic regions, including the islands of the Arctic archipelago, is well established and there is no dispute concerning this matter. No country has asserted a competing claim. . . . The government is not aware of any maps allegedly disputing Canadian sovereignty over certain Arctic lands. . . . Canada's sovereign rights over the continental shelf in the Arctic follows from Canada's sovereignty over the adjacent lands, and again there is no dispute on this matter. No country has asserted a competing claim to the resources in question; no country has challenged Canada's claim on any other basis, and none can do so under international law.[12]

However, when referring to the waters of the Arctic archipelago, the government's position was less clear. Here the Prime Minister quoted the 1958 statement of the then Minister of Northern Affairs: 'The area to the north of Canada, including the islands and the water between the islands and areas beyond, are looked upon as our own, and there is no doubt in the minds of this government, nor do I think was there in the minds of former governments of Canada, that this is national terrain.' But instead of reaffirming this claim the Prime Minister's statement weakened the Canadian position by noting that

> . . . not all countries would accept the view that the waters between the islands of the archipelago are internal waters over which Canada has full sovereignty. The contrary view is indeed that Canada's sovereignty extends only to the territorial sea around each island. . . . Such differences, of course, would have to be settled not on an arbitrary basis but with due regard for established principles of international law.

Reaction by opposition spokesmen to this position was less than enthusiastic, and concern over the government's position on Arctic sovereignty was raised in the House of Commons on a number of occasions. In addition, the report to the Commons on 16 December 1969 of the Standing Committee on Indian Affairs and Northern Development expressed the opinion that 'the waters lying between the islands of the Arctic Archipelago have been, and are, subject to Canadian Sovereignty historically, geographically and geologically.'[13] Unfortunately the Trudeau administration rejected pressures to declare complete sovereignty over the

Arctic even though it realized that this geographical area constitutes the one remaining region where Canadian territorial integrity might be directly challenged. However, once the dispute with the United States over the Arctic anti-pollution legislation became public, the Canadian diplomatic note to Washington outlined Canada's claim in more forth-right terms: 'With respect to the waters of the Arctic Archipelago, the position of Canada has always been that these waters are regarded as Canadian. . . . [T]he Canadian Government cannot accept any sugges-tion that Canadian waters should be internationalized.'[14]

According to government spokesmen a major Arctic issue was the heightened concern and awareness of the need to protect the fragile environment. The dangers were aptly expressed by Pierre Trudeau in a Toronto speech on 15 April 1970.

The Arctic ice-pack has been described as the most significant surface area of the globe, for it controls the temperature of much of the Northern Hemisphere. Its continued existence in unspoiled form is vital to all mankind. The single most imminent threat to the Arctic at this time is that of a large oil spill. Not only are the hazards of Arctic navigation much greater than are found elsewhere, making the risk of breakup or sinking one of constant concern, but any maritime tragedy there would have disastrous and irreversible consequences. . . . Involved here, in short, are issues which even the more conservative of environmental scientists do not hesitate to describe as being of a mag-nitude which is capable of affecting the quality, and perhaps the con-tinued existence, of human and animal life in vast regions of North America and elsewhere.[15]

During the early 1970s this theme appeared in the majority of statements and speeches on the Arctic by members of the Trudeau administration. Furthermore it became explicitly linked to the sovereignty theme as the government perceived the need for extensions of existing Canadian law and regulations. Otherwise Canada's ability to exercise sovereignty in the Arctic would be seriously weakened.

In order to protect territorial integrity in the Arctic, Parliament approved the Arctic Waters Pollution Prevention Act and amendments to the Territorial Sea and Fishing Zones Act in 1970. The Arctic legislation provided for the creation of a 100-mile anti-pollution zone and contained provisions for shipping standards within the zone. The geographical region covered the Canadian Arctic islands from the Canada-Alaska boundary to 100 miles into the Beaufort Sea in the west to equi-distant points between Greenland and the Queen Elizabeth Islands in the north-east and for 100 miles into the Davis Strait in the east: i.e., the Arctic islands were in effect circumscribed, where possible, by a 100-mile contiguous control zone over which the Canadian government claimed jurisdiction in order to protect the environment. In introducing the legislation the government disclaimed any desire to extend Canadian sovereignty in the North, and at a press conference on 8 April 1970 the Prime Minister argued that the Arctic legislation 'is not an assertion of sovereignty, it is an exercise of our desire to keep the Arctic free of pollution and by defining one hundred miles as a zone within which we are determined to act, we are indicating that our assertion there is not one aimed towards sovereignty but aimed towards one of the very important aspects of our action in the Arctic.'[16]

Government spokesmen consistently agreed with the view that the Arctic legislation did not constitute a declaration of expanded sovereignty claims.[17] By itself this interpretation may have some validity, but when combined with the amendments to the Territorial Sea Act, which claimed a twelve-mile limit drawn from straight base lines (headland to headland) and the closure of traditional high-seas fishing zones in the Bay of Fundy, Gulf of St Lawrence, and Queen Charlotte Sound to all except the Americans, a somewhat different picture emerges. The practical effect of the twelve-mile limit in the Arctic was to create a Canadian controlled eastern 'gateway' to the Northwest Passage between Young and Lowther Islands in the Barrow Strait. Coupled with a similar western 'gateway' through the Prince of Wales Strait, which existed under the old three-mile limit, Canada could legally control access to the navigable waters of the Arctic archipelago. This was clearly understood by the Prime Minister, as his statement on 17 April 1970 to the House noted: 'Since the 12-mile territorial sea is well established in international law, the effect of this bill on the North-west Passage is that under any sensible view of the law, Barrow Strait, as well as the Prince of Wales Strait, are subject to complete Canadian sovereignty.'[18] Mr J. A. Beesley, then Legal Adviser for the Department of External Affairs, expressed a similar view before the Standing Committee on External Affairs and National Defence: 'In the case of Barrow Strait ... the 12-mile territorial sea has the effect of giving Canada sovereignty from shore to shore. To put it simply, we have undisputed control—undisputed in a legal sense—over two of the gateways to the Northwest Passage.'[19] Understandably the two pieces of legislation raised a host of issues in the sphere of international law, including the right of innocent passage, the status of the waters of the Arctic archipelago, freedom of the seas in the Arctic, the right of functional specialized jurisdiction, custodianship, and acquisitive versus non-acquisitive claims.[20]

Since a number of countries had previously extended their territorial sea to twelve miles the government considered the probability of legal challenges to a Canadian twelve-mile limit fairly remote, but this was not the case with the Arctic pollution legislation. In fact the Arctic legislation broke new ground in international law and constituted an important departure from prevailing legal norms. The Minister for External Affairs, Mitchell Sharp, claimed that the Act 'should be regarded as a stepping-stone toward the elaboration of an international legal order which will protect and preserve this planet Earth for the better use and greater enjoyment of all mankind;'[21] while Colin Gray has observed that it constituted 'a genuinely forward-looking attempt to bring maritime legislation into step with the ecological need and with expert ecological opinion.'[22] As the Arctic legislation was unilaterally attempting to make international law in an area where none existed, and as concerns were expressed that maritime powers could bring challenges before a conservatively orientated International Court of Justice, the government filed a reservation rejecting acceptance of the Court's compulsory jurisdiction. Even though the reservation became a source of criticism both at home and abroad, it constituted a reasonable legal precaution.

As the Arctic legislation was primarily directed, at least in the short run, at the United States and American corporations in the North, the U.S. response, both officially and unofficially, strongly opposed the Canadian initiative. Reactions varied: there were challenges to the authority of the government to legislate, fears that other countries might follow suit, concern that the application of international law would be adversely affected, and claims that the Trudeau administration acted solely out of consideration for Canadian sovereignty. In fact once the U.S. administration became aware of Canadian intentions several rounds of top-level discussions were held between officials of the two countries. And at one point President Nixon phoned the Prime Minister to intervene personally. When it became clear that a compromise would not emerge the U.S. State Department released a diplomatic note that claimed that 'international law provides no basis for these proposed unilateral extensions of jurisdiction on the high seas, and the U.S.A. can neither accept nor acquiesce in the assertion of such jurisdiction.'[23] This in effect constituted a challenge to the right of Canada to undertake unilateral action on this issue, and some American scholars such as Richard Bilder argued in less diplomatic fashion that 'Canada's right to establish regulations aimed at preventing such pollution...remains—less than clear....[W]hile there seems fairly broad international agreement that the waters of the Arctic Ocean itself are "high seas", the status of the various other waters north of the mainland has not been established.'[24] The U.S. was equally perturbed about the possibility that if the Canadian position remained unchallenged then other countries might be encouraged to adopt unilateral measures. Thus the State Department note pointed out that 'we are concerned that this action by Canada if not opposed by us, would be taken as precedent in other parts of the world for other unilateral infringements of the freedom of the seas.'[25] In addition the note urged Canada to submit to compulsory international jurisdiction and to work through multilateral forums. Bilder agreed, but suggested that 'given Canada's enactment of this legislation, its many protestations of commitments to the concept of international measures ring somewhat hollow. Unless Canada is prepared to rescind or limit its far-reaching legislation, there seems comparatively little left for an international conference to negotiate.'[26] Furthermore V. P. Nanada of the Denver College of Law claimed that 'Canada's unilateral action would perhaps not be conducive to creating international law. Past trends show that efforts at creating international law of the sea by unilateral action have not been fruitful. The hazard of creeping jurisdiction and expansionism on the part of other countries is real and grave.'[27]

Americans perceived that sovereignty and independence issues accounted for Canada's unilateral action, as the Arctic Waters Pollution Prevention Act was 'related to mounting domestic pressures for assertion of Canada's national identity in the face of continuing trends towards political, economic, and cultural dominance by the United States.'[28] Leigh Ratiner of the U.S. Defense Department shared the opinion that the Trudeau government bowed to 'the groundswell of popular sentiment underlying Canadian claims of sovereignty over the entire Arctic,' while American businessman E. Hayes, in distorting the content of the legislation, observed that "Grab" is not a very nice word, but it is difficult to find another that is equally descriptive of an assertion of sovereignty in the ocean a hundred miles from the base line.'[29]

In light of these views official Canadian statements concerning the intent of the legislation need to be treated cautiously. Taken together the overall thrust of the two pieces of legislation appears congruent with the declared desire to upgrade the sovereignty theme, particularly with respect to protecting territorial integrity. Even though the legislative bills were intended to operate in different jurisdictional spheres, they share underlying sovereignty objectives and should be viewed from this perspective.

With time American protests over unilateral action in the Arctic, both official and non-governmental, became less vociferous. As the heated debate of 1970-71 between Canada and the United States faded into the background the Trudeau administration conveyed the impression that problems relating to territorial integrity in the North had been resolved. In effect Arctic issues that could bear on Canadian-American relations, other than the Mackenzie Valley pipeline, assumed only minimal importance in Ottawa. Nevertheless the U.S. government has remained opposed to the Arctic Waters Pollution Prevention Act, and Washington has maintained pressure on Ottawa officials to rescind or modify the 1970 legislation. Thus the government should expect future challenges to Canadian Arctic sovereignty and more than legislation may be required to protect Canadian interests.

LAW OF THE SEA AND MULTILATERALISM

The unilateralism of the Canadian approach to Arctic sovereignty can be contrasted with the multilateralism adopted in negotiations relating to most law-of-the-sea issues. Even though successive Canadian governments have resorted to unilateral action and bilateral agreements in order to protect Canadian interests, particularly in the fishing industry, a willingness to employ multilateral forums has been the norm. The Intergovernmental Marine Consultative Organization has provided a forum for the negotiation of marine pollution standards, while the International Commission of the Northwest Atlantic Fishery has attempted to establish fishing quotas and regulations. More importantly Canada has actively participated in the Third United Nations Conference on Law of the Sea, which has addressed itself to the establishment of revised law-of-the-sea regimes in such areas as the breadth of the territorial sea, freedom of navigation, and marine pollution, as well as the management and distribution of the world's ocean resources. To date two rounds of discussions have been completed — the first in Caracas during the summer of 1974 and the second in Geneva during the spring of 1975. A third, and hopefully final, round has been scheduled for New York during the spring of 1976.

The outcome of the Third Conference on the Law of the Sea will have a profound impact on the future use of the 70 per cent of the earth that is ocean space, and a law-of-the-sea package is essential in order to avoid chaos. Current legal regimes are based on the 300-year-old principles of state sovereignty and freedom of the seas, but over the last two decades unilateral action has indicated the need for revised regimes. While the first conference on the Law of the Sea in 1958 reached agreement on the exploitation and exploration of the continental shelf, no agreement emerged on limits to the territorial sea and establishment of exclusive fishing zones. The same situation arose during the second conference on the Law of the Sea in 1960 as the traditional views of the maritime powers prevailed. However by 1974 nearly sixty countries had proclaimed a twelve-mile territorial sea and exclusive fishing zones — in some cases out to 200 miles. In addition, the danger of depletion of the living resources of the sea had become a reality. These factors, along with the 1970 United Nations declaration that the resources of the seabed belong to the common heritage of mankind, emphasized the need for change.

Needless to say Canada has an important stake in the outcome of the current negotiations and considerable diplomatic and political energy has gone into efforts to protect Canadian interests. The government presented a position paper to the Standing Committee on External Affairs and National Defence on 6 November 1973 that called for 'a radical modification of the law of the sea to take into account present-day political, economic and technological realities.'[30] This reflected the perceived inter-est and needs of a coastal state, and constituted a departure from earlier policies that often agreed with the interests of the major maritime states. Since Canada has one of the world's longest coastlines, an extensive continental margin off the east coast, an environmentally fragile Arctic, an active fishing industry, and relies on foreign shipping for transporta-tion of overseas exports, the interest shown by the government in the law of the sea seemed justified.

The November 1973 paper to the Standing Committee on External Affairs and National Defence spelled out Canada's view on the six major issues that have been discussed at the Third Conference on the Law of the Sea—living resources of the sea, mineral resources, navigation, scien-tific research, protection of the environment, and jurisdiction over the seabed.[31] In general the conceptual framework adopted was functional: 'Canada has not sought to assert total sovereignty over wide areas of the marine environment but instead has pursued a functional approach whereby no more jurisdiction would be exercised than would be required to protect its specific interests.' With regard to living resources Canada should be permitted 'to claim (a) *exclusive sovereign rights* in the manage-ment and harvest of all living resources within 200 miles off its coast, as well as (b) *preferential rights* in respect of such resources in areas adjacent to this zone', that is, to the edge of the continental margin. In addition, a species approach meant that coastal states should maintain exclusive rights over sedentary species such as crabs; obtain exclusive management and conservation rights, as well as preferential harvest rights, over coastal species; obtain exclusive management and harvesting rights over anad-romous species such as salmon, and establish international arrangements for wide-ranging species such as tuna and whales. For non-living resources the government favoured retention of the 1958 convention adopted at the First Conference on the Law of the Sea: that is, for mineral and hydrocarbon exploitation Canada 'claims and exercises rights over the whole of the continental margin comprising not only the physical continental shelf but the continental slope and rise as well.'

Not surprisingly the government urged acceptance of a twelve-mile territorial sea, but supported the maritime powers on passage through international straits. However Canada argued that the Northwest Passage was not an international strait for navigation purposes and should be exempted. The navigation issue was considered to be closely linked with the protection of the environment, as coastal and strait states should insist on the control of anti-pollution standards. According to the government paper 'coastal states should be empowered to prescribe and enforce their own anti-pollution standards, to the extent necessary, over and above the internationally agreed rules, not only in their territorial waters but also within the areas of jurisdiction beyond.' In the area of marine scientific research arbitrary restrictions should be avoided and knowledge should be shared, but 'coastal states should have the right to control and, where necessary, disallow such activities by foreign states or their nationals.' Finally the mineral resources of the seabed should be considered the common heritage of mankind and shared by all countries in the world.

For the most part the Canadian position reflected a strongly nationalistic view, and in those cases where domestic interests tended to conflict with the common-heritage principle the former prevailed. In fact the functional approach allowed the government to make more extensive jurisdictional claims in those areas deemed most important than would have been possible with a 200-mile economic zone. For example Canada claimed fisheries management and control over some species beyond a 200-mile zone, and claimed exclusive harvest rights for salmon regardless of ocean space. Similarly the claim to non-living resources to the edge of the continental margin exceeded a 200-mile zone by 400 miles in some cases. Since approximately 80 per cent of the known resources are located within 200 miles off shore, the Canadian position left precious little to be allocated under the common-heritage rubric. In light of the desperate plight of many third-world countries and the ever-widening economic gap between developed and developing states, the initial Canadian position seemed excessively acquisitive.

The government's position rather shrewdly anticipated the response of interested parties within Canada, but a number of objections emerged in testimony before the Standing Committee on External Affairs and National Defence.[32] The 12 March 1974 statement by the Fisheries Council of Canada supported the position on anadromous species, but also urged fishery jurisdiction to the edge of the continental margin. Mr Alex Hichman, Newfoundland's Justice Minister, in presenting a brief on 3 May 1974 rejected the species approach in favour of exclusive management and fishing rights to the edge of the continental margin or for 200 miles, whichever was greater, as 'efforts on the east coast of Canada to protect the eastern Canadian fishermen at this time, are . . . abysmal to say the least.' The brief of the Pacific Trollers' Association agreed that a 200-mile fishing zone 'is not going to protect all of shelf related resources on either coast,' even though the statement made on 12 March 1974 noted that it would 'force fishermen of all nations to harvest the resources in such a management zone in an orderly manner.' With the rather sad economic and technological state of the Canadian fishing industry, compared to major fishing nations, these arguments received a sympathetic hearing.

The petroleum, mining, and shipping interests also made presentations to the parliamentary committee. The 23 April 1974 Imperial Oil brief agreed with the stated government objectives, but the company found 'it difficult to obtain a feeling for the Canadian Government's priorities.

There is no doubt in our minds that Canada must establish its priorities and be prepared to give way on certain lesser ones in order to gain those of prime importance.' Needless to say Imperial Oil recommended that priority be given to extending coastal-state jurisdiction to the edge of the continental margin beyond 200 miles. The Noranda Mines brief recommended an international transitional arrangement for the research and development of seabed resources as their statement on 25 February 1974 argued: 'the control of the marketing of metals in any way, would result in an international, world-wide cartel and must be avoided. This would depress the market on metals obtained from land resources.' The Canadian Chamber of Shipping brief of 20 March 1974 expressed concern about 'restrictive measures being developed at the Conference to the detriment of Canada's extensive export and import seaborne trade.' The brief strongly supported retention of the right of innocent passage in territorial waters as well as the traditional freedom of the high seas. This corresponded with Ottawa's view, but the proposal that 'flag state' jurisdiction could most effectively ensure environmental protection for coastal states ran counter to government opinion, as countries that register vessels have not always insisted that strict standards be maintained. If nothing else, the briefs to the Standing Committee on External Affairs and National Defence reflected the varying, and in some cases conflicting priorities of domestic interests.

Canadian officials realized that the law-of-the-sea negotiations would be complicated and lengthy. Any initial optimism for an early international agreement quickly dissipated during the Caracas discussions as the 138 countries coalesced into different groups. The more than one hundred developing countries used the loosely co-ordinated 'Group of 77' as a forum for negotiating a common position. In addition African, Latin American, western European, and eastern European states occasionally met as geographical groupings. Cutting across these regional lines was a group of some fifty landlocked and shelflocked states, a group of maritime powers, and the coastal-state group. Along with such countries as Australia, Norway, Britain, India, Chile, and Mexico, Canada fell into this latter category. In terms of specific issues many coastal states shared views somewhat similar to Canada's; major maritime states tended to resist encroachment on the principles of freedom of the seas and more specifically on passage through international straits; and shelflocked states advocated narrow areas of national jurisdiction. Underlying these diverse interests, differing views by the developed and developing states over the common-heritage component of law of the sea generated further disagreements.

Some delegates left Caracas with a sense of frustration with the rate of progress as headway varied in each of the three main working committees. Committee I, charged with drafting articles regarding the international seabed area, focused almost exclusively on principles relating to the exploration and exploitation of resources. A major source of disagreement emerged as the developed countries advocated that exploitation be left to states and corporations, that the regulatory powers of any International Seabed Authority be limited, and that there be no interference with production or price controls; while the developing countries argued for an authority to exploit the seabed area with wide discretionary powers including production controls. Committee II dealt with the more traditional law-of-the-sea issues such as the territorial sea, fisheries, the continental shelf, and navigation. According to P. A. Lapointe, the Alternate Deputy Representative on the Canadian delegation, the committee made 'great strides toward a general accommodation'[33] as the majority of states, including the United States and the Soviet Union, accepted in principle a twelve-mile territorial sea with a further 188-mile economic zone. However the major maritime powers, particularly the United States, continued to demand the right of free transit through international straits. Issues related to the protection of the environment, scientific research, and the transfer of technology fell within the purview of Committee III. Despite some progress the controversial issues of coastal-state versus flag-state jurisdiction, warship immunity, dispute procedures including compensation and intervention rights remained unsettled. Thus while Mr Lapointe observed that the conference 'succeeded in making progress on a number of basic issues and in identifying more clearly the parameters of the eventual solution',[34] considerable compromises would be required.

To some extent the Geneva session from 17 March to 10 May 1975 provided the necessary forum for compromises to emerge as delegates accepted in principle a three-tier concept: that is, a 200-mile economic zone; an area beyond for the common heritage of mankind; and the management, use, and preservation of ocean space. Coupled with the 200-mile economic zone was general acceptance of a twelve-mile territorial sea. While conflicting interests remain just below the surface of the discussions, each of the three main committees presented informal single negotiating texts that could be considered at the March 1976 meetings. While the three unified texts could be substantially modified or even rejected at New York, they carry considerable moral weight and could represent the framework for a comprehensive law-of-the-sea package.

The Geneva texts indicate that most of the major Canadian objectives initially outlined in the November 1973 position paper have been incorporated into the working documents for the New York meetings. However problems remain in a number of controversial areas. First the texts reject the view that individual states can establish, within the 200-mile economic zone, pollution standards higher than internationally approved standards. This represents a setback for Canada, except that geographical regions that encompass severe climatic conditions or where marine pollution could cause major ecological damage are exempt. This amounts to *ex post facto* recognition of the Arctic Waters Pollution Prevention Act and seems to justify Canada's unilateral action in 1970. Second, non-living resources beyond the 200-mile economic zone fall within the common-heritage rubric, but provision exists for some form of revenue-sharing arrangement. In all probability Canada will have to settle for this compromise as the majority of participating states will not agree to complete Canadian control over mineral resources to the edge of the continental margin where it exceeds 200 miles. Third, and most significantly, exclusive state-fishery resources are limited to the economic zone, even though special provisions may be agreed upon for salmon. In effect this represents the most Canada can hope to attain, but less than that demanded by the Canadian fishing industry. Yet on balance the government's chief negotiator, J. A. Beesley of the Department of External Affairs, correctly observed that 'Canada has a lot to be happy about.'[35]

Considering the complexities of the issue, plus the wide range of competing and diverse international interests, the Caracas and Geneva sessions of the Third Conference on the Law of the Sea made sufficient progress to justify Canada's multilateral approach. In fact it was not uncommon for the delegates of other countries to comment that Canada's position seemed to be unnecessarily acquisitive, and some observers went so far as to classify the Canadian position as being excessively greedy. Should the conference fail, however, the government will be forced to take unilateral action, and ministerial statements held open this option. For example at the close of the Caracas conference the Minister of Economic Expansion, Donald Jamieson, stated that from Canada's perspective 'it makes far more sense to get international agreement than take unilateral decision(s) which may not be as beneficial in the long run.'[36] Yet in a speech on 12 December 1974 at St John's the Minister observed that Canada might have to declare a 200-mile sovereignty zone: 'obviously a unilateral solution is an option that can't be rejected forever. It would have to be considered if future circumstances warranted it.'[37] During the spring and fall of 1975 ministers continued to advocate a multilateral approach, but increasingly referred to possible unilateral measures. In part the government intended to pressure recalcitrant states into accepting the Canadian position and at the same time mollify Canadian fishing interests. The latter demanded that immediate steps be taken to protect their industry in the face of diminishing returns. Not surprisingly Mr MacEachen warned during a press conference in Geneva that 'we are not ruling out unilateral action before completion of the total process of sea law.... That still remains an option – probably a more lively option than at the end of Caracas.'[38] Despite this possibility the main thrust of the Canadian position remains an attempt to reach agreement multilaterally with a comprehensive law-of-the-sea treaty and thus government action in this sphere contrasts rather sharply with the approach adopted in the Arctic.

APPROACHES TO SOVEREIGNTY AND CONTROL CAPABILITIES

While unilateralism and multilateralism represent contrasting approaches for the protection of Canadian sovereignty, linkages between the two exist. This is particularly true in areas encompassing international law, which is often based on some form of unilateral state action that then becomes the accepted norm. Protestations to the contrary, unilateralism may be required in order to change the basis of international law or to stress the need for negotiations within multilateral forums. From this perspective Gotlieb and Dalfen argue that 'in the last analysis, national jurisdiction and international responsibility pose no dichotomy between them, but, rather two elements in a more complete and appropriate response.'[39] This may be correct, but why is unilateralism employed in one instance and multilateralism in another, and what rationale is there for the adoption of either approach?

According to Canadian government spokesmen unilateralism in the Arctic and on the twelve-mile limit was the only approach possible to meet an immediate problem, because the world community, and more specifically the United States, did not agree with the Canadian position. For example, in response to the U.S. State Department's note of April 1970, the government pointed out that 'Canada takes second place to no nation in pressing for multilateral solutions to problems of international law.... The Canadian Government has long been concerned about the inadequacies of international law in failing to give the necessary protection to the marine environment and to ensure the conservation of fisheries resources.'[40] But because of the inability to reach satisfactory multilateral solutions and because of the inadequacy of existing international law, unilateral measures were deemed necessary. Mr L. LeGault of Exernal Affairs summed up this view as follows: 'Canada cannot abdicate its responsibility for the protection of its territory, and Canada cannot wait for the slow and difficult development of international law to afford that situation. Canada moreover has thoroughly tested the climate for international action against marine pollution ... and has found it seriously wanting.'[41] Despite American claims to the contrary, government spokesmen were on firm ground in arguing that attempts to reach multilateral agreement on issues relating to Canadian territorial integrity had been unsuccessful. One need only turn to the inability of the First and Second Law-of-the-Sea Conferences to reach accord on the breadth of the territorial sea and the breadth of contiguous zones for limited jurisdiction, and to the 1969 Brussels Intergovernmental Marine Consultative Organization Conference, which refused to adopt preventative as distinct from remedial and liability measures on marine pollution, to appreciate the Canadian viewpoint.

In addition several other factors should be taken into account. In the case of the Arctic Waters Pollution Prevention Act officials stressed the uniqueness of the geographical area and the need to extend the boundaries of existing international law to meet changed circumstances. Without unilateral action the probability of altering marine-pollution law seemed less likely and the Geneva text on the law of the sea showed this to be the case. The extension of the territorial sea to twelve miles clearly dovetailed with the pollution legislation and, in many respects, had the same effect as a more extensive sovereignty claim. However there was also the need to help protect a beleaguered fishing industry, and the application of baselines on the headland-to-headland principle made a considerable difference.[42]

The multilateral approach to law of the sea can be partially explained by the fact that it encompasses a much wider range of issues than the functionally more specific action taken in the Arctic, and unilateral action would lead to a breakdown in negotiations as well as the possibility of increased anarchy in the ocean space. Since Canada is in a minority with respect to its extensive claims on fisheries and the continental margin, an international accord would protect the Canadian claim in a situation where the major fishing states such as Japan, the Soviet Union, Portugal, France, Spain, as well as the states with commercial interests such as the United States and West Germany, would probably defy unilateral claims. That is, the stakes are higher for law-of-the-sea issues, at least in the short run, with a greater number of potential transgressors than in the Arctic.

Another factor influencing the government's law-of-the-sea approach has been differences in the American and Canadian positions. Both countries support the right of coastal states to manage living resources within the 200-mile economic zone and both agree on exploitation of mineral resources on the continental shelf. On the question of scientific research within the economic zone, however, the United States advocates complete freedom for research vessels while Canada would require coastal-state consent. No agreement exists on the powers of an International Seabed Authority, as the United States argues that exploitation should be left to individual states while Canada believes the Authority should engage in exploitation. On pollution matters Canada feels that the coastal state should establish standards to protect its marine environment, while the American position states that this should be left under flag-state jurisdiction. Most significantly the United States strongly urges the right of innocent passage through international straits because its military and security considerations are paramount. Canada understands the American viewpoint, but in addition to rejecting the U.S. view that the Northwest

Passage is an international strait, argues that the coastal state has the right to protect its environment.[43] Consequently unilateral action could result in the United States directly challenging Canadian sovereignty on a wide range of law-of-the-sea issues. The other alternative would be for Canada to modify its position and negotiate special arrangements with Washington, but this option should only be pursued if the Third Conference on the Law of the Sea fails.

In the final analysis the viability of unilateral versus multilateral measures must be assessed with considerable care. The advantages of pursuing objectives via multilateral forums seems to be at least three-fold: agreements are more likely to be accepted by the international community; they are more likely to last; and there is normally less need for enforcement and control mechanisms. Yet the disadvantages, as reflected in law-of-the-sea issues such as the need to compromise on principle and substance, as well as the lengthy negotiating process, often make unilateral measures appear more attractive. The Arctic Waters Pollution Prevention Act and Territorial Sea legislation of 1970 suggested that the unilateral approach enables the nation-state to act on important measures of principle and substance; involves no lengthy negotiations even though international consultation is generally advisable; and allows for prompt and specific solutions. However, balanced against this is the possibility that members of the international community will object and directly challenge unilateral measures. In addition the image of the nation-state within the international system can be damaged; and finally unilateralism requires greater enforcement and control mechanisms. On balance unilateralism seemed appropriate in the Arctic case, just as multilateralism seems most appropriate with respect to law of the sea. However in both cases the real shortcomings are related to the lack of adequate enforcement capabilities.

The Trudeau administration has tended to adopt unilateral measures in those areas, especially the Arctic, where the capability of other nation-states to challenge the Canadian position is not that apparent, at least in the short run. At the same time sufficient resources have not been allocated to ensure in the long run that Canada will be able to exercise adequate control in those areas where sovereignty claims have been made. For example it would seem that the lack of means to enforce claims is an important factor inhibiting unilateral action on law-of-the-sea issues. Mr. Jamieson's St John's speech noted that 'there are also practical reasons to doubt the effectiveness of unilateral action at this time. . . . [W]e would find it extremely difficult and enormously costly to enforce a unilateral declaration against countries that might very well decide they had no choice but to challenge Canada's action.'[44] This is absolutely correct, but even with an internationally agreed upon law-of-the-sea treaty, Canada lacks the means to exercise control over a 200-mile economic zone. On 20 November 1974 Conservative M.P. Donald Munro argued in the House of Commons that Canada lacks an adequate enforcement capability: 'Nothing in the budget suggests that we shall acquire that capability.... Canada's coast guard is inadequate even for patrolling and enforcing jurisdiction over our existing territorial waters.'[45] Multilateralism may reduce the level of required capabilities, but such capabilities are still needed and to date no long-range program has been announced by the government to cope with this shortcoming.

In some respects the Arctic represents the more acute case for control mechanisms. Unfortunately the Trudeau administration has conveyed the impression that sovereignty challenges in the North have been resolved by the 1970 legislation and consequently a future enforcement capability can be minimized. Cabinet ministers and senior officials in External Affairs and National Defence hold the view that no immediate security threat exists in the Canadian Arctic and that the economic viability of the region is not fully known. Based on these premises it is not considered necessary to allocate financial resources to augment the existing inadequate presence in the North. This line of reasoning should be seriously disputed: any other country in the world that claimed as extensive a geographical region as the Canadian Arctic would automatically declare such a region a security zone and attempt to exercise adequate surveillance and control. Politicians and officials realize that if challenges arise and/or if commercial quantities of hydrocarbon resources are located it will take several years to augment existing control capabilities. Yet no action of substance seems to be contemplated and the present deficiencies increase the probability of challenges to Canadian jurisdiction.

The Department of National Defence has been given the explicit task of exercising surveillance and control; *Defence in the 70s* ranked 'the protection of our sovereignty' as the first defence priority. Yet the dilemma faced by the Armed Forces can be readily understood by the references in the White Paper to the lack of capability in the North: 'surveillance over Arctic lands and waters can be carried out by long-range patrol aircraft but at present is limited by light and weather conditions. Surveillance by ships is restricted to ice-free periods of the year. Because of the areas involved, general ground surveillance by land forces is not practicable.' Similarly, 'Canada...has only very limited capability to detect submarine activity in the Arctic. It might be desirable in the future to raise the level of capability so as to have subsurface perimeter surveillance, particularly to cover the channels connecting the Arctic Ocean to Baffin Bay and Baffin Bay to the Atlantic.' Or again: 'the present naval ships cannot operate safely in ice-covered waters, or above 65° N latitude at any time of the year.'[46] During the early 1970s the Defence Department appeared to place greater emphasis on protecting northern sovereignty by increasing Argus flights over the Arctic regions, by deploying naval vessels in northern waters during the summer months to a greater extent than in the past, by establishing a Northern Region Headquarters at Yellowknife, and by placing more emphasis on ground training under Arctic conditions.

Not surprisingly the Defence Department lacks the proper equipment to implement existing defence priorities adequately. With the budgetary crisis of late 1974 Arctic surveillance was downgraded, and Defence Minister Richardson temporarily cancelled the Argus flights in the North. This suggests that the Minister is willing to pay lipservice to the priorities in the 1971 White Paper, but since sovereignty tasks are considered quasi-military they are deemed of secondary importance when compared to the more traditional military functions such as NATO and NORAD. Neither Mr Richardson nor most of his senior officials express any real desire to reallocate existing resources to meet the declared priorities, and thus Canada's military presence in the North is downgraded in the face of financial difficulties.

Ideally Canada should acquire a surface and sub-surface military capability in the North, but this would involve the acquisition of at least two nuclear submarines and some form of fixed-bottom surveillance and identification system to cover the appropriate channels and entrances to the Arctic. One can appreciate why such options are controversial in view of the high cost and Ottawa's belief that a military threat will not materialize. As an alternative some officials argue that a satellite system would suffice, but such a system could not replace the actual physical presence required should intrusions occur. This became clear in late summer 1975 when, without permission and undetected, a Polish schooner sailed some 350 miles into Arctic waters. The Defence Department was unable to maintain contact with the vessel to ensure that it was leaving Canadian territorial waters after it had been requested to do so. This example tended to reinforce the need to replace the Argus maritime-patrol aircraft. In fact there should be at least one operational air unit located in the Arctic for surveillance and control as well as for search-and-rescue purposes.

Even if Ottawa continues to reject the requirement for a continuing military presence in the North, and a headquarters unit does not meet the need, the same arguments hardly apply when it comes to a non-military presence. At a minimum an expanded icebreaker fleet is essential to ensure the enforcement of the Arctic legislation, and to date there have been few indications that the government is willing to move in this direction. Even though the Canadian Coast Guard has five major icebreakers, none were specifically designed for winter operations in the Arctic and the difficulties with ice conditions encountered by the C.C.G.S. *Macdonald*, which accompanied the S.S. *Manhattan*, pointed out the limitations of deploying underpowered icebreakers in the North. As in other areas involving the allocation of resources for the purposes of safeguarding sovereignty, there does not appear to be sufficient understanding of the need for Arctic icebreakers. For example the Maritime Sub-committee of the Standing Committee on External Affairs and the National Defence argued in its 1970 Report that 'some additional capability is needed only if maritime surface transport of oil proves to be technically and commercially attractive.'[47] A more realistic opinion has been expressed by Captain T. C. Pullen, R.C.N. (Retd), who questions whether Canada is capable of implementing and enforcing the 1970 legislation, and also argues that if it does not expand the icebreaker fleet Canada will be abdicating its maritime responsibilities.[48] It should also be remembered that once the American *Polar Star* icebreaker program is completed the United States will have the means to support operations in the North and could challenge Canadian legislation and regulations.

Unfortunately the government's record with respect to fisheries protection is also deficient. It would appear that the Fisheries Service of the Department of the Environment, with a total fleet of some eighty-two fisheries-protection vessels, had an enforcement capability prior to the 1970 Territorial Sea legislation. Yet the 1970 Maritime Report of the Standing Committee on External Affairs and National Defence noted that of the vessels located in the Atlantic region eighteen are designated for inshore patrol, seven for inshore and intermediate patrol, including the new twelve-mile limit, and two special-class vessels for the twelve-mile limit. Of a more serious nature, however, was the observation that 'only the two offshore special class vessels had the capability of enforcing the new offshore closing lines.'[49] All told, according to one observer, only six of the patrol vessels can remain at sea for any length of time and these vessels must operate off both coasts. The Standing Committee on External Affairs and National Defence Report certainly indicates that an augmented fleet is required to patrol the twelve-mile territorial sea, to say nothing of a 200-mile economic zone. To help overcome the obvious shortcomings the Defence Department in December 1974 designated the twelve destroyers stationed in Halifax as fisheries-protection vessels. This was the only possible short-run solution and clearly increased Canada's surveillance capability. Yet using 4,000-ton destroyers with crews of 250 is not an effective measure because of their high operating costs, and Canada should not be in a position where it is forced to employ such vessels for fishing-patrol purposes. The action taken in December 1974 indicates that the enforcement deficiencies are obvious to Ottawa. This, in part, accounts for the reluctance of the government to adopt unilateral measures, and one can appreciate the warnings by cabinet ministers concerning a lack of control capabilities should a 200-mile economic zone be adopted. However it is hard to understand why no action has been undertaken to rectify the situation. As of the summer of 1975 no long-term equipment program had been announced to ensure the protection of Canadian fishing interests.

The current difficulties in effectively enforcing the regulations of the International Commission on Northwest Atlantic Fisheries are a portent for the future.[50] For the past several years there has been a continuing problem with foreign vessels, particularly Soviet vessels, exceeding Commission quotas in international waters. During 1974 the unwillingness of Soviet officials to supervise fishing quotas led to the decision to designate the naval destroyers as patrol vessels. Even so, over-fishing has continued and on 28 July 1975 east-coast ports were temporarily closed to Soviet fleets, but were reopened in early September when agreement in principle to resolve the dispute was reached with the Soviet Union. During this period Ottawa was also actively engaged in bilateral fishing negotiations with Spain, Portugal, Norway, and Poland. At the special meeting of the International Commission on Northwest Atlantic Fisheries in Montreal on 22-8 September 1975, the Canadian view prevailed as most officials realized that quotas had to be reduced in order to ensure the future of the fishing stock. This contrasted with the regular spring session in Edinburgh where Canada's request for a 40 per cent reduction, with preferential Canadian quotas, was rejected. By the end of 1975 Canada's diplomatic activity and negotiations in the fisheries sphere appeared to be producing a number of constructive results.

However it should not be assumed that a 200-mile economic zone can be solely protected by bilateral agreements or by multilateral treaties either within the Commission framework or via a law-of-the-sea treaty. A real danger exists that Ottawa will complacently assume that only a limited enforcement capability is required once agreements have been negotiated. In fact just the opposite argument can be made — that preferential Canadian quotas must be protected by means of enhanced maritime-patrol capabilities. It would appear that the Trudeau administration often correctly perceives the need for concrete action but then claims that declared objectives or diplomatic agreements constitute a sufficient response. The need for means to implement and enforce agreements seems to be consistently forgotten once the diplomatic negotiations have been completed.

Enforcement capabilities are further handicapped by competing spheres of jurisdiction within the Canadian governmental structure. The Defence Department, with its Argus and Tracker patrol aircraft and destroyers, has been given the task of protecting Canadian sovereignty but considers this to be of secondary importance. The Canadian Coast Guard Service within the Ministry of Transport is responsible for ice-breaking, but officials argue that an Arctic capability is too expensive and less crucial than icebreaking on the St Lawrence and Great Lakes. The Department of the Environment has jurisdiction for fisheries protection, but has not allocated sufficient resources to develop an ocean-going patrol fleet. The Department of the Solicitor General through the RCMP Marine Services also has responsibility for marine operations. Overlap and duplication is obvious, but interdepartmental committees have been unable to rationalize the marine components of the four major departments involved. From all appearances the Cabinet has been unwilling to intervene directly even though in early 1975 the Treasury Board set up an Interdepartmental Task Force to define sovereignty priorities and work out cost estimates for sovereignty purposes. Despite such activity, it is unlikely that organizational changes will result, and the prospect of integrating the four maritime services remains meagre. Until some form of integration is realized the effectiveness of Canada's enforcement capability will remain deficient.

BRIDGING THE GAP

The Trudeau administration realized that sovereignty issues could not be ignored and recognized that policies would have to be developed to meet challenges to Canadian sovereignty. In the case of the Arctic, unilateralism turned out to be the most appropriate approach, while on law-of-the-sea issues the benefits of multilateralism seem to outweigh unilateral action. While there are some grounds for basing Canadian policy on exclusive sovereignty claims, the functional approach for the Arctic and for the law of the sea seems suited to the variegated sovereignty demands being put forward. In a number of important respects the functional approach has allowed the government to make more extensive claims, particularly in the law-of-the-sea area, than would a statement of exclusive sovereignty. While there may be reasonable grounds to criticize the government for its 'gradualist' rather than 'activist' approach, the general thrust of stated objectives is in the right direction.[51]

However the sovereignty theme has had a somewhat disconcerting effect on Canadian-American relations. Even though the sharp public exchanges of the early 1970s are no longer heard, and the U.S. position on the law of the sea increasingly reflects important Canadian viewpoints — a twelve-mile limit and a 200-mile economic zone — there are still a number of bilateral differences. Washington disagrees with Canada's Arctic policy and has expressed a desire to negotiate changes in the Arctic Waters Pollution Prevention Act. Differences also exist on some law-of-the-sea issues such as anti-pollution measures and the Seabed Authority. A number of these bilateral disagreements will be difficult to solve and more will arise in the future. Thus it should be realized that the majority of prospective challenges to Canadian sovereignty will be initiated either by the U.S. government or by U.S. multinational enterprises. To acknowledge this possibility need not be considered anti-American. Unfortunately there appears to be some reluctance within Ottawa to accept this viewpoint, but relying upon the reservoir of friendly relations with our neighbour to the south is not a realistic approach for resolving future disputes. In addition there are bound to be continuing challenges from other countries when a 200-mile economic zone is finally adopted.

Whether a unilateral or a multilateral approach is adopted the same central problem remains: the need to bridge the gap between declared objectives on the one hand and enforcement capabilities on the other. Here the record of the Trudeau administration has been dismal, as the government gives the impression that diplomatic agreements will be observed. This may be the norm and multilateral arrangements may be more desirable, but Canada must acquire the means to support its jurisdiction with respect to sovereignty issues. To this end the following programs and recommendations, in descending order of priority, should be seriously contemplated.

1. The reorganization and integration of the four marine services responsible for maritime surveillance and control. One department should be assigned exclusive responsibility, because the required resources and manpower are generally downgraded when placed alongside other functions assigned to Defence, Transport, Environment, and the Solicitor General.

2. An augmented surface-patrol fleet for enforcing fishery and pollution regulations to cover a 200-mile economic zone. The fleet size would have to be determined in relation to the coverage desired, but at least twenty seagoing-patrol vessels of sufficient size and speed to cope with modern fishing trawlers would be the minimum. This program should be commenced immediately in light of the lead time required for the first vessels to become operational.

3. An increased air-surveillance capability for the Arctic and both coasts. The long-range maritime-patrol aircraft program should cover this need, providing a sufficient number of aircraft are purchased to perform this task in conjunction with other designated military functions such as anti-submarine warfare.[52] A medium-range patrol aircraft, such as the de Havilland Dash 7, could be employed if a northern air base is authorized.

4. The immediate development of an Arctic icebreaker program along the lines suggested by the last chapter in this volume, including at least two class-7 vessels that would be able to operate in the North for at least eight months of the year. With a minimum seven-year lead time needed for developing these vessels, immediate approval for such an icebreaker program is essential. Feasibility studies should also be undertaken for a possible class-10 icebreaker that could operate year round in the Arctic.[53]

6. For the post-1985 period there will probably be a need for a fixed-bottom surveillance system in Hudson Strait, Lancaster Sound, Prince of

Wales Strait, and probably M'Clure Strait. This function could be partially performed by orbiting satellites, but if commercial submarines are developed for Arctic transport the fixed-bottom system becomes more important.

7. With increased Arctic development there may be a requirement, at least for research purposes, for a submarine capability, and this option should not be completely disregarded. At least there should be continuing feasibility studies for such a requirement even though military needs will probably remain minimal.

Obviously the cost of developing an adequate and continuing long-term enforcement capability would be considerable. Yet Canadian sovereignty, and more particularly the country's territorial integrity, cannot be protected solely by treaties and legislation. The Cabinet has the responsibility to foster a sense of national identity and unless our claims to sovereignty are protected that sense of identity will be impaired. The gap between declared policy and the means to enforce that policy remains to be bridged.

NOTES

[1] See Bruce Thordarson, *Trudeau and Foreign Policy* (Toronto, 1972).

[2] The same objectives and priorities formed the basis of the 1971 Defence White Paper — Government of Canada, *Defence in the 70s* (Ottawa, 1971).

[3] Government of Canada, *Foreign Policy for Canadians* (Ottawa, 1970), pp. 8-9.

[4] Mitchell Sharp, 'Canada-U.S. Relations: Options for the Future', *International Perspectives* (Autumn 1972), p. 13.

[5] *Foreign Policy for Canadians*, p. 15.

[6] *Defence in the 70s*, p. 11.

[7] Brian Roberts, rapporteur, *The Arctic Ocean* (Ditchley, 1971), p. 9.

[8] For example see Donald E. Milsten, 'Arctic Passage — Legal Heavy Weather', *Orbis*, xv, 1971-2.

[9] Colin S. Gray, *Canadian Defence Priorities: A Question of Relevance* (Toronto, 1972), p. 128.

[10] *Ibid.*, p. 126.

[11] House of Commons, Standing Committee on External Affairs and National Defence (hereafter cited as SCEAND), *Minutes of Proceeding and Evidence*, no. 26, 12 February 1969, p. 942.

[12] House of Commons *Debates*, 15 May 1969, p. 8720. See p. 8721 for opposition reaction.

[13] House of Commons, Standing Committee on Indian Affairs and Northern Development, *Minutes of Proceeding and Evidence*, no. 1, 16 December 1969, p. 6.

[14] See House of Commons *Debates*, 17 April 1970, p. 6029.

[15]Quoted in L. LeGault, 'Canadian Arctic Water Pollution Prevention Legislation', in Lewis M. Alexander, ed., *The United Nations and Ocean Management*, Proceedings of the Fifth Annual Conference of the Law of the Sea Institute, June 1970, University of Rhode Island, Kingston, p. 295.

[16]Office of the Prime Minister, Transcript of Press Conference, 8 April 1970, p. 2.

[17]See Mitchell Sharp, 'Preserving Canada's Arctic Environment', Statement to the House of Commons, 16 April 1970, ss no. 70/5 and LeGault, *op. cit.*, p. 297.

[18]House of Commons *Debates*, 17 April 1970, p. 6015.

[19]SCEAND, no. 26, 29 April 1970, p. 18.

[20]The legal arguments are interesting, complex, and not central to this paper. See Donat Pharand, *The Law of the Sea of the Arctic* (Ottawa, 1973) and William V. O'Brien and Armando C. Chapelli, 'The Law of the Sea in the "Canadian" Arctic: The Pattern of Controversy', *McGill Law Journal*, 19, no. 3, 1973, 322-66 for part I and 19, no. 4, 1973, 477-542 for part II.

[21]Sharp, *op. cit.*

[22]Gray, *op. cit.*, p. 139.

[23]See House of Commons *Debates*, 15 April 1970, p. 5923.

[24]Richard B. Bilder, 'The Canadian Arctic Waters Pollution Prevention Act', in Alexander, *op. cit.*, p. 206.

[25]House of Commons *Debates*, 15 April 1970, p. 5923.

[26]Bilder, *op. cit.*, p. 218.

[27]See Alexander, *op. cit.*, p. 332.

[28]O'Brien and Chapelli, *op. cit.*, p. 328.

[29]For both statements see Alexander, *op. cit.*, pp. 307 and 327.

[30]SCEAND, no. 30, 6 November 1973, p. 32.

[31]For quotes from the government's position paper see footnote 30.

[32]For references to various briefs see SCEAND. nos 1, 11, 15, and 16, 12 March, 23 April, 3 May, and 7 May 1974.

[33]P. A. Lapointe, 'Law of the sea advanced but much remains to be done', *International Perspectives* (November/December 1974), p. 21.

[34]*Ibid.*, p. 24.

[35]Toronto *Globe and Mail*, 10 May 1975.

[36]Halifax *Chronicle-Herald*, 29 August 1974.

[37]Toronto *Globe and Mail*, 13 December 1974.

[38]*Ibid.*, 9 May 1975.

[39]A. E. Gotlieb and C. M. Dalfen, 'National Jurisdiction and International Responsibility: New Canadian Approaches to International Law', paper presented to the First Annual Conference of the Canadian Council on International Law, 13 October 1972, p. 55.

[40]House of Commons *Debates*, 17 April 1970, p. 6028.

[41]LeGault, *op. cit.*, p. 299.

[42]Implementation of the twelve-mile territorial sea and the enlarged fishing zones required negotiations with the European fishing nations. During 1972 agreements were concluded with Britain, France, Denmark, Portugal, and Spain for termination of fishing in the outer nine miles and in the Gulf of St Lawrence.

[43]See Donald J. Slimman, 'The Parting of the Ways: Canada-United States Differences on the Law of the Sea', *Behind the Headlines*, XXXIII, no. 6 (April 1975) ; Ann L. Hollick, 'Canadian-American Relations: Law of the Sea', *International Organization* (Autumn 1974), 28, no. 4, 755-80; and R. M. Logan, *Canada, the United States and the Third Law of the Sea Conference* (Montreal-Washington, 1974), for detailed discussions.

[44]Toronto *Globe and Mail*, 13 December 1974.

[45]House of Commons *Debates*, 20 November 1974, p. 1515.

[46]*Defence in the 70s*, pp. 18 and 21.

[47]SCEAND, Tenth Report, 1970 (Report of the Committee on Maritime Forces), p. 28. Also see Colin S. Gray, *Canada's Maritime Forces*, Wellesley Paper no. 1, January 1973, Canadian Instiitute of International Affairs, Toronto.

[48]T. C. Pullen, 'Canada and Future Shipping Operations in the Arctic', *Canadian Defence Quarterly*, III, no. 2 (Autumn 1973), 8-13.

[49]SCEAND, Sub-committee on Maritime Forces, p. 11.

[50]See Peter Z. R. Finkle, 'Canadian Foreign Policy for Marine Services: An Alternative Perspective', *Journal of Canadian Studies*, X. no. 1 (February 1975), 10-24.

[51]See Franklyn Griffiths, 'Canadian Sovereignty and Arctic International Relations', in this volume.

[52]The decision to purchase 18 Lockheed Orion aircraft will augment current surveillance capabilities, but it is not clear that the surveillance and control role for the Armed Forces will remain a priority. Recent government statements indicate that the NATO role has been assigned greater priority than the protection of Canadian sovereignty. See footnote 2.

[53]See John W. Langford, 'Marine Science, Technology and Arctic Sovereignty', in this volume for a discussion of icebreakers and marine-support systems.

5 THE MILITARY TASK: SOVEREIGNTY AND SECURITY, SURVEILLANCE AND CONTROL IN THE FAR NORTH

by J. Gellner

If any proof were needed that the primary mission of the armed forces of a sovereign state is to support national policies and to assist in the achievement of national objectives, and that readiness to fight in a war is only a subsidiary function (relevant as far as it helps attain the main purpose), it is provided by Canada's military engagement north of 60. Virtually no 'defence' task in the literal sense of the word is involved. What is involved, is on one hand the assertion of Canadian sovereignty over an area of land and sea of some one-and-a-half million square miles where the normal manifestations of national dominion are not, and cannot be, always present, and on the other hand the safeguarding of Canadian interests in a security zone that is common to the middle-power Canada and the super-power United States. This second mission is the less important from the purely Canadian point of view. It did, however, become significant earlier than the mission to protect Canadian sovereignty, and it will thus be as well to deal with it first.

The function of the 'glacis' in fortifications of earlier days was to force the assailants to expose themselves—to view and to fire—well before they reached the defenders' main positions. Canada north of 60 is the glacis of 'fortress North America'. There was no notion of any such thing until after the Second World War: the United States shared with Canada what a Canadian representative at the League of Nations rather disingenuously called, back in 1923, a 'view from a fire-proof house'. The need for a glacis, more urgent obviously for the United States than for Canada, arose only upon the introduction into the arsenals of the big powers of the intercontinental bomber, an event that coincided in time roughly with the beginnings of the Cold War.

For years thereafter there was a direct and marked relationship between the capabilities of the Soviet long-range bomber force and the width of the North American glacis. At the beginning of the fifties the United States began to construct the Pinetree Line, a string of radar stations for early warning and for control of defensive weapon systems along its northern borders. The Line provided a glacis for the United States of about 200 miles' width against the conceivable attacker of the day, the Soviet Tupolev Tu-4 bomber, which had a cruising speed of just about that many miles an hour. In August 1951 Canada agreed to the extension of the Pinetree Line into its territory. In the eastern part of the continent in particular this widened the U.S. glacis to around 600 miles, and gave the main population centres of eastern Canada a glacis of 250 miles or so. By then jet bombers were being developed both in the United States and in the Soviet Union with cruising speeds up to two-and-a-half times greater than those of their piston-engined predecessors. In 1954 the Soviet Myasishchev Mya-4 bomber first flew. That same year, on 27 September to be precise, the U.S. and Canadian governments announced that they had decided to build a chain of early warning radar stations right across the continent, roughly between the Arctic Circle and 70° north latitude, the DEW line. There was now to be a solid glacis 1,500 miles wide on the average in front of the main U.S. and Canadian anti-aircraft defences, and even wider in front of the bases of the U.S. nuclear-bomber force designed to act as deterrent to an attack — a glacis that even a jet aircraft would take three hours to traverse.[1]

The NORAD (North American air defence) Agreement, concluded between the United States and Canada on 12 May 1958, merely institutionalized what already existed, a joint control of the glacis or strategic forefield of North America, a control that the U.S. government considered indispensable on military grounds, and that the Canadian government admitted to be unavoidable on political, and at least desirable on military grounds. After all, if there was a military threat to North America — and the duty of those responsible for national security to see to it that preparations are made to counter the *worst* eventuality rendered sophisticated arguments of whether in fact a threat did or did not exist largely irrelevant — then it was certain that it was directed against the whole of the continent. It was thus only logical to oppose to the threat a continental defence system.[2]

Throughout, for Canada, the one factor that remained of paramount importance in any consideration of the pros and cons of continental defence was the insistence of the United States on a secure strategic forefield. The accident of their geographical position compels certain lesser powers to pay careful heed to the special security requirements of big powers. That Canada is in this position vis-à-vis the United States has been acknowledged by responsible Canadian political leaders for at least thirty-five years now, ever since the Ogdensburg Declaration of 18 August 1940 (which first set out the task to 'consider in the broad sense the defence of the north half of the western hemisphere'), and the creation of the U.S.-Canadian Permanent Joint Board on Defence. It was acknowledged again by all political parties—though rather reluctantly and with reservations by the spokesman for the New Democratic Party—in early 1973, in the debate preceding the second renewal of the NORAD Agreement. For the ruling Liberal Party, Defence Minister James Richardson called it 'really *unthinkable* that we would not be participating [in North American air defence] in some form', and left it at that. The Progressive Conservative defence critic, Mr George Hees, was more specific: 'We are obliged to play our part in the air defence of the continent.... If we shirk our duty, the United States will come in and do it for us. There is no question in my mind of that.' This point was also conceded by Mr Hees' counterpart in the NDP, Mr Douglas Rowland: 'There is the question that if we don't maintain our association the United States will want to move in and do what we are now doing, anyway.'[3] Where Mr Rowland parted company with his opposite numbers in the bigger parties was that he maintained that Canada should bow out of NORAD whatever the consequences, because to his mind the organization itself no longer made sense. In his opinion the bomber threat, if there ever was one, had vanished in the missile age. Since Canada was not participating in anti-ballistic missile defence,[4] its continued participation in joint North American air defence was really a waste of scarce resources, human and material. This facile—and let it be said right away, rather simplistic—argument was used before in the House of Commons,[5] and is generally being used by Canadian opponents of the NORAD connection (and in many cases, of *any* connection with the United States).

In this case, too, it is rather futile to speculate (as some have done) on whether or not the United States would in fact 'move in' if it came to the conclusion that Canada was not doing enough to assure the security of the glacis, and if so, *how* it would do it. As responsible Canadian political leaders have emphasized many times in the past, and as the Secretary of State for External Affairs of the day (Mr Mitchell Sharp) so succinctly put it in a speech on 14 December 1970, the 'central problem facing Canada (is) how to live distinct from but in harmony with the United States, the greatest power on earth.' There is simply no way of getting around that problem, least of all by non-co-operation.

The simple fact is that the U.S. need for tight control over the strategic forefield, and the corresponding (though no doubt less stringent) Canadian security requirement in the same area, have not changed as the result of the advent of new weaponry. What has changed are some of the means by which these requirements are met. And if one examines these means one by one, one invariably finds that they still depend on the availability of Canadian land, Canadian sea, and Canadian air space. They fall, very broadly speaking, into four main categories.

1. Early warning of penetrations of the air space over the strategic forefield, and active defences capable of intercepting and, in the extreme

case, destroying intruders. Such penetrations do in fact occur. Thus in 1973 the then Vice-Chief of the Defence Staff testified before the House of Commons Standing Committee on External Affairs and National Defence that about four times a year Soviet bombers on their way to Cuba test NORAD defences by coming 'quite close' to Canadian territory on the Atlantic side. And he added: 'If we didn't react, they might come closer.'[6] Against atmospheric intrusions (as distinct from spatial, by ballistic missiles and orbital vehicles), NORAD maintains its two radar lines, DEW and Pinetree, rather thinned out in recent years; a decreasing number of interceptor-fighters and surface-to-air missiles; and the necessary electronic and computerized weapon-control facilities such as SAGE (semi-automatic ground environment) and BUIC (back-up interceptor control).[7] This is the extent of what one may broadly (though perhaps not entirely accurately) call NORAD's anti-bomber defences.

2. Co-operation in the detection and tracking of ballistic missiles and orbital vehicles, though not in *active* defence against them (as far as there can be any).[8] The three stations of the Ballistic Missile Early Warning System are outside Canadian territory, at Clear, Alaska, Thule, Greenland, and Fylingdales Moor, Yorkshire, England. Their rearward communications, however, some 225,000 miles of land and undersea telephone cable and microwave radio relay circuitry, go to a large extent through Canada, and data from the Ballistic Missile Early Warning System are automatically transmitted to National Defence Headquarters in Ottawa.[9] Canada also takes part in the NORAD-operated Space Detection and Tracking System, which keeps tabs on everything man-made that orbits the earth, from still-operating satellites to debris left from all kinds of space launches.[10]

3. Efforts aimed at tightening control over the glacis of 'fortress North America', and possibly extending it outwards from its present practical limits set by the reach of the DEW line radars. This involves, in particular, the partial transfer of early warning and interception control from the ground to the air (AWACS-airborne warning and control system), and experimentation with over-the-horizon backscatter radar (OTH-B). As for the former, the Canadian government has taken a cautious, wait-and-see approach, probably because of the very high cost of the system. By contrast Canada has done its share fully in the development and tests of OTH-B, in particular in operation *Polar Cap III*, which involved OTH-B transmissions from Hall Beach, on Melville Peninsula, and receptions at Cambridge Bay, Victoria Island. These two localities are about 600 miles apart, at about 68° north latitude.[11]

4. Control of the land and waters, open and icebound, north of 60. As for the land, only periodic surveillance is required to prevent any possible illicit activities, such as orographic surveys or the installation of automatic beacons (e.g. for navigational purposes) by a foreign power in what is

largely uninhabited wasteland. As for the sea, in the east only Hudson Strait and Foxe Channel, entrance ports to large expanses of inland waters, and the Davis Strait, which affords access to the Northwest Passage, can be used by surface ships, under certain conditions. In the west there is really only the Beaufort Sea. In between, offering a tenuous connecting link between the latter and the Davis Strait, there is the Northwest Passage itself: the line Lancaster Sound — Barrow Strait — Viscount Melville Sound, and finally either north (M'Clure Strait) or south (Prince of Wales Strait and Amundsen Gulf) around Banks Island and into the Beaufort Sea. The Passage is, according to the route taken, between 1,000 and 1,200 miles long, and surface ships can progress through it only slowly even in the best of circumstances. Thus all that is needed from the purely defence point of view is again the kind of aerial surveillance suited to the control of the *terra firma* north of 60. Illicit underwater and/or under-the-ice passages by warships are quite another matter. Submarines require at least twenty fathoms (120 feet) of water for safe submerged operation. That much is available in several sounds and straits of the Canadian Arctic archipelago. Nuclear submarines have negotiated the Northwest Passage without surfacing.[12] What is officially called a 'limited sub-surface system to give warning of any unusual . . . activity' beneath Arctic water and Arctic ice is currently being tested.[13] It may be based on sonar-buoy barriers capable of storing up information; this information would in due course be summoned (called up) by a reconnaissance aircraft, and any indication of the presence of a submarine in the area would thus be received. An educated guess could then be made as to its probable course. Appropriate warnings could be given, and perhaps an interception effected, by some means not yet quite clear at this moment, at least not to this writer, possibly at the next sonar-buoy barrier.

All these activities will take place because they *must* take place; this at least, it is hoped, has been made clear already by what was said earlier. The question only is to what extent Canada will engage itself in this work.

In this respect the position taken by the Canadian government is unequivocal. In his statement of 3 April 1969 on future Canadian defence policy, Prime Minister Trudeau emphasized that 'we shall endeavour to have those activities within Canada which are essential to North-American defence performed by Canadian forces.' By saying this he went a step — a very long step — further than the House of Commons Standing Committee on External Affairs and National Defence, which, a few days earlier in its Fifth Report, only ventured so far as to say: 'It has been argued before the Committee that Canadian defence expenditures can be substantially reduced because of the fact that Canada's geographical proximity to the United States makes it necessary for the United States to defend Canada in order to defend itself. This has been referred to as the "free ride" theory. The Committee does not accept this theory. On the contrary, it is convinced that Canada must be prepared to incur reasonable expenditures for its own defence in order to maintain its independence and freedom of action as a nation, and to ensure that Canadian interests are taken into account when continental defence measures are being taken.'[14]

That same statement of 3 April 1969 also established as Canada's first defence priority 'the protection of our sovereignty'.[15] The Prime Minister drove that point in, only days afterwards, on 12 April in a speech to the Alberta Liberal Association in Calgary: 'Our first priority in our defence policy is the protection of Canadian sovereignty, *in all the dimensions.*'

This over-riding concern—a concern that makes the government not only ready but eager to perform most, and if this were possible, all the tasks connected with the control of the glacis of 'fortress North America' —is understandable in the context of the times. As set out elsewhere in this book, Canadian sovereignty in the vast area of the Arctic archipelago is not uncontested, and indeed not everywhere certain; to a degree it depends on actions that create factual situations that can be interpreted as proving 'effective occupation' by Canada. Such actions were always necessary to safeguard Canadian rights; they have merely become more urgent now that the Canadian Arctic has become of more than just strategic importance. Thus an earlier instance of a most opportune assertion of Canadian sovereignty occurred in connection with the operation of the DEW line. The latter was built between 1954 and 1957, entirely at U.S. expense. It has been operated by a U.S. corporation, the Federal Electric Company. The manned stations of the Line are, however, commanded by Canadian officers, who are supported by small Canadian administrative staffs. This arrangement—a few Canadians at the head of what are really U.S. installations—has been classed as merely symbolic, but it is much more than that. It has been rightly pointed out that 'as a result of the DEW Line agreements, Canada secured what the United States had up to that time assiduously endeavoured to avoid, namely, an explicit recognition of Canadian claims to the exercise of sovereignty in the Far North.'[16]

This then gets us through the area of overlap and fully into the discussion of the other of the two principal Canadian military tasks in the far North, the assertion of sovereignty *per se*, that is, entirely for political and legal reasons, without any strategic aim.

In regions where most of the forms of the exercise of state administration normal in temperate climes—roads, postal service, regular policing, and such—are missing, sovereignty is not something that can be taken for granted. Thus opportunities for asserting it should be seized when they present themselves. Since the enunciation of a new Canadian defence policy in early 1969, it is this consideration that has provided the main impetus for the 'Canadianization' of military activities and those supportive of the military in Canada north of 60. An example is the take-over, between 1970 and 1972, of the Arctic weather stations formerly operated jointly with the United States: at Resolute Bay on Cornwallis Island; Mould Bay on Prince Patrick Island; Isachsen on Ellef Ringnes Island; Alert and Eureka on Ellesmere Island. Unless one quibbles over who is really in charge of the DEW line stations, there is now no U.S. installation in Canada north of 60, and certainly no U.S. military installation.

If the amount of Canadian military activity in the far North in the past few years were plotted on a graph, it would show a line that was ascending slowly and with an occasional flattening into a plateau but by and large steadily increasing.[17] True, fewer than 500 Canadian servicemen are permanently stationed north of 60. On the other hand transient movements, sometimes connected with a stay of weeks and even months, are relatively frequent. The following list is not complete – and cannot be because tasks are tackled as they crop up – but it covers the principal activities.

(i) Regular personnel/air cargo flights to Inuvik in the Mackenzie River delta, Resolute on Cornwallis Island, Alert on Ellesmere Island, and Frobisher Bay on Baffin Island.

(ii) Irregular flights, mainly for re-supply and the support of exercises, from main bases in the South, and from Resolute, to various stations in the far North.

(iii) Reconnaissance over-flights, on an average once every ten days, by Argus (Canadair CP-107) aircraft of Maritime Command using Frobisher Bay and Inuvik as advanced bases.*

(iv) Regular ground exercises by company-size units (Operation 'New Viking'). They were being intensified after a permanent Arctic Training Centre was established at Churchill in April 1974, supplementing the small 'New Viking' winter headquarters that had already operated there. The exercises themselves fan out from Churchill and Resolute and, with appropriate air support, cover a great deal of Arctic ground.

(v) Construction work done by military engineers. This involves such things as the building of bridges (across the Ogilvie and the Eagle Rivers, on the new Dempster Highway linking Dawson City in the Yukon with Fort McPherson at the root of the Mackenzie River Delta) and of airstrips (at the native settlements of Pangnirtung, Chesterfield Inlet, Pond Inlet, Whale Cove, Igloolik, and Cape Dorset, all in the eastern Arctic).

---

*These flights were suspended for reasons of economy in late 1974. When this caused some public stir, the government announced that the early resumption of the flights was planned, and they have in fact been resumed, though on a somewhat lesser scale.

A Canadian Armed Forces plane over ice-covered water.
Courtesy Department of National Defence

(vi) Search-and-rescue operations when the need arises — which happens more and more often as commercial activities expand in the far North. (In Canada, search and rescue is entirely a military responsibility, with civilian agencies and individual volunteers drawn in as required.) To this will no doubt now be added pollution control — the first serious incident after the enactment of the Arctic Waters Pollution Prevention Act, the accidental pumping into the sea of a huge amount of diesel oil at Saglek on the Labrador coast, occurred south of 60, but only just.

(vii) Occasional sea and air exercises, as a rule combining training with some national development and/or scientific tasks. Into this category come, for instance, the extended cruise in Arctic waters of the operational support ship H.M.C.S. *Protecteur* in the late summer of 1973; the reconnaissance flights by the Air Reserve, mainly over regions where new commercial activity is in progress; and, on the spectacular side, the air-lifting to and recovery from the North Pole of a scientific party that, apart from more scholarly activities, planted the Canadian flag at the Pole both on and under the ice. It should be noted, though, that enterprises like these are restricted by the lack of icebreaking capabilities in the fleet, and by the limitations of the aircraft with which the Air Reserve are equipped.

Finally, even though one can hardly call them a military organization, mention should at least be made of the Canadian Rangers, some 1,600 native hunters and trappers who act as unpaid militiamen. They are issued with a bolt-action rifle and 100 rounds of ammunition a year — which they no doubt use in the course of earning their livelihood — and are supposed to observe and report any unusual activity in the regions where they live and through which they travel. Even if it were not for the regrettable gradual urbanization of the Eskimo (in the sense that they are becoming increasingly dependent on the services provided in industrial society), the military value of the Canadian Rangers would be minimal. The main benefit lies in the ties that membership in the organization forges between the native population and the apparatus of the state, still somewhat foreign to them.

With the possible exception of that listed under (iii), these seven types of military activity in the far North are all oriented towards specific objectives, the achievement of which would pay dividends even if there were not the additional motive of underpinning a claim to sovereignty by proving 'effective occupation'. On the other hand the primary purpose of the Argus flights is no doubt to show the flag. The aircraft is designed for anti-submarine warfare, and carries electronic equipment appropriate to that mission. It is not equipped for all-weather, day and night reconnaissance. Visual observation of the ground — especially if it largely consists of looking at vast expanses of snow-covered hummocks and of solid or broken ice — would hardly justify ten- to twelve-hour patrols in aircraft in which one flying hour costs anywhere between $1,500 and $2,000, and that carry crews expensively trained for much more complex tasks. Still, under the circumstances even showing the flag is probably worth the effort and the cost involved.

The Armed Forces are, of course, not the only government agency working in the far North, but merely the one most engaged there and thus most visible. In terms of providing 'effective occupation', the Royal Canadian Mounted Police with its scattered outposts, and even more the Northern Health Service of the Department of Health and Welfare, which maintains more than a hundred medical installations from hospitals to nursing stations, are probably more significant than are the Armed Forces. Even security functions are shared to a degree with the Marine Services Division of the Ministry of Transport, (which through the Canadian Coast Guard controls the icebreakers that the fleet lacks), and will be with the Department of the Environment once the responsibilities are sorted out for enforcing the Arctic Waters Pollution Prevention Act and, in the high latitudes, the Territorial Sea and Fisheries Zones Act. The point is, though, that 'National Defence has . . . ultimate responsibility to ensure that overall an adequate surveillance and control capability exists for the protection of Canadian sovereignty and security.'[18] The Department is the co-ordinating agency in this field.

The need for co-ordination had already been stressed in the report of the Sub-Committee on Maritime Forces of the Standing Committee on External Affairs and National Defence, the so-called Penner Committee (after its chairman, Mr Keith Penner, M.P.).[19] It recommended a more precise structure than the rather pragmatic one that the government subsequently opted for, with non-military activities (admittedly only maritime surface, these being in the particular case the subject of inquiry) assigned to 'an enlarged Canadian Coast Guard . . . acting as an autonomous government agency'. The commanding officers of its vessels would have 'concurrent authority' with the captains of Canadian warships and military aircraft 'for the enforcement of Canadian sovereignty and extra-territorial jurisdiction against non-military violation'.[20] Of particular interest is the third of four reasons given by the Penner Committee for its recommendation that there be a clear division between military and non-military tasks and the consequent responsibilities for the performance of those tasks: 'The increasing potential use of maritime forces to enforce sovereignty and extra-territorial jurisdiction against non-military violation or exploitation, *possibly by Canada's military allies* [emphasis added] as well as others, may make it desirable on occasion for non-military maritime forces to be able to carry out police type functions, thereby avoiding any military implications'.[21] This was 1970, and the Committee was quite obviously impressed — and influenced in its considerations — by the U.S. challenge to Canadian sovereignty over Arctic waters.

By and large the government's solution to the problem of many fingers in the surveillance-and-control pie — leaving things as they were, but giving National Defence 'ultimate responsibility', and consequently establishing 'Canadian Forces' operations centres on the East and West coasts which will work closely with the civil departments to coordinate surveillance and control activities'[22] — would appear to be preferable, because more flexible, than the arrangement advocated by the Penner Committee. The organization has yet to be put to any serious test. There has thus been no opportunity to judge how it may work under stress.

When it comes to asserting sovereignty through 'effective occupation' the question necessarily arises, 'How much is enough?' The answer will obviously have to be based on law and on facts. The former remains a contentious issue in international legal circles. As to the latter, given the kind of country Canada north of 60 is, there can really be no serious doubt that all the ingredients of 'effective occupation' are present that one could reasonably expect to find under the circumstances. In particular, Canada has established in the lands and the waters it claims as its own an organization capable of making Canadian law respected. No other power has at present that capability. The people living in the area, whether permanently or temporarily, consider themselves governed by Canadian law. What physical presence there is of representatives of the state is no doubt sufficient, at least at the present stage of development of the region. It would appear, then, that challenges to Canadian sovereignty would have to be based not on the lack of 'effective occupation', but rather on general principles of international law or — though this would be difficult to imagine — on historical rights. That much at least can perhaps be deduced even from what was said in this chapter about Canadian military activities in the far North.

Even so, a challenge to sovereignty, whatever may be its basis, can obviously not be taken lightly. It has been contended that 'the greater the use that other states make of Arctic waters, the more secure will be Canada's claim to jurisdiction, provided that the waters are subject to Canadian control.'[23] The argument was that foreign operators would in that case become as dependent on the assistance of the Canadian Coast Guard, and generally on the services provided by the Canadian Ministry of Transport, as the S.S. *Manhattan* had been during her famous 1969 voyage through the Northwest Passage. This should not be taken for granted. The *Manhattan* had the mass needed to break through heavy ice but much too little thrust in proportion to her mass. Icebreaking tankers with the right combination of mass and thrust have been on the drawing boards in the United States for some years. There, too, a new class of big and powerful icebreakers is under construction, the first of which, the

Polar Star, was commissioned in 1974. If she had been available in 1969, she could probably have easily done the job that the Canadian Coast Guard icebreaker *John A. Macdonald* did more laboriously for the S.S. *Manhattan*. Also, the first cargos of lead/zinc have been shipped from Little Cornwallis Island through the eastern portion of the Northwest Passage in smaller icebreaking ore carriers, which do not need assistance in the short navigation season and under normal conditions. It is entirely conceivable that ships sailing under a foreign flag might ply the Northwest Passage without giving a fig for Canadian regulations — unless Canada enforces them, and this will require both the means and the will.[24]

This is not to say that the difficulties of surface and under-the-ice navigation in the Arctic should be minimized. It is still a tricky and hazardous business. This was established, in such a way as to silence those overly enthusiastic, in a thorough survey conducted in the second half of 1970 by the Canadian scientific ship *Hudson* working, at various times, with three smaller Canadian support vessels and the U.S. Coast Guard cutter *Edisto*. On that occasion the bottom of the Beaufort Sea was charted using side-scan radar (which gives a three-dimensional picture). The bottom was found to be dotted with massive cones of antediluvian ice ('pingoes') reaching up to forty feet beneath the surface, and gouged by shifting ice 'keels'. The hazard to navigation constituted by the pingoes is obvious. The significance of the ice keels is that they make the laying of underwater/under-the-ice pipelines impossible. As a result of that survey the Canadian government is said to be 'now very reluctant to have ships travel through the North-West Passage. Also, it cannot allow pipelines (as now conceived) on the continental shelf. One tanker ripped open by a pingo or one offshore pipeline sliced by an ice keel could disrupt the fragile ecological balance of much of the Arctic.'[25]

Even so, the likelihood is that the pressure of world demand for raw materials, and perhaps the requirements of the North American economy as well, will make the Northwest Passage an important and much-frequented waterway, and this in the relatively near future. It can also be safely assumed that the natural riches of the Canadian Arctic archipelago, riches that have already been tapped and are just beginning to be exploited, will be moved out mainly in ships. There is no alternative to the huge bulk carriers for the transportation of ores. For instance a company like Baffinland Iron would expect to extract ultimately several million tons of ore a year from its deposits at Mary River in North Baffin. This and other iron ore found on either side of Foxe Basin, on western Baffin Island, and on Melville Peninsula would not of course be shipped through the Northwest Passage, but it would have to pass through other Arctic waters that are also under Canadian sovereignty or special jurisdiction: Foxe Channel, Hudson Strait, lower Davis Strait. The lead/zinc that Cominco is already mining on Little Cornwallis Island will have to go entirely through the Northwest Passage; Cominco apparently has plans to step up production to at least 200,000 tons a year as quickly as it can be done. Oil, too, would have to go in tankers, since carrying it by pipeline from an island well to the mainland, except where the intervening channel was very narrow, would present insuperable difficulties: the oil would have to be heated to flow freely through the pipe. With natural gas the situation is not as critical, though the relative merits of pipelines as against liquefaction on site and transport by ship are being studied.[26] In any case, as pointed out earlier, the laying of underwater/ under-the-ice pipelines in Arctic waters is in many places simply not feasible.

Transit through Arctic waters will have to be strictly regulated if a mockery is not to be made of the Arctic Waters Pollution Prevention Act and if the accidental blocking of narrow navigable channels (e.g. in Barrow or Prince of Wales Straits) is to be prevented. Special standards of sea- and ice-worthiness for ships using Canadian Arctic waters may be set and compliance with them checked by inspections at the entrances to the waterways. Regular users may be issued with an equivalent of the 'navi-certs' of old. There may be regulations concerning speed, periodic reporting, emergency anchorage, and what not. In view of the very great hazards involved, it is likely that the employment of licensed pilots would be made obligatory in the Northwest Passage.

It is entirely possible that a foreign power may decide to flout these regulations — or perhaps, more likely, comply with most of them tacitly but refuse to submit to inspection, go through reporting procedures, or embark a pilot, so as not to admit that Canada has sovereignty over those waters. Thus a U.S. bulk carrier may sail serenely through the Passage, alone or preceded by a *Polar-Star*-class icebreaker, which, like all the armed U.S. Coast Guard vessels, is a warship in fact though not within the definition of one under international law.[27] As for real foreign warships, submarines (the most likely to use the Arctic passages) could do so only submerged, and thus *would* do so, even though international law prohibits it in territorial waters. Yet the narrows of the Northwest Passage come under the description of territorial waters if for no other reason than that they are less than twenty-four miles wide, shore-to-shore, in a few places: Canada claims under the Territorial Sea and Fishing Zones Act a territorial sea extending twelve miles and this in any case is becoming widely accepted worldwide.

What Canada would do if its jurisdiction in Arctic waters were challenged by surface ships that ignored Canadian regulations, or by submarines transiting unreported and submerged, has been widely discussed. It has been stated flatly that Canada 'has no choice but to confront, with whatever symbol of authority is appropriate, any challenge to the legislation now passed.'[28] This is all very well, but how would this be done in practice? If the offender were a U.S. surface ship, a diplomatic protest would hardly serve any purpose since the United States resists on principle pertinent Canadian claims to exclusive jurisdiction. If the offender were a Soviet submarine, a similar Canadian *démarche* in Moscow would no doubt elicit no more than a denial that the submarine was there.

The alternative then would be enforcement: arresting the offending surface ship or compelling it to turn back at the inspection point, intercepting the submarine and forcing it to surface and to submit to regulations. The second eventuality can be put aside for the present: as pointed out earlier, Canada has no capability for detecting, let alone intercepting, a submarine proceeding beneath the Arctic ice; ways and means of doing that are so far only being studied. As has also been stated, Canada possesses no naval icebreakers, and only three major Coast Guard ships of a class that can be used for policing the Arctic waterways. There is none on the Pacific coast for possible work in the Beaufort Sea and at the western entrances of the Northwest Passage. Nor are there, as far as is known, any immediate plans for the construction of polar icebreakers, only for four vessels to increase the fleet of major icebreakers in the St Lawrence Gulf and River from a skimpy two to six.[29]

As for surveillance of the waterways from the air, Canada has at present no long-range reconnaissance aircraft capable of doing their job in every weather or in darkness—this, too, has already been said earlier. The acquisition of long-range patrol aircraft capable of all-weather, day/night reconnaissance has been approved and the type selected, but deliveries can only begin in two years or so, at best. It is thus entirely possible that a big oil spill in Arctic waters, ecologically particularly dangerous because the oil might be trapped underneath the ice and might then foul up the waters for years, could go undetected for days and even weeks. Stand-by facilities for combating pollution are meagre, to say the least. The Armed Forces would have to do the job, or at any rate most or all of the heavy work connected with it, and they do not have enough aerial transport, fixed-wing and rotary-wing, even for the manifold tasks they are already saddled with. The same applies to Search and Rescue, where facilities are already badly stretched. One trembles to think of what would happen if one of the many big airliners that now traverse the Canadian Arctic on regular flights came down in the wastelands, stranding 200 or more passengers clad in street clothes and physically and mentally unequipped to withstand the rigours of the far North, passengers who would thus have to be brought out in a matter of hours. If in addition the Arctic waterways became more frequented, the existing search-and-rescue organization would certainly have to be considerably strengthened.

It is indeed difficult to understand the apparent reluctance of the Canadian government to face the inevitable consequences of the 1970 legislation in terms of making preparations and procuring equipment. One cannot but get the impression of a blithe belief in high places that all that would be needed would be to assert sovereignty and to arrogate special jurisdiction, without any thought of the possibility that declarations of rights may have to be backed by enforcement. If this was indeed how the situation was viewed in Ottawa — and whether it was or wasn't, we do not really know — then chances were taken that one day it will be difficult to justify.

The danger is that Canada may be caught in a time squeeze. Aircraft suitable for search and rescue, some of which could perhaps double in pollution control, could no doubt be bought virtually off the shelf, most probably in the United States. The long-range patrol aircraft, on the other hand, will, as has already been mentioned, not be available before early 1978, although it will be a model already flying. To start now designing and constructing polar icebreakers of an advanced type would mean that the first of them would be delivered about 1981 at the earliest, and perhaps later than that. Yet most of that long lead time would be past by now if the decision to provide the means of enforcement had been taken concurrently with the decision to enact the laws that were expected to require those means.

In the meantime, embarrassing precedents could be set, and whether they are or not will largely depend on developments on the international scene. The urge to resist encroachments on the freedom of the sea may become stronger in Washington. Troubles with Panama may make it desirable for the United States to have, for strategic reasons, an alternative route for its warships from the Atlantic to the Pacific, one that, at least where submarines are concerned, may not be any more difficult than the more straightforward but considerably longer route around Cape Horn. Similar considerations of strategic mobility may make Moscow eye with favour the Arctic passages as a line of transit for its submarines. Commercial operators may find Canadian regulations too onerous and too expensive to comply with in a competitive market, and they may have the backing of their governments. Any number of situations may arise in which a foreign government, especially that of a great power, faced with the choice of challenging Canadian sovereignty in Arctic waters and thereby incurring Canada's wrath, or maintaining friendly relations, may choose the former. In that case it would be up to Canada to avert the setting of a precedent by countering the challenge properly. Always assuming that the Canadian government of the day summons up the courage for such a confrontation, it will be *then* that the paucity of available means of enforcement will be shown to be a serious handicap.

It is certain that the faster the economic development of the Canadian far North, the more costly it will be to protect Canadian sovereignty there 'in all the dimensions', as Prime Minister Trudeau promised in his (already quoted) Calgary speech of 12 April 1969. In the absence of unequivocal backing by institutions of international law – after the failure to achieve agreement at the Law of the Sea Conference at Caracas in 1974, and the follow-up meeting at Geneva in 1975, prospects are rated as rather dim – Canadian diplomacy could be faced with the increasingly difficult task of blunting challenges to, and forestalling encroachments on, Canadian sovereignty in Arctic waters. As for the Canadian military, there can be no doubt whatsoever that they will have their hands full looking after that first priority of Canada's defence policy.

NOTES

[1] Considerations of the effectiveness of the glacis in terms of the actual protection it provides against incursion by aircraft are not germane to the subject of this study and are consequently omitted.

[2] For a closely argued case against the necessity, as perceived by the U.S. government in the fifties, to build a vast continental air-defence system, see Samuel P. Huntington, *The Common Defence* (New York, 1961); for an argument of the largely emotional-moralistic kind against U.S.-Canadian military co-operation, see John Warnock, *Partner to Behemoth: The Military Policy of a Satellite Canada* (Toronto, 1970).

[3] Quoted by Terrance Wills in two successive articles in the Toronto *Globe and Mail* of 6 and 7 February 1973.

[4] The U.S. instrument of (first) renewal of the NORAD Agreement, a note of 30 March 1968, contains the proviso: 'It is also agreed by my Government that this Agreement will not involve in any way a Canadian commitment to participate in an active ballistic missile defence.' The important qualifier 'active' is all too often overlooked.

[5] For instance, by four committee members dissenting with the Ninth Report (on North American defence) to the House of the Standing Committee on External Affairs and National Defence, *Minutes of Proceedings and Evidence*, 26 June 1969. The records of that at one time very active parliamentary committee will hereafter be cited as SCEAND, *Proceedings*.

[6] SCEAND. *Proceedings*: Testimony of Lieutenant-General A. C. Hull, 13 April 1973.

[7] Between 1958 and 1972 the number of Pinetree Line stations was reduced from 193 to 99, of DEW line stations from 57 to 32, of regular interceptor-fighter squadrons from 65 to 14; the BOMARC unmanned interceptors were phased out; testimony of the Commander-in-Chief, NORAD (General McKee) before an investigating sub-committee of the U.S. House of Representatives Committee on Armed Services (92nd Congress, 1st session, Washington, 1972). See also the statement of Secretary of Defence Melvin R. Laird before that Committee, 17 February 1972.

[8] See above, footnote [4].

[9] NORAD fact sheet, *The Ballistic Missile Warning System*, (NORAD Public Affairs Office, Colorado Springs).

[10] 1971 Defence White Paper, Government of Canada, *Defence in the 70s*, (Ottawa, 1971), p. 26.

[11]*Defence in the 70s*, p. 30, and oral information from National Defence Headquarters/ Defence Research Board. For a clear outline of current thinking on North American defence, see Major-General W. K. Carr, 'The Components of a Modernized Aerospace and Defence System', *Canadian Defence Quarterly/Revue Canadienne de Défense* (hereafter cited as *Defence Quarterly*), IV (Summer 1974).

[12]In this connection it is of interest to note that for the first of two submerged passages of U.S. nuclear submarines 'the Americans had asked permission which we promptly granted; for the second, they didn't ask permission, but we gave it anyway in the same terms' — no doubt a wise move on Canada's part to safeguard its sovereignty rights. Oral information provided during the discussions of a Study Group on Canadian-United States Defence Relations and their effect on Canadian-U.S. relations in general, Ottawa, 10 February 1970.

[13]*Defence in the 70s*, p. 18, and oral information from National Defence Headquarters/ Defence Research Board.

[14]SCEAND. *Proceedings*: Fifth Report to the House, 26 March 1969.

[15]This has been stated again and again since then (incl. in *Defence in the 70s*, p. 16), to the point that it has become a kind of gospel of Canadian defence thinking.

[16]Robert Sutherland, 'The Strategic Significance of the Canadian Arctic', in R. St. J. Macdonald, ed., *The Arctic Frontier* (Toronto, 1966).

[17]For a brief description of the manifold activities of the Canadian Armed Forces in the far North (with a sketch map showing the main localities and lines of communication), see Brigadier-General R. M. Withers, 'Defence Requirements "North of Sixty"', *Defence Quarterly*, I (Summer 1971). The specific data come from the regular news releases of the Information Services of the Department of National Defence and from a special fact sheet (dated 3 July 1974) kindly supplied to the author by that agency.

[18]*Defence in the 70s*, p. 11.

[19]SCEAND. *Proceedings*: Tenth Report to the House, 26 June 1970.

[20]*Ibid.*, Section 11.6, 'Organizational Considerations'.

[21]*Ibid.*

[22]*Defence in the 70s*, p. 11.

[23]Colin S. Gray, *Canada's Maritime Forces: Duties and Capabilities*, unpublished paper, 1972, available at the Canadian Institute of International Affairs, Toronto.

[24]For an interesting discussion of the problems involved, with some challenging perceptions, see Captain T. C. Pullen (who was the Canadian representative aboard the S.S. *Manhattan* during her 1969 voyage), 'Canada and Future Shipping Operations in the Arctic', *Defence Quarterly*, III (Autumn 1973).

[25]*Canada Today/D'Aujourd'hui*, V (February 1974).

[26]Pullen, *op. cit.*

[27]For that definition and its implications, see SCEAND. *Proceedings*: Testimony of Professor Pharand of the University of Ottawa, 13 May 1970.

[28]Colin S. Gray, *Canadian Defence Priorities: A Question of Relevance* (Toronto, 1972), p. 143.

[29]Pullen, *op. cit.*

6 CANADA'S ARCTIC AND ITS STRATEGIC IMPORTANCE

by T. A. Hockin and P. A. Brennan

Canada's Arctic is vital to the strategic interests of the United States. Its need to defend itself and to deter Soviet military attack across the North Pole has led to a considerable American military interest in our Arctic, and has made it imperative for the United States to fill whatever military vacuums may exist there. This imperative, combined with the vital position the Arctic will play in providing much-needed oil and gas for the American economy, means that the quiet Canadian Arctic emerges as a key strategic area in any global assessment of American security.

The strategic interests of the United States in the Canadian Arctic are discussed elsewhere in this book (see chapter 5). Turning to the Soviet interests in its Arctic, the first point to make is that they are even greater than the American. The Soviet Arctic is much closer to the Soviet industrial heartland than is the North American (Canadian) Arctic to the industrial and population centres of the United States. Therefore it makes sense for the Soviets to pay considerable attention to their defensive strategy in the Arctic, as far north as it is possible for them to go, and to back up with military force their claims to sovereignty over the Soviet 'sector' of the Arctic ocean and landforms, including not only the islands close to the Soviet mainland but also those closer to the Pole, like Franz Josef Land, where they maintain weather-reporting facilities and defensive early-warning systems.[1] It is estimated by American observers that Soviet early-warning systems against ICBM and manned-bomber attack are situated across their northernmost perimeter in much the same manner as the American/Canadian DEW line and the Ballistic Missile Early Warning System are in the North American Arctic.[2]

The northeast passage or, as the Soviets call it, the Northern Sea Route, passing through the Arctic coastal waters of the Soviet Union from Atlantic to Pacific, is of considerable strategic significance. The passage is vital for maintaining and re-supplying early-warning sites and military bases, particularly those established on the Soviet Arctic islands. Numerous north/south river-transportation systems across the breadth of the

Soviet Union connect to the Northern Sea Route for direct domestic transport, notably for heavy machinery or other bulky freight,[3] and thus make this corridor vital for economic reasons as well. Nor should other aspects of the Northern Sea Route for military transport be overlooked.

The Northern Sea Route is completely within Soviet territorial waters. It is a relatively secure route for moving ships and submarines from the principal base at Murmansk to the Pacific and back. The Arctic Ocean is therefore of central importance to Soviet global/naval strategy.

Some informed observers, notably American Commander Robert Herrick, have maintained that the Soviet naval presence in the Arctic is mainly defensive – to protect important air-defence and ICBM installations in the Murmansk-Archangel area.[4] Certainly the Soviets maintain a high level of maritime defence in their Arctic waters. During a recent NATO naval exercise in the northern waters off Norway adjacent to the Barents Sea, the Soviets gave ample evidence of their defences there by patrolling the region with Bear and Badger aircraft as well as numerous ships and submarines.

Yet in a broader perspective their essential strategic task may be to use the Northern Sea Route as part of a pattern to develop Soviet influence on a global scale and to carry the Soviet SLBM (submarine-launched ballistic missile) threat to the Atlantic and Pacific coastal areas of the U.S. as well as to other, more distant, areas that can be reached by sea. It is well known that since the Second World War, but particularly since 1962, the Soviet Union has been expanding its naval, merchant marine, and fisheries fleets until their numbers are now formidable. The Soviet Union is the fastest-growing global maritime power since the Second World War, and closely rivals, if it does not surpass the United States in dominating the world's oceans. The possibility of Soviet dominance becomes even more ominous to the Americans when they consider that most of the Soviet naval ships are new, heavily armed with the latest missile weapons, and likely to remain effective well into the 1980s. Although the Soviet naval build-up is most evident at present in the Mediterranean Sea and in the Indian Ocean, it is known that Soviet submarines do patrol both coasts of North America. Soviet naval ships are relatively rare on the Atlantic so far, but Soviet trawlers, merchantmen, oceanographic, and electronic-spy ships abound.

The Soviet Union maintains many naval bases, but a quick survey of the main ones on the Baltic Sea, Black Sea, and the Sea of Japan (Vladivostok), indicates that their access to the oceans is through straits controlled by nations friendly to the United States—Denmark, Norway, Turkey, and Japan. The Murmansk-to-Archangel area contains the principal Soviet northern military air and sea bases (the whole of the Kola Peninsula and Inlet, Severo-dvinsk west of Archangel); the adjacent Barents Sea is the year-round sally port through which Soviet naval units can reach the Greenland-Iceland-United Kingdom gap, and thence the open

Atlantic. The whole region is of the utmost strategic importance to the Soviet Union, both defensively and offensively. The Soviet naval base at Providenija at the mouth of the Bering Strait reflects the Soviet concern for the strategic value of this exit opposite Alaska. Providenija acts not only as a stop-over base for refuelling and support on the long route to or from Murmansk, but also has the capacity to provide naval defence in the Straits area, at least during the summer and fall shipping season when vital Soviet re-supply is undertaken from the Archangel-Murmansk area to Pacific ports, particularly those that are not connected to European industrial Russia by rail.

The Davis Strait and northwest passages through the Canadian Arctic archipelago also might be used by the Soviets for the passage from the Arctic to the Atlantic of nuclear submarines carrying ballistic missiles (SSBN). The feasibility of this passage has been demonstrated by American nuclear submarines. The Arctic ice, great portions of which are under Canadian jurisdiction, could also provide Soviet SSBNS with protective cover from which to launch their missiles. The advantage here is quite clear. From their Arctic bases Soviet SSBNS can advance to Arctic Ocean attack stations against North America generally, the NORAD sites in the Arctic in particular, without having to run the American-Allied anti-submarine defences at the three exits. Thus the Canadian Arctic has strategic significance for the Soviet Union as a potential area for SSBNS to operate in and to exit from the Arctic towards their attack stations along the U.S. east coast. In this three-way strategic game, the United States has an interest in preventing Soviet SSBN egress from any of the three Arctic exits, including of course the exit through the Canadian Arctic. Compared to the extent of debate in Canada about NATO and NORAD, it is striking how little has been said about this equally relevant political-military confrontation in Canadian territory.

U.S. MILITARY CAPABILITIES IN THE MARITIME ARCTIC: THE STRATEGIC IMPLICATIONS

U.S. military capabilities in the maritime Arctic can be divided into three categories: air reconnaissance, nuclear submarine operations, and ice-breaking.

AIR RECONNAISSANCE

American air reconnaissance over the Arctic is carried out to detect the movement of ice and of Soviet ships. Two methods are employed: manned long-range flights, usually designated as weather-observation missions, and *observation satellites*. The former method, relying primarily on P-3 Orion long-range aircraft, now has been practically supplanted by satellites for Arctic observation, but still can serve for anti-submarine warfare surveillance, attack, and control purposes. Anti-submarine warfare Orion patrols are still operated from the U.S. Naval Operations Base at Keflavik, Iceland, mainly over the Greenland-Iceland-United Kingdom gap, the North Atlantic, and the eastern Canadian Arctic (Baffin Bay). Articles appearing in the *U.S. Naval Institute Proceedings* of August 1969 and June 1970 comment on these activities. In both articles U.S. naval aviators make direct references to the strategic importance of submarine traffic in the Arctic. Lieutenant Commander D. Luehring, U.S.N., comments:

> ...[Soviet] nuclear submarines may transit the [Arctic] areas virtually at will. While the entrances to Baffin Bay, west of Greenland, [in the Canadian archipelago] are narrow and shallow, the transpolar route might still be of considerable utility in effecting Atlantic deployments of [Soviet] nuclear submarines through the Norwegian Sea or Denmark Strait, and corresponding Pacific Ocean deployments from any northern base in the Soviet Union.[5]

The strategic implications of these air reconnaissances are quite clear; the extent to which the Arctic ice pack can be used as a cover for Soviet SSBN activity can be determined precisely, not only in the Canadian Arctic but in the entire polar region. Of course the same information could be used by the U.S. to deploy its SSBN forces to the best anti-submarine and strike advantage. Icebreaker-supported Arctic shipping carrying strategically important commodities can also benefit immensely from such information.

NUCLEAR SUBMARINE OPERATIONS

The principal American military weapon in the Arctic, both for offensive and defensive purposes, is the nuclear submarine. Although it is not known—or at least not publicized—what the capabilities of Soviet nuclear submarines (SSN's) are, it can safely be assumed that they at least match those of the American submarines. The publicized exploits of American submarines navigating under and through the obstacles of the pack ice and polar cap, and through each of the three Arctic exits, make it clear just how versatile and potentially effective the nuclear submarine can be in the Arctic.

In August 1957 the American nuclear submarine *Nautilus*, under Commander W. R. Anderson, U.S.N., proceeded submerged under the polar ice cap to within 180 miles of the geographical North Pole, thus confirming Stefansson's 1922 prediction of Arctic submarine navigation. In July and August of 1958 the *Nautilus*, under the same command, proceeded from the Bering Sea, under the ice cap, across the top of Arctic Canada and Greenland, surfacing at the pole and exiting into the Atlantic by way of the Greenland Sea, thereby demonstrating the practical feasibility of submarine operations in the Arctic and introducing the region to an era of unprecedented strategic importance.[6] In March 1959, Commander Calvert took the submarine *Skate* through the Arctic and surfaced at the Pole. Some observers surmise it must have passed through the Soviet sector en route to the Pole, presumably undetected. Until then access to the Arctic had been gained through the Greenland-Iceland-United Kingdom gap in both winter and summer, and had also been accomplished three times through the Bering Strait, but only in the ice-free season of summer.

In 1960 all-season access to the Arctic through all three entrances was demonstrated by American submarines. In the winter of 1960 the American nuclear submarine *Sargo* proceeded submerged through the Bering Strait, under the ice cap to the Pole, and returned to the Pacific by the same route. Although the passage was executed through the strait with some difficulty, it did demonstrate that this particular access to the Arctic was definitely passable in all seasons to nuclear submarines. In the summer of the same year the *Seadragon*, under the command of G. P. Steele, Cdr U.S.N., sailed from the Atlantic to the Pacific under the Baffin Bay ice pack submerged through the Northwest Passage, and returned to the Atlantic by the same route. Thus the *Seadragon*'s voyage added the third and last of the three Arctic exits.

The implications of these voyages for the Canadian Arctic should not be overlooked. The fact that a serving Canadian officer, Commodore O.C.S. Robertson, R.C.N., was aboard the *Seadragon* during its transit of the Northwest passage indicates that the Canadian government must have given at least implicit approval for this penetration of Canadian sovereignty, and must have understood the strategic implications for the Canadian Arctic resulting from the passage. All these implications were reemphasized in 1962 by the *Skate*'s passage to the Arctic from the Atlantic northward through the Davis Strait and the Kennedy and Robeson Channels between Greenland and Ellesmere Island. It returned by way of the Northwest Passage (M'Clure Strait, Viscount Melville Sound, Barrow Strait, Lancaster Sound, Baffin Bay) into the North Atlantic. It must be assumed that any nuclear submarine, American or Soviet, is capable of passing through the Canadian Arctic as well as through the other two Arctic exits in the course of its attempt to achieve offensive or defensive strategic objectives.

ICEBREAKING

The other type of American military capability in the Arctic is, of course, maritime surface-icebreaking operations. A question that should be discussed at the outset is whether or not the United States icebreakers are 'military' units, that is warships. American icebreakers, whether armed or not, have military and strategic functions, particularly in operations in the Arctic.

Before 1966 the United States Navy operated five icebreakers that were 'military' vessels or warships, both because they were designated as such by the U.S. government and assigned to the Department of Defence, and because they were armed. By December 1966 all five had been transferred to the U.S. Coast Guard under the Department of Transport.[7] The decision to make the transfer was probably prompted by a desire to centralize control and expertise of icebreaker operations in one service, and to a certain extent to 'de-militarize' the icebreakers' official status by placing them under a 'civilian' department of the United States Government. Commander K. B. Schumacher, U.S.N., observed in his 1969 article, 'Studies for the New Icebreakers', that

> The United States is the only other country [besides Sweden] that has icebreakers operated by an armed service, and we are the only nation that mounts weapons on these ships. Late in 1968, we began to remove the guns from them.[8]

The removal of the guns might have been a further attempt to 'de-militarize' the icebreakers, and might have been prompted by the 1967 Soviet refusal of 'innocent passage' through the Vilkiskiy Straits to the U.S.C.G. icebreakers *Edisto* and *Eastwind*. The Soviets clearly regarded the icebreakers as 'warships',[9] not without good cause. Not only were they armed but, although their ostensible purpose in being there was for oceanographic research, their real purpose was to establish the 'internationality' of the Arctic Ocean beyond the twelve-mile limit of Soviet sovereignty, thus challenging the Soviet 'sector' claim upon which the strategically vital Northern Sea Route as a defence route was and is based. In essence the mission was a strategic 'probe', and the icebreakers attempting to carry it out were suitably regarded as 'military'. It is well known, of course, that the United States Coast Guard is a military force. The comments of Rear Admiral J. W. Moreau, U.S.C.G., are instructive on this point:

> The Coast Guard military readiness posture must be maintained and supported. There are far too many persons who want to convert the Coast Guard into a non-military force. To do so would deprive our nation of a valuable defence force — an armed force that has distinguished itself throughout America's proud history.[10]

With respect to the Coast Guard's icebreakers themselves, Commander Schumacher has observed:

> The United States employs icebreakers primarily for support of commerce, military operations, and scientific expeditions. Our fleet includes

eight polar icebreakers [1969]. Since World War II, the strongest emphasis in the Arctic has been on military duties, such as breaking the path for the ships needed for the construction and support of the DEW line radar stations across Canada and Greenland, and the BMEWS installation at Thule, Greenland.[11]

Speaking of the Soviet icebreakers, he notes further:

Although they carry no guns, Soviet icebreakers have definite military significance, just as do their 'trawlers' operating off our coasts.[12]

He is suggesting, of course, that the military or non-military character of a vessel is not determined by the presence or absence of armament, but by the purpose to which the vessel is put. Even if the *Polar Star*, the new American polar icebreaker launched in January 1974, is unarmed, its future missions in the Arctic after coming into service sometime in 1975 will undoubtedly be related to military and strategic objectives, just as the functions served by other American icebreakers have been and will continue to be military in nature.

As officially designated in the *Budget of the United States Government*, the functions of the U.S. Coast Guard are:

1. search and rescue;
2. aids to navigation (lights, buoys, electronic navigation systems);
3. merchant-marine safety;
4. U.S. marine-law enforcement;
5. oceanography, meteorology, and polar operations;
6. military readiness and operations;
7. general support (of U.S. national policy).[13]

The strategic implications of the operations of U.S. Coast Guard icebreakers in the Arctic can be related to these seven official Coast Guard functions.

U.S. Coast Guard search-and-rescue operations in the Arctic do not rely on icebreakers but almost exclusively upon aircraft.[14] The regions served by the American Rescue Coordination Centres at Elmendorf Air Force Base, Anchorage, Alaska, and at Keflavik, Iceland, are outside, but bordering on, the Canadian Arctic. The Rescue Coordination Centres at Edmonton, Trenton, and Halifax share the responsibility with Canada for search and rescue in Arctic Canada.[15] With greater maritime and air activity in and over the Arctic, the frequency of search-and-rescue missions, both American and joint Canadian-American, is bound to increase. Brigadier General R. M. Withers, in his 1971 article 'Defence Requirements North of Sixty', made clear his understanding that improvement and expansion of Canadian search-and-rescue facilities in the Arctic will soon be necessary to keep up with the increasing demand, both potential and actual.[16] Because U.S. resource requirements and activities in the Canadian Arctic have direct strategic importance to the United States government, it is reasonable to expect the Americans to extend their Coast Guard's support and search-and-rescue coverage to those activities. With respect to the enforcement of U.S. maritime regulations or international agreements, the U.S. Coast Guard icebreakers have a significant role to play, which potentially at least is strategically significant, but not to any appreciable extent in the Canadian Arctic. Canadian law enforcement and sovereignty surveillance in the Arctic, meagre as it is, does prevent the Americans from carrying out their own patrols through that region using aircraft or icebreakers, at least for the present. Nevertheless the general strategic potential of American icebreakers for enforcing national sea frontiers and national maritime regulations in ice-bound waters cannot be dismissed lightly, particularly when the potential transgressor happens to be Russian. This fact was dramatically illustrated in January 1972 by the U.S. Coast Guard icebreaker *Storis*, which was operating in the central Bering Sea. The Soviet fisheries factory ship *Lamut* and stern trawler *Kolyvan* were apprehended inside the Alaskan reaches of the U.S. contiguous fishing zone near St Matthew Island, and escorted under arrest to Adak. Its icebreaking capacity in the ice-covered seas and the very real threat of its guns made it possible for the *Storis* to foil several attempts by the Soviet ships to resist arrest and to escape.[17]

The U.S. Coast Guard Arctic icebreakers have already made significant contributions to military operations and can be expected to do so again in the future. The following statement on the U.S. Coast Guard icebreaker operations attests to the military significance of their contributions. The U.S. Department of Transport *Sixth Annual Report* (FY 1972) states:

> Coast Guard icebreakers continued to serve this nation's interests in the Arctic and Antarctica during FY 1972. In the Eastern Arctic and Antarctic, two ships facilitated the annual re-supply of U.S. defence installations and supported various scientific investigations benefitting such activities as the International Ice Patrol and U.S. Navy defence oriented research. Three icebreakers deployed to the western Arctic in the summer months and one in the winter to conduct such diverse investigations as ecological research, geological surveys, and defence oriented research.

After the initial DEW line construction period (1954-7), when resupply was conducted almost entirely by U.S. ships, the servicing of sites in the Canadian Arctic was taken over by the Canadian government. Thus resupply of the U.S. base at Thule, Greenland, is the only remaining function for the U.S. Coast Guard icebreakers in the high Arctic except for resupply of nuclear submarines operating in the Arctic, thus contributing to their potential effectiveness.

The United States is undertaking a replacement program for its icebreaker fleet. Seven *Wind* class ships were built between 1943 and 1947, and the latest, the *Glacier*, (a slight enlargement of the *Wind* design) in 1955. Since that time most nations interested in icebreaking have built or acquired larger and stronger icebreakers, particularly the Soviet Union, so that by the late sixties the eight American icebreakers were aged, unreliable, and outclassed. The Soviet icebreaker fleet, by way of contrast, is still the largest in the world, although the launching of the U.S.C.G. *Polar Star* promises to increase significantly U.S. capabilities. Moreover the Soviets have continued their ambitious icebreaker-building program. With the commissioning of the nuclear-powered *Arktika*,[18] and with other vessels in the planning or construction stages, the Soviets will maintain indefinitely a large fleet of icebreakers consistent with their vital national and strategic interests in the icebound waters of the Northern Sea Route. The United States, on the other hand, will be hard-pressed to meet its minimum icebreaking requirements over the next five to ten years, merely because of the lack of ships. The *Wind* class ships, with two exceptions, are presently being phased out of service, not only because of their advanced age and mechanical unreliability, but also because '[T]heir hulls are constructed of a form of steel that becomes more brittle as the temperature sinks, a fact that was learned only as the state of the metallurgical art progressed after their launching.'[19] In reply to a written question from Senator M. Stevens before the U.S. Senate Sub-Committee on Coast Guard and Navigation for the First Session of the 92nd Congress, 30 March 1971, Admiral Chester R. Bender, Comdt U.S.C.G., stated: 'All remaining six *Winds* are rapidly approaching the end of useful service. They are already unreliable. Of the six, we plan to decommission four by 1975.'[20] This was apparently the only official rationale offered by the Coast Guard for the icebreaker-replacement program. However it isn't a bad guess to suggest that the Congressmen and Senators who were considering Coast Guard icebreaker appropriations were persuaded to a favourable decision largely because of the embarrassing performance of the then-existing fleet.

Admiral Bender went on to explain the Coast Guard's icebreaker-replacement program, which essentially consists of renewing the machinery of the *Northwind* and *Westwind* to extend their usefulness for at least five years, renovating the *Glacier* so that it be able to operate well into the 1980s, and building four replacement icebreakers.[21] One, the 400-foot *Polar Star*, was launched in January 1974 and will be in service in 1975; the other, approved in the 1973 Budget, is presently under construction and is expected to be launched in 1976. The remaining two are not yet approved for construction but are planned for completion before 1980.

The following excerpt from U.S. Budget statements indicate the official icebreaker-replacement program objectives. The 1971 Budget states:

> The Coast Guard's facilities modernization program includes construction of a modern polar icebreaker and six medium-range helicopters. With this new equipment, the Coast Guard will be able to improve its search and rescue, *polar navigation support*, and maritime law enforcement services.[22]

And the 1972 Budget repeats the program objectives:

> The traditional roles of the Coast Guard in search and rescue, polar transportation and aids to navigation will be enhanced by equipment and facility modernization. . . .

In these Budget statements there is little if any mention of military operations in relation to the icebreaker program. It appears, from these primary sources at least, that polar transportation and search and rescue constitute the primary objectives of the icebreaker program. Yet the military functions described above will be served as well by the new icebreakers, probably more efficiently in fact.

The U.S. Coast Guard icebreaker fleet for the next few years will therefore consist of four ships; the re-engined *Northwind* and *Westwind*, the *Glacier*, and the *Polar Star*. Even with the increased capacity of the *Polar Star*, and rotation of crews, it seems unlikely that the U.S. icebreaker fleet in the late seventies will meet the demand. Moreover, noting the difficulties involved in persuading Congress to fund large and expensive programs, Captain How of the U.S. Coast Guard observed, 'the program to fund two additional breakers may find itself in great difficulty.'[23]

Even so, the capabilities of the two new icebreakers do have clear implications for the Canadian Arctic. The *Polar Star* and her as yet unnamed sister ship will each have almost twice the power of Canada's biggest icebreaker, the *Louis St Laurent*. This suggests that the ice of the Canadian Northwest Passage will no longer pose an obstacle to American attempts to demonstrate the 'internationality' of those waters as an ocean shipping route for the strategically important resources of the North. In fact the U.S. Secretary of Transportation, Claude S. Brinegar, was explicit at the launching ceremony of the *Polar Star*: 'With the opening of the Alaskan oilfields, the ship will play a dominant role in helping the movement of Arctic supplies and equipment.' Without adequate icebreakers of its own, Canada may be forced to sit back and watch the United States navigate the Northwest Passage freely and establish the validity of its claim that these are international waters.

It is now possible to draw some tentative conclusions about the implications for the Canadian Arctic raised by the American offensive and defensive strategic objectives in the Arctic generally. Table I summarizes those strategic objectives, indicates the military operations necessary in order of importance, and states the relation of each to Canada in terms of American interest in free passage through, or military operations in, Canadian Arctic waters. In the case of both free passage and military operations, the principal American concern is to establish and maintain the international character of the Canadian Arctic waters, or alternatively to establish a military presence there by agreement with, or in conjunction with, Canada. It should be readily apparent from Table I that the

TABLE I.

U.S. Strategic Objectives in the Arctic	U.S. Forces	Interest in Canadian Arctic	
Offensive		Passage	Operations
1. SLBM attack on all Soviet strategic targets	SSBN	L	P
2. SLBM attack on Soviet Air & BMEWS	SSBN	L	P
3. SLBM attack on all Soviet SSBN bases	SSBN	L	P
4. Attack Soviet shipping on Northern Sea Route	SSN – AGB	L	P
5. Attack Soviet naval traffic Northern Sea Route	SSN – AGB	L	P
Defensive			
1. ASW against Soviet SSBNs	SSN & Bottom Sonar	N	N
2. Protect U.S. military re-supply missions	SSN – AGB	N	N
3. Protect U.S. strategic resource shipping	SSN – AGB	N	N

Code:
SLBM – submarine-launched ballistic missile
SSBN – ballistic missile nuclear submarine
SSN – nuclear attack submarine
AGB – polar icebreaker – armed
BMEWS – Ballistic Missile Early-Warning System
ASW – anti-submarine warfare
N – necessary
L – likely
P – possible

American military strategic interest in the Canadian Arctic is mainly defensive, but that American interest in free passage and military operations in the Canadian Arctic for offensive strategic objectives is both likely and possible.

EMERGING ECONOMIC IMPERATIVES

'Welcome to the world's largest and most expensive addition to the Ice Follies,' smiled the Chairman of the Board of Humble Oil as he briefed the press on the 1969 Arctic voyage of the American ship, the S.S. *Manhattan*. The effect of that voyage—the traversing of the Northwest Passage—on Canadian sovereignty, to say nothing of its effect on Canadian domestic and foreign policy, has more or less disappeared from view.

Out of sight, however, is not necessarily out of mind or out of shipbuilding yards. It is true that since the voyages of the S.S. *Manhattan* not much attention has been given to the Northwest Passage, and challenges since then to Canadian sovereignty in that area have not been physical so much as confined to legal briefs at conferences on the law of the sea.

The Canadian press generally has not directed much attention in the last few years to any possibility of American or Soviet or Japanese tankers or icebreakers plying the waters of the Northwest Passage. Recent announcements from the oil industry indicating that pipelines appear to have the 'economic edge at present'[24] over using icebreaking tankers as a solution to the oil-transportation problem have lulled Canadian consciousness about this possibility. Let us remember, however, that Humble Oil announced on 21 October 1970—well before oil prices skyrocketed—that the use of icebreaking tankers to transport crude oil from Alaska's North Slope to American markets was commercially feasible, even if it decided to suspend its icebreaking-tanker studies by choosing to concentrate its efforts on pipeline alternatives. In this announcement Humble suggested that work on the development of Arctic tankers could be resumed on short notice if economic factors or other circumstances warranted it.[25] The company's Arctic marine studies indicated that icebreaking tankers could move North Slope oil through both the Northwest Passage to the American east coast and through the Bering Strait to the west coast. Humble also announced at that time that preliminary design studies for icebreaking tankers had been completed by Newport News Shipbuilding and Dry Dock Company. The studies were based on a 1,250-foot ship of 300,000 dwt, capable of year-round Arctic operations without icebreaker assistance. Humble also suggested that the use of such giant icebreaking ships would require construction of an off-shore loading terminal in the Arctic waters of the Beaufort Sea. Feasibility and basic design studies on the terminal's facilities were completed in early 1970. On 21 October 1970 Mr J. A. Wright, Humble Oil's Board Chairman, suggested that

the two Arctic voyages of the S.S. *Manhattan* were highly successful in providing valuable data for our studies concerning the various transportation alternatives for moving Alaskan crude oil to U.S. refineries. We now know that icebreaking tanker transportation is a workable alternative, and this gives us much greater flexibility in meeting future transportation needs.[26]

The needs of the American oil companies are often viewed as co-extensive with American strategic interests. This paper, while neither attacking nor supporting this contention, recognizes the considerable symmetry between American military assessments of the importance of the Arctic and the needs of the American oil giants. Now almost all Americans see the growing dependence of the United States on Middle East oil, as one member of the American Coast Guard saw it over three years ago, as a problem that 'threatens to upset the delicate power balance between the superpowers. The current trend of steadily increasing oil imports will reach a crucial level of dependence at some time in the near future.' That was written by Captain W. S. Cass for the United States Naval Institute *Proceedings* in January 1973. Several months before his suggestion became fact with the advent of the OPEC squeeze on industrialized countries, he defined the critical level of dependence as 'that level of oil imports which if denied would seriously threaten U.S. national security.' Most Americans consider that the United States is already at that level.

The threat implicit in the possibility of OPEC's interrupting vital oil supplies has several potential implications for American strategic interests. Intimidation from OPEC has ranged from subtle pressure for the U.S. to take a specific position to overt pressure for its withdrawal of support of Israel. That pressure at times reached a point where, in the words of Captain Cass, it amounted to 'a deliberate effort to reduce the capability of the United States to support super power status'. It is not surprising therefore that naval and oil interests in the United States have seriously examined the probability of a successful all-out program to develop Alaskan and other Arctic oil and gas as an alternative to what it sees as a critical dependence on the goodwill of the OPEC countries.

In order to carry out an extensive program to develop Alaskan oil there must be sufficient recoverable oil in the area; technology adequate to explore for oil and develop production; sufficient trained personnel available for exploration and development; and, key to Canadian interests in the North, an adequate transportation system. Although it is far from conclusive that there is sufficient oil, Captain Cass and others feel that all these assumptions can be classed as reasonable. Naturally Captain Cass, as a naval officer, sees the transportation question as the key to a success-ful venture. To assume that an adequate transportation system can be developed is to raise more questions than are usually asked in discussions of the Alaskan and Mackenzie Valley pipelines, for example. If the Alaskan pipeline is completed it will deliver in the neighbourhood of only 600,000 barrels a day; planned additional pumping stations may be able to raise this capacity to two million barrels per day by 1980. The competi-tive proposal for a Canadian pipeline down the Mackenzie Valley would only be able to deliver a similar volume. Why, then, the interest in pipelines instead of icebreakers? The decision to select a pipeline system instead of an icebreaker-tanker system turned basically on the estimated time required to complete the system. Also, in the words of Captain Cass, 'potential controversy with Canada over use of the Northwest Passage also weighed against the icebreaker-tanker system.' A most crucial factor in deciding to go for pipelines however was that the technology was as yet undeveloped for the icebreaker-tanker system. In addition, research and development had not proceeded far enough to solve the difficult prob-lems of offshore loading facilities.

Yet the icebreaker-tanker system will emerge before long. Evidence, while not conclusive, supports the view that the decision not to go ahead with the icebreaker-tanker system was taken in the belief that the Alaska pipeline would be adequate for the present development of Prudhoe output until further fields in Alaska are discovered and developed. Then, however, the American objective of a secure supply of energy from domestic sources will require the capacity to transport approximately six million barrels per day by 1978, and an icebreaker-tanker system then becomes an attractive possibility. Such a system would be more flexible than building more pipelines. To begin with, the location of future oil deposits is not yet known — and tankers can move around while pipelines have to be built in one place. Secondly, a pipeline must be fully com-pleted before it can start transporting oil, while a tanker system can start transporting upon completion of the first unit. Finally, the volume of production of new oil deposits is unknown and the capacity of a tanker system can be continually increased as ships are added. Also the risks in building a major tanker system are not as great as the high cost of tankers might suggest, since large exploitable deposits of oil are almost certain to be discovered somewhere in the Arctic.

Tankers are not risk-free, however. The problem with tankers is not simply the physical challenge of icebreaking but the danger of pollution and environmental damage. It is widely recognized that accidents will result in greater environmental damage in the Arctic than in more temper-ate zones. The risks to the environment inherent in pipelines have been thoroughly aired in both Canada and the United States in the discussion of the Alaska Pipeline and the Mackenzie Valley Pipeline. However the threat of tanker operations to the ecology of the Arctic has received nothing like the same amount of close inspection.

We will find of course that American oil companies will not be inarticulate on this subject. They will argue that the limited evidence available suggests that a major tanker spill may be easier to handle in the Arctic than in the open sea because the heavy ice acts as a containment boom and prevents the rapid spread of oil. They will claim as well that although Arctic temperatures are low, pooled oil can be burned with a small residue of inert carbon if it is ignited quickly, within one or two days. The oil companies will also argue, in any discussion of risk, that sufficient protection of an icebreaker tanker can be assured by heavy plating of the hull.

Icebreaker tankers are extremely expensive, massive machines. However the relatively high cost of icebreaker tankers for the Arctic is offset to some degree by the reduced round-trip time from the Arctic to the United States compared with trips from the Middle East to the United States. Thus a fewer number of tankers would be required to carry the same volume of oil. It should also be remembered that the oil companies recognize that a successful Arctic-tanker system would tend to hold import prices considerably below Middle East oil sources particularly if OPEC retains its cohesion and its present importance in the U.S. market.

American interest in developing a major transportation facility in the Arctic has existed at least since the 1960s not only for oil and gas but for minerals as well. In September 1967, when a new polar section was dedicated at the National Archives building in Washington D.C., Representative William Anderson, Commanding Officer of the *Nautilus* during the 1958 transit of the Arctic, spoke at the ceremony. He suggested that large cargo nuclear submarines could bring out the rich mineral reserves of northern Canada and that this ought to be a prominent objective of American ship construction and naval development. He forecast that cargo nuclear submarines 'will ply between the far east and Europe via the north pole, cutting the sea distances almost in half.'

The prospect of submerged traffic in Arctic waters poses a problem for American policy-makers. The law of the sea requires that a submarine operate on the surface while on innocent passage through the territorial waters of another country. A coastal nation should not, however, interfere in any way as long as the innocent passage is through waterways normally used for international navigation between two parts of the high seas. The problem for the Americans is that it is impossible for a submarine to proceed on the surface through ice-covered straits.

Still, the Americans continue to be undaunted by the prospect of major vessels plying the Northwest Passage. To understand why, the S.S. *Manhattan* voyage must be put in perspective. It was not the first trip through the Passage; several smaller vessels had made it before, and although the

150,000 ton S.S. *Manhattan* got through, the passage has not automatically opened to commercial shipping. The S.S. *Manhattan* travelled at the best time of year. She was never intended to be the prototype of a future commercial vessel; she was a tanker adapted for an experiment. In December 1969 the *Imperial Oil Review* stated:

> She was a floating laboratory with a fortified hull, propellers, keel shafts and rudder, a special icebreaker prow and a load of sophisticated electronic equipment. Big though she is, the *Manhattan* would be dwarfed by the specially built 250,000 ton ships contemplated for future Northwest Passage service. This partly explains why she bogged down five times on the westbound trip.

In 1969 Humble Oil speculated that various companies would have twenty-five or thirty huge icebreaking tankers in the passage by 1975. This speculation has proved to be ill-founded, but who is to tell whether five years from now it might not become a reality?

Imperial oil asked in its *Review* what this will mean to Canada.

> [This] could turn the dream of an open Canadian north to reality. The worst part of the route, in terms of the old, hard-pack ice, is off Alaska. From Melville Sound east of Baffin Bay in other words, in that part of the route lying due north of most of mainland Canada – there is open water during part of the year. Thus even in winter its ice is rarely more than a year old. Canadian oil tankers could utilize this route.

> So could Canadian minerals – our northern copper, lead, silver, zinc, iron ore. Powerful new tankers, icebreakers and icebreaking techniques could even turn Churchill into a year-round port for the prairies . . . geographically our north is the hub of the top of the world. Banks Island is roughly equally distant from London, Tokyo and New York. A regular sea lane through the passage would cut thousands of miles from traditional shipping routes. The traffic could bring harbours, terminals, entire communities into the Canadian north.

By far the largest potential, an estimated eighty billion barrels of undiscovered oil, lies in the *frontier areas*, primarily the Arctic and Atlantic basins. Of this potential about 80 per cent lies offshore, much of it in areas where the technology to drill for and develop the resources is far from perfected. Yet it is clear that the need for energy is so pressing that the search for these potential reserves will continue to be carried on intensively in this decade. The Canadian Arctic provides two prospective producing areas: the Beaufort area, which is the mainland around the Mackenzie River Delta and the adjacent shallow waters of the Beaufort Sea; and the islands of the high Arctic and the waters between them. In 1974 the *Imperial Oil Review* reported that in the Beaufort area the oil industry had drilled a total of sixty-six wells of which four found oil and eleven found gas;

fifty-one were dry. There was an important discovery at Atkinson Point in 1970. Imperial found oil at Mayogiak six miles east of Tuktoyaktuk in 1971 and at Iruoik also in the Mackenzie Delta in 1972. Imperial has also drilled for gas at Taglu and Mallik. Other companies have drilled gas wells in the Beaufort area. Although Imperial admits that the oil found so far is insufficient to warrant commercial development, the gas finds are described as significant by Imperial President J. A. Armstrong. Sixty-seven wells have been drilled in the Sverdrup Basin. Two drilled by Panarctic (45 per cent owned by the Canadian government) on Ellesmere Island and Thor Island found oil, but neither is rated significant. However twelve gas wells have been drilled and have indicated six significant gas pools. Panarctic is currently drilling the deepest and most expensive exploratory wells in the North, to 18,000 feet, in the Drake Point gas field on northeastern Melville Island.[27]

Even though Humble Oil decided not to use tankers for moving North Slope crude oil, the voyage of the *Manhattan* has shown that the use of sea transportation for the development of resources in the Arctic may, in the words of Captain T. Pullen 'be just around the corner rather than a vague dream for the future.'[28] World-freight patterns could be altered by this new shipping route. The implications for a new trade route through the Arctic are tremendous, says Dr Assur of the Colder Regions Research and Engineering Laboratory. 'I wouldn't be surprised that within a short time some nation will eventually build a ship that will go through. More than likely such ships will operate north of the Canadian Arctic islands rather than through the North West Passage. Within our lifetime this will happen.'[29]

Already the expected new American icebreakers, according to the U.S. Naval Institute's *Naval Review* for 1974,

> should have no trouble operating 240 to 270 days per year, the same men don't have to be aboard all the time. Therefore a plan is being considered to assign crews of 150% of normal complement so that part of the ship's company can always be on leave or assigned to shore duty in the ship's home port.

The American position on the law of the sea as it affects the Arctic is clearly in conflict with Canada's position. The United States has unequivocally stated that its willingness to accept twelve miles as the limit of the territorial sea is contingent upon agreement on the right of free transit and overflight through and over international straits. This issue is critical for the United States, and for other major maritime nations for that matter. The United States is well aware that if the territorial limit is increased to twelve miles, over a hundred straits now navigable as high seas would be territorial seas. Maritime nations, and in this case we must include Canada, argue however that if the territorial limit were increased to twelve miles this would pose no problem for the United States because the right of innocent passage would protect it. However the right of innocent passage does not solve the problems of the United States because the state having jurisdiction over the strait, in this case Canada, is ultimately the judge of what is innocent and what is not. It is clear that the Americans are confronted with a difficult situation. It is unquestionable that aircraft and submerged submarines would not enjoy the right of innocent passage if the terms of the territorial-sea convention set down in Geneva in 1958 were applied. American naval officers chafe at the lack of mobility this restriction implies. To quote Commander R. C. Knott of the U.S. Navy in *U.S. Naval Institute Proceedings* of March 1973:

> Clearly the mobility of U.S. forces cannot be subjected to the whims of straits states, yet it is equally clear that such states have legitimate concerns which must be addressed.[30]

The United States has always relied on its location athwart the two great oceans of the world for its security and its ability to protect its influence as a world power. Commander Knott of the U.S. Navy has put the American position and its strategic significance as ominously and candidly as anyone to date.

> Americans discovered early that the oceans not only provided them with in depth protection but also with the means of making common cause with others who have similar interests no matter how distant they may be. On the other hand those who would threaten these interests are effectively deterred because they know that the military, industrial and economic might of the United States can be quickly employed anywhere in the world. This geographic advantage coupled with sea and air power provides the United States with the capability to move men and equipment on and over the sea for great distances at a moment's notice as well as the ability to furnish continuous logistics support for sustained military operations of any kind or size.[31]

It should be expected then that the U.S. position on all law of the sea issues will be influenced to some degree by the imperative of such considerations.

NOTES

[1] The Soviet position on sovereignty over their 'sector' of the Arctic is thoroughly examined in Donat Pharand, *The Law of the Sea of the Arctic* (Ottawa, 1973).

[2] For a sampling of non-official but informed American and NATO interpretations of the

Soviet strategic interest in the Arctic, see O. P. Araldsen, Capt. R.N.N., 'The Soviet Union and the Arctic', *USNIP* (June 1967), 48-57; T. J. Laforest, Capt. U.S.N., 'Strategic Significance of the Northern Sea Route', *USNIP* (December 1967), 56-65; G. E. Synhorst, Capt. U.S.N., 'The Soviet Strategic Interest in the Maritime Arctic', *USNIP* (May 1973), 88-111.

[3] Synhorst, *op. cit.*, 97.

[4] R. Herrick, Cdr U.S.N., *Soviet Naval Strategy* (Annapolis, Md., U.S. Naval Institute, n.d.).

[5] D. Luehring, L/Cdr U.S.N., 'The Never-Never Sea', *USNIP* (August 1969), 142-6.

[6] W. R. Anderson, Cdr U.S.N., *Nautilus-90-North* (Cleveland, 1959).

[7] G. R. Boling, 'The Coast Guard's Navy Icebreakers', *USNIP* (January 1968), 134.

[8] K. B. Schumacher, Dcr-U.S.N., 'Studies for the New Icebreakers', *USNIP*, Naval Review Issue (1969), 220.

[9] S. M. Olenicoff, 'Territorial Waters in the Arctic: The Soviet Position', RAND Corporation Paper no. R-907-ARPA (July 1972), pp. 21-2.

[10] J. B. Moreau, R/Adm U.S.C.G., 'The Coast Guard in the Central and Western Pacific', *USNIP* (May 1973), 294.

[11] Schumacher, *op. cit.*, 218.

[12] *Ibid.*, 220.

[13] U.S.A., *Budget of the U.S. Government* (Washington, 1972), p. 123.

[14] R. A. J. Ranieri, Cdr U.S.N., 'Angels in the Snow: SAR in the Arctic', *USNIP* (January 1974), 103-5.

[15] A chart of Canadian search-and-rescue regions is reproduced as Appendix '0' in Colin S. Gary, *Canadian Defence Priorities: A Question of Relevance* (Toronto, 1972), p. 268.

[16] R. M. Withers, Brig./Gen., 'Defence Requirements North of Sixty', *CDQ*, I (Summer 1971), 41-3.

[17] Moreau, *op. cit.*, 277-9.

[18] 'Icebreaker Arktika Under Construction', *Vodnyy Transport* (25 October 1973), as translated in *USNIP* (June 1974), 122-3.

[19] A. B. How, Capt. U.S.C.G., 'The Guard Approaching the Century's End', *USNIP*, 100, (May 1974), 92.

[20] U.S.A., Senate Sub-Committee on Coast Guard and Navigation, *Hearings on U.S.C.G. Appropriations*, 92nd Congress, 1st Session, 30 March 1971, pp. 57-8.

[21] *Ibid.*, p. 58.

[22] U.S.A., *Budget of the U.S. Government*, FY 1971, p. 119.

[23] How, *op. cit.*, 102.

[24] Humble Oil and Refining Company *News Release*, 21 October 1970, p. 1.

[25] *Ibid.*, and Humble Oil and Refining Company *News Release*, 16 April 1971, *passim*.

[26] W. K. Carr, M/Gen., 'Toward a Modernizing North American Air Defence System', *CDQ*, II (Spring 1973), 9.

[27] *Imperial Oil Review*, LVIII (1974), 29.

[28] Gray, *op. cit.*, pp. 10-11.

[29] *Ibid.*, pp. 9-10.

[30] R. C. Knott, Cdr U.S.N., 'Who Owns the Oceans?', *U.S. Naval Institute Proceedings* (March 1973), 68.

[31] *Ibid.*

7 THE POLICY DIMENSION
by P. C. Dobell*

The Arctic frontier has only sporadically attracted general attention in Canada, and the public's knowledge of the region is generally vague and often romanticized. Canadians take the Arctic for granted as an integral part of their national heritage, an established portion of the map of Canada. Only when that assumption has been called into question have strong feelings erupted, as the reaction to the S.S. *Manhattan*'s voyages demonstrated. Public and press throughout the country pressed for vigorous action. Faced by an implicit challenge to Canadian control in the Arctic, and pushed by an aroused public and Parliament, the government acted and Parliament responded in an unprecedented manner by giving unanimous approval to the Arctic Waters Pollution Prevention Bill (1970).

What neither the public nor Parliament fully appreciated were the difficulties facing the government in pursuing Canadian claims. Earlier pronouncements on the subject of Canadian Arctic sovereignty by both Conservative and Liberal governments in Ottawa had been confusing, woolly, and often contradictory, and none of these governments had clearly set out on what basis Canadian claims were made or to what extent they might extend to the Arctic waters as well as to the mainland and the Arctic islands. Sometimes the sector principle had been espoused, at other times the archipelagic principle, or the principle of effective occupation had been taken up. This uncertainty indicates that no principle in international law established an unassailable claim. Because of the unusual physical features of the Arctic it was even unclear how the ordinary rules of law would apply. Should ice be treated as *land*, particularly if it were part of the permanent ice-pack, or as frozen *water*? Could the Arctic waters be classed as an ocean like other oceans? Would recognition of archipelago claims mean that the waters between the islands

---

*Research for this chapter was carried out by Carol Seaborn. The article was completed in December 1974.

could be treated as internal Canadian waters, or would each island be considered as having a territorial sea?

During the S.S. *Manhattan* controversy the Canadian government proceeded on the assumption that Canadian sovereignty over the Arctic land territory could not be legally challenged. Prime Minister Trudeau asserted that 'the Arctic mainland and islands form an integral part of Canada and we have extended to them the administrative, legislative and judicial framework which applies to all parts of Canada.'[1] He appeared to be basing the claim to Arctic lands on the 'effective occupation' principle. But what tactic to employ for the waters, there being no accepted means for a state to occupy water?

Established international law, with its emphasis on freedom for navigation, clearly favoured states engaged extensively in shipping. The United States, as the world's greatest maritime power, put forth arguments designed to accord merchant vessels the right of innocent passage, stressing that it was in the interests of everyone to have the greatest possible area of freely navigable waters. It maintained that the Arctic ocean was 'high seas' in the legal sense and subject to the usual regime of the high seas like any other ocean. The 1969 voyage of the S.S. *Manhattan*, despite the Canadian government's concurrence and co-operation, constituted an implicit challenge to any Canadian assertion of its right to control the Northwest Passage. There were many both in and out of Parliament who saw this voyage as a possible precursor, should oil be found in great quantities on the Arctic islands or in Arctic waters, to stronger challenges to Canadian Arctic sovereignty. The Opposition and the House of Commons Standing Committee on Indian Affairs and Northern Development strongly urged the government to declare 'that vessels passing through Canada's Arctic Archipelago are and shall be subject to the sovereign control and regulation of Canada.'[2] The government resisted making an outright claim of sovereignty to the waters, unwilling to risk a challenge to the drawing of baselines, or asserting that these were internal waters on the basis of the archipelagic principle. Strong contrary views had been expressed in international circles, but particularly in Washington, against either measure, and the government feared that an outright assertion to the Arctic waters might provoke a broader challenge and call into question other aspects of Canada's northern jurisdiction for which it was believed a successful sovereignty claim had already been gradually established through a number of steps.

Instead the government chose a course of action that asserted only the jurisdiction necessary to control passage of vessels sailing through the Arctic waters of the Northwest Passage. By claiming a twelve-mile territorial sea Canada was able to assert effective control over the two narrowest points of the Northwest Passage, Barrow Strait and Prince of Wales Strait. This still left the problem of the rest of the passage being treated as

THE POLICY DIMENSION | 123

an international waterway of the 'high seas' unreservedly open to commercial ships of all nations. The pollution-control legislation was adopted as a device for gaining control without the need to assert sovereignty. At the same time as it submitted the legislation, the government was careful to put on record that 'Canada has always regarded the waters between the islands of the Arctic archipelago as being Canadian waters. The present government maintains that position.'[3] Nothing was being given up. The government's action was an extension of jurisdiction, not a claim to sovereignty, an assertion of effective control without the confrontation that a claim to sovereignty might have produced. As the legal adviser of the Department of External Affairs said later in reference to a question regarding international opposition to the Canadian position: 'It is desirable to present as small a target as possible, to make it irrelevant to have test cases and test passages for example',[4] and this was indeed what the government chose to do. The tactic was ingenious and the new concept was particularly difficult to challenge since the emphasis was on protection and responsibility for the ecology.

The government nevertheless felt its position on the pollution legislation[5] to be sufficiently vulnerable to cause it to place a reservation on its acceptance of compulsory jurisdiction of the International Court of Justice. This reversal of Canada's former policy with regard to the International Court of Justice had not been an easy one for Cabinet to take and it had been the subject of vigorous debate between ministers. Traditional Canadian policy had been one of strong commitment to international law and order. Canada had sought to perfect and strengthen international mechanisms, to be a model of international behaviour in this regard. For years at the United Nations Canada had urged other states to remove the reservations they had placed on the Court's jurisdiction. The Pearson government had resisted limiting the Court's jurisdiction even to protect the extension of Canadian jurisdictional claims for fishing zones. In deciding in favour of this reservation the Trudeau government made a major break with the past, persuaded that this was the only safe way for Canada to proceed. The concept in the legislation was too innovative, the Court too conservative, and existing international law in this area either inadequate or nonexistent.

Humble Oil's decision in the fall of 1970 to forego further work on commercial tankers for the North meant that the immediate challenge to Canadian Arctic sovereignty had passed. Other immediate prospects for foreign shipping through the Northwest Passage were negligible. Nevertheless since the pollution legislation was passed in 1970, a number of policies have been adopted and steps taken by the Canadian government directed not only at strengthening the jurisdictional assertions put forth in 1970 concerning Arctic waters, but also at reinforcing Canadian claims to Arctic sovereignty that the government hoped were well-established and over which there was no dispute in 1970. Action has been taken on the multilateral level, the bilateral level, and the domestic level.

In international legal deliberations since 1970 the attention of Canada's legal advisers has been focused primarily on the broad issues to be discussed at the Third Law-of-the-Sea Conference. The main discussions were held in the preparatory meetings leading to the Conference, including the UN Seabed Committee, and in the Caracas and Geneva sessions of the Conference in 1974 and 1975. Related discussions also took place within the UN Conference on the Human Environment, the London Ocean Dumping Conference, and the London Intergovernmental Maritime Consultative Organization Conference. While Canada's Arctic concerns did not play a highly visible role in the discussions and preparations, most of the issues had important implications for Arctic sovereignty.

The relevant issues for which Canada sought confirmation or support concerned an extension of the territorial sea to twelve miles, the right of coastal states to prevent passage of a foreign vessel in their territorial sea if the passage would result in pollution, an arrangement concerning navigation through international straits that would permit coastal states some measure of control over the transit of ships in the interest of security and environmental protection, and finally a legal definition of waters within an archipelago that would accord the archipelagic state certain rights. There are obvious implications in each of these areas for Canada's claims to Arctic sovereignty and jurisdiction. If the Third Law-of-the-Sea Conference reached agreement on any of these questions in terms that differed from Canadian policy, the government's position might be undermined. Conversely if Canadian positions were to gain international endorsation, its claims would be unquestionably confirmed. In the absence of any agreement, Canada would continue to be dependent on its present unilateral initiatives.

An important Canadian defensive measure, set out in the government's 1973 position paper prepared for the Law-of-the-Sea Conference, stated that any international agreement about straits used for international navigation would not be applicable to the Northwest Passage 'since it has not been used for international navigation'. Closely related was the government's disclaimer in the same paper that any international agreement about the special status of archipelagic waters would 'not apply directly to the Arctic archipelago which is a coastal one'.[6] Later, at the Conference itself, Canada sought approval for its definition of an archipelagic state as a group of interconnecting islands 'that form a geographical, economic and political entity' and that would, according to J. A. Beesley, the head of the official Canadian delegation, enable Canada to claim the Northwest Passage as an internal waterway.[7] Canada also argued that islands as well as continental states should be given territorial rights. Canada was playing it all ways in order to be sure.

Because of the inter-relatedness of many issues, the 1973 position paper pointed out that Canada would seek an 'umbrella' treaty aimed at controlling specific sources of pollution over the whole marine environment. This objective, which was related to gaining recognition for the Arctic-waters-pollution legislation, was to be further reinforced by the Canadian stand that 'coastal states should be empowered to prescribe and enforce their own anti-pollution standards over and above the internationally agreed rules, not only in their own territorial waters but also within their areas of jurisdiction beyond.'[8] It was this question of the right of the coastal state to adopt special measures for the prevention of pollution in particularly sensitive areas of the marine environment that was to be a special concern of Canadians at the next Law-of-the-Sea Conference.

At the 1973 London Intergovernmental Maritime Consultative Organization Conference, Canada was successful in defeating attempts to restrict the coastal state's right of enforcement of pollution prevention to its territorial sea. In general, from a legal and jurisdictional point of view, Canada was satisfied with the resulting convention on Prevention of Pollution from Ships, which gave coastal states certain rights to enforce new environmental standards. Canada had pushed for a provision that would enable states to adopt stricter standards 'where environmental conditions warranted exceptional measures such as in the Canadian Arctic.'[9] This provision only narrowly failed to secure the required majority and had support even from ship-owning countries like Greece, Liberia, and Norway—witness to the effectiveness of the Canadian delegation's 'lobbying'.

Another approach taken by the government to gain international support for the Arctic legislation consisted of a series of consultations with the other Arctic states and several non-Arctic states aimed at persuading them to attend a conference that would consider navigational safety and pollution control in Arctic waters.[10] When it became evident that this effort would fail, the government tried to work out the basis for a multilateral convention for Arctic waters, which concerned states could sign without having to participate in a conference. This idea also proved unsuccessful. At the same time, in an effort to gain acceptance of the Canadian pollution regulations, the government sent technical experts 'very widely all over the world' to hold consultations intended so far as possible to work out regulations acceptable to other states, which Canada would promulgate under the Arctic Waters Pollution Prevention Act.[11]

Canada actively sought support for its Arctic legislation and for the idea of an Arctic international conference from the Soviet Union, because it is both a superpower and the state with the largest Arctic interests. Approaches were made during the Prime Minister's trip in May 1971. The Russians appeared to have no objection to the pollution legislation for the Canadian Arctic (Mr Beesley later used the term 'acquiesced'[12]). But to the

Prime Minister's argument as to 'why we thought it would be useful to have an international gathering, not with a purpose to abdicate in any way our rights as Arctic nations or coastal states in the Arctic but to involve other nations in forms of international agreement on these matters',[13] the Soviet reply was negative. The Prime Minister reported that he had told the Soviet Union frankly that Canada needed international law to support its policy and that it would be in their interests to support Canada in this international-multinational approach, but that the Russians had 'just stonewalled [the argument]'.[14] They were no doubt wary that their own exclusionist views of their Arctic regions might be called into question. On the same trip the Prime Minister laid the groundwork for an agreement, subsequently announced in August 1971, for the establishment of a Canada-U.S.S.R. joint working group on Arctic scientific research. By 1974, however, co-operation had not advanced very far in this area.

As far as bilateral discussions with the United States were concerned, a Department of External Affairs spokesman reported in May 1973 that there was still disagreement with the United States regarding both the status of the Northwest Passage and the validity and desirability of the Canadian Arctic-pollution legislation.[15] But he emphasized that Canada had 'spent a tremendous amount of time and energies working out an agreed approach with the United States and it is not out of the question even now.'[16] In spite of this somewhat optimistic appraisal, it is difficult to see how such an agreement could be reached outside the multilateral context of the Law of the Sea Conference.

Canada's bilateral efforts with Denmark were more successful. In December 1971 an agreement was concluded between the two countries regarding the line dividing the continental shelf between the Canadian Arctic islands and Greenland, thus permitting exploration and exploitation of the natural resources in accordance with the 1958 United Nations Convention on the continental shelf.

At the domestic level a series of steps were taken after the spring of 1970 that were intended to give evidence of a vigorous Canadian exercise of jurisdiction in the North. The objective of such measures was to reaffirm and strengthen the existing Canadian claims to sovereignty on land. At the same time it was hoped that by stepping up activities in many areas a claim to sovereignty over the ice and perhaps even waters would be gradually woven until there would be no possible basis for a successful challenge. It was to be the doctrine of 'effective occupation' manifested in a multitude of ways.

First the flag was to be flown symbolically in the Arctic. The government invited the Queen of Canada to pay her first official visit to the Arctic in July 1970. Welcomed by the Governor General and the Prime Minister at Frobisher Bay on Baffin Island, she flew deep beyond the Arctic Circle, visiting Inuit communities as far north as Resolute Bay. Yearly trips to the Arctic were organized by the government for diplomats stationed in Ottawa. These trips gave foreign representatives visible demonstrations of the Canadian presence in the North; even more important, the diplomats' acceptance of the invitations confirmed Canada's sovereignty in the area. Another earnest of Canadian activity, albeit mainly symbolic, was the 'Canadianization' of the Hudson's Bay Company, which had over 200 stores in the North serving remote Inuit and Indian communities. The company headquarters were moved from London (England) to Winnipeg.

A number of measures were taken to establish a Canadian military presence in the North. In the 1971 Defence Department's White Paper *Defence in the 70s*, top priority was accorded to the defence of Canadian sovereignty, the role being mainly one of 'surveillance and control'.

> The government's objective is to continue effective occupation of Canadian territory and to have a surveillance and control capability to the extent necessary to safeguard national interests in all Canadian territory, and all airspace and waters over which Canada exercises sovereignty or jurisdiction.[17]

Under the heading 'external challenges' the paper indicated that the North presented special problems of administration and control because of 'the growth of commercial interest in the resource potential of the area'.[18] Non-military responsibilities were now clearly included in the Armed Forces' northern duties. The announcement in the paper that the Defence Research Board was undertaking research into a modest subsurface monitoring system to increase Canada's very limited capability to detect submarine activity in the Arctic showed a concern for a possible security challenge in this area. In 1970 Yellowknife was selected as the headquarters for northern military activities. A program of training of armed forces personnel under Arctic conditions was considerably expanded, and increased air surveillance and year-round land and tactical air exercises were instituted. The modest number of men and equipment involved in these operations seem to confirm that the emphasis was primarily on a visible presence rather than a response to security challenges.[19] Canadian-based DEW line posts from Cape Dyer in the eastern Arctic to Cape Parry in the west were 'Canadianized' in 1970, with each site being placed under a Canadian military commander responsible for the operational role of the site. Of a more direct and practical benefit to northern communities and development activities, the search-and-rescue operations conducted by the Armed Forces in the North were stepped up.

One of the measures introduced by the Defence Department was to arrange periodic flights by Argus long-range patrol aircraft over the

Arctic. Known as 'sovereignty flights', they were intended to demonstrate indirect occupation of the Arctic. A halt in these flights because of budgetary difficulties in late 1974 caused concern in Parliament and the press; they were subsequently restored. It is open to doubt whether the Defence Department was wise in introducing these flights in the first place. The Argus is a sophisticated anti-submarine warfare aircraft carrying a large and specialized crew. The aircraft are based on the east and west coasts, and because the time spent flying to the Arctic is so long there is little on-site flying time. Moreover the Argus is a poor instrument for the job. It depends primarily on its crew for spotting, and in uncertain weather and the short hours of daylight in winter they can see little. Even in sparsely inhabited parts of the Arctic the best form of intelligence comes from the local inhabitants, reported through RCMP outposts. In fact so much is this the case that the Defence Department has been obliged to seek information from civil authorities in order to locate and observe exploration or development sites, a routine aspect of the broader mission of surveillance and control of northern, and particularly offshore activities. The original decision seems therefore to have been taken primarily to satisfy public concern and gain support for the Armed Forces in a time of budget cut-backs. For the high Arctic, regular Department of National Defence supply flights to Alert provide the necessary coverage and evidence of indirect occupation. It is difficult to see how a reduction in the number of these 'sovereignty flights' would prejudice Canadian claims to sovereignty in the Arctic.

Alarmists point to the risk of a surprise landing being used as a claim by another state to occupy a part of the Canadian Arctic. But the test this would pose would be whether the government would be prepared to use force if necessary to evict the trespasser. The enormous problems of supply in the Arctic would make this a major undertaking. Any forward base would be extremely vulnerable to air action. So it would seem that in this area also the defence authorities cannot be faulted for the limited attention they have been giving to the Arctic.

The government has continued to demonstrate its responsibility for the northern native peoples by an ever-increasing number of measures related to their health, education, and community life, programs that were supervised by the Department of Indian and Northern Affairs. This department is charged not only with all matters related to the Indians and Inuit people north of 60, but with the responsibility for economic development and administration of government in the North. A substantial program for surveying Arctic waters has been undertaken and plans for the construction of a year-round highway down the Mackenzie were announced in 1973. However construction on this latter project was halted after only nine months' work, apparently because the environmental impact had not been adequately assessed. A special commission was set up under the

Territorial Lands Act to hold public hearings and to investigate the environmental and socio-economic implications of the construction and operation of a major pipeline in the Territories.

Further legislative action allowed the government to control other aspects of northern life. The Canada Shipping Act was amended in October 1970 to provide stiff penalties for commercial shipping that polluted Canadian territorial waters north of 60, waters not already within the shipping-control zone under the Arctic Waters Pollution Prevention Act. In 1972 the regulations under this latter Act were promulgated and the shipping-safety control zones prescribed in detail. The pollution-prevention regulations set out strict specifications for construction and equipment of vessels, their areas of permissible operation, as well as navigational and anti-pollution requirements. For a time after promulgation it appeared that the stringency of the measures had frightened shipping insurers from offering reasonably priced insurance rates for northern-bound vessels. This difficulty was resolved, however, when statistics revealed no serious accidents, collisions, or sinkings of vessels during five years of ever-increasing shipping in the eastern Arctic.[20] However apart from shipping to Hudson Bay and resupply operations throughout the Arctic, there still is no regular shipping north of 60.

Nor did the regulations appear to hamper grain ships coming through Arctic waters to the Hudson Bay port of Churchill to fill their holds for European markets, although regulations for this summer traffic were not particularly stringent. No charges have yet been laid under the Arctic Waters Pollution Prevention Act, which is administered by the Ministry of Transport.

A popular line of criticism concerning the defence of Canadian sovereignty in the North centres on the potential role of multinational oil companies now exploring for Arctic oil and natural gas. Richard Rohmer, the best known of these critics, has accused the government, in his book *The Arctic Imperative*, of virtually giving away Arctic resources to American corporations for ridiculously low permit and exploratory fees. By allowing American-owned companies to explore and find gas and oil in the Arctic, he asserts, Canada has more or less committed itself to the sale of these resources to the United States.[21]

Rohmer's thesis—that Canada will not have the political will to resist United States pressure for Canadian Arctic oil and gas—is based on opinion rather than fact. Actually Canada is well protected by a whole series of instruments, regulatory bodies, and legislation, providing the government has the will to use them. The 1958 Geneva Convention on the continental shelf gives Canada sovereign rights over the continental shelf in the Arctic for the purposes of exploration and exploitation of its natural resources. Only companies incorporated in Canada and therefore fully subordinate to Canadian law are permitted to work in the Canadian Arctic. In cases where companies carrying out such activities on the northern shelf or elsewhere in the Arctic are foreign-owned, they operate under Canadian permit and license and in so doing expressly recognize Canada's sovereign rights. Moreover all applications for the export of Canadian gas and oil must be approved by the National Energy Board, which provides a second line of defence. The reaction of some United-States-owned exploration companies to recent Board rulings limiting or prohibiting the export of oil and gas has been to threaten to transfer exploration activity to other parts of the world, and in some instances actually to do so. This suggests that these companies believe the present government has the means and the will to retain Arctic oil and gas for Canada. Rohmer would presumably argue that the government's resolve may weaken in the face of such threats, but this is of course only a matter of opinion.

The Canadian government also decided some years ago to form a large consortium to conduct exploration in the Arctic. The government holds 45 per cent of Panarctic Oils Limited shares, and four senior civil servants are on its board of directors. This opens the perspective of major government participation in any oil and gas exploitation in the Arctic. The construction of all ports and airports in the North must have the approval of the Ministry of Transport. Guidelines prepared by several departments have been issued establishing requirements for ownership and operation of pipelines, and for certain necessary ecological safeguards. There are additional legislative controls: the Territorial Lands Act, the Northern Inland Waters Act, the Federal Wild Life and Land Use Act, all provide the government with various levers to control northern technological development. Finally the provisions of the Arctic Waters Pollution Prevention Act and its regulations allow the government very broad powers to control shipping in Arctic waters. It is hard to reach any conclusion other than that the government is exercising powers that enhance Canadian claims to sovereignty in the North and that it has equipped itself with adequate instruments with which to meet most foreseeable economic challenges.

Although there appear to be no imminent, overt challenges to Canadian Arctic sovereignty, there exist certain areas where questions remain unsettled or unclear. The seaward extension of the Yukon-Alaska boundary in the Beaufort Sea is a problem that has not yet been solved, and might become acute if oil were to be found in the area. The Yukon-Alaska land boundary is at the 141st meridian west longitude. By the regulations issued under the 1970 pollution legislation,[22] the Canadian shipping-zone demarcation is set at this line extended seaward across the continental shelf. While an academic authority has expressed an opinion that the Americans might question such a boundary assertion and instead suggest a median-line division of the shelf, thus augmenting the zone under U.S. jurisdiction,[23] the Canadian government has not yet taken any position. The issue has not in fact been taken up, and there are other unsettled maritime boundaries on the east and west coasts, the resolution of which have a clear priority over the Yukon-Alaskan boundary question.

Ice islands pose another problem. Composed of durable ice, they vary greatly in size and drift slowly around the Arctic Ocean, generally in a clockwise direction, at about one to two miles a day. Both the Americans and Russians have occupied several of these islands for years at a time. What rules of sovereignty apply to ice islands? The case involving Fletcher's Island, or T-3, a U.S. research station since 1951, became a point in question. This ice island had apparently been first sighted by a Canadian Air Force plane in April 1947.[24] A bizarre murder case on the island in May 1971, involving an American-born citizen and a Mexican-born U.S.-domiciled man, posed a delicate jurisdictional problem. For Canada the implications concerning sovereignty were complex. If the ice island were to be treated as 'high seas' the case would be tried before a U.S. domestic court. If however the defence lawyers' argument — that T-3 was subject to a sovereignty claim (that ice was land) — was to be upheld, this could be viewed as strengthening Canada's position of having jurisdiction over the ice between the Arctic islands.[25] In the event, a note added to the federal government's expression of opinion on the subject evaded the central issue:

> The Canadian government continues to reserve its position on the question of jurisdiction over the alleged offence but would not object to having the drifting ice formation in question treated as a ship for the purposes of the particular legal proceedings concerned in order to facilitate the course of justice, and if it is considered necessary for the purpose of the legal proceeding in question, the Canadian government waives jurisdiction.[26]

The government clearly did not see any advantage, at that time and on such a relatively minor issue, in making a claim on which it might be challenged. But beyond this case emerged a broader question. What challenges to Canadian sovereignty are represented by these ice islands drifting in and out of the Canadian Arctic archipelago? What can be done about such a challenge? It is a thorny legal problem for which answers can hardly be given until the Law-of-the-Sea Conference has drawn conclusions on some of the more basic questions.

Artificial islands formed for the purpose of exploring for oil and gas constitute another anomaly. Can territorial waters or national jurisdiction be progressively extended by making gravel islands where none existed? On this issue there were already indications at the Law-of-the-Sea Conference that international legal opinion is generally agreed that artificial structures should be under the control of the coastal state. This would ensure that they could not serve as instruments for challenging northern sovereignty if constructed by companies not incorporated in Canada. If this view is formally adopted in a convention emerging from the next Law-of-the-Sea Conference, Canada's position in the Arctic will have been further strengthened.

Another area of uncertainty arises from submarine activity in the Arctic. Canada has done a little research on Arctic submarine-detection techniques, but no system has been installed because systems based on soundings or acoustics are ineffective due to noise caused by grinding ice and the vulnerability of the system to ice movement. Certainly both the United States and the Soviet Union have nuclear-powered submarines capable of travelling under Arctic ice. In addition the General Dynamics Corporation of the United States has advocated the use of commercial submarine tankers for which it has done preliminary studies, but no prototype has yet been built and no serious interest has yet been shown in the idea as a technique for transporting Arctic oil. In any event, if a company were to proceed with such a scheme to transport Arctic oil, it would undoubtedly not make the investment to build such tankers without first securing the approval of the Canadian government for using such a transportation system. There would thus be no challenge to national sovereignty.

This leaves undetected foreign military submarines as a possible threat. The presence of foreign submarines in Canadian territorial waters in the North cannot in itself be thought of as a challenge to Canadian Arctic sovereignty.[27] However if such submarines were to ply constantly through the Northwest Passage without detection or challenge, this would constitute a threat both to the Canadian assertion of jurisdiction for pollution regulation and to Canada's contention that the Passage is not an international strait on the grounds that it has never been used as a passageway for international navigation. Under the 1958 Geneva Convention, foreign submarines are required to surface when passing through the territorial waters of another state. Since in the first Law-of-the-Sea Conference in 1958 the territorial sea remained at three miles, this meant that submarines only had to surface in straits less than six miles wide. Thus the present international law does not require submarines to surface in the Northwest Passage even if ice conditions permit it. Where states have extended their territorial limits to twelve miles, as Canada has done, the major naval powers have resisted the attempt to apply the principle to straits of less than twenty-four miles.

The question of how much submarine traffic if any is traversing the Passage remains. Visual sightings are not feasible and fixed acoustic systems have not reached a dependable level of accuracy. Another nuclear submarine could do the task, but it is an extraordinarily expensive listening platform. A less expensive platform might be a fixed system supplemented by a small underwater vehicle for local use only.

Without the means of determining how much submarine traffic there is, the extent of the threat cannot be judged. Given the danger of the route, owing to the existence of such ice formations as 'pingoes' and 'keels', and the fact that the Passage does not lead to any submarine staging ground, traffic can be presumed to be infrequent, and voyages are probably undertaken primarily to test equipment and give crews experience in under-ice navigation. Nevertheless the government should be concerned to obtain information about such traffic. Experiments with fixed-detection systems should be pressed, as these are the cheapest way at this stage of gaining the needed information.

Some Canadians have been critical because the government has not enlarged its fleet of icebreakers for the North despite the American icebreaker-construction program. Again the judgement appears to have been made in Ottawa that widespread and extensive commercial development in the Arctic is unlikely in the near future. The dangers and hazards of the waters themselves are regarded as the best safeguard of Canadian sovereignty. Nevertheless the resupply operations for Arctic-exploration companies and Arctic settlements have grown steadily. The existing Canadian icebreaker fleet is not large enough to break up the ice for all the supply ships that go into the Arctic in the summer, and that must make the most of the very limited period of navigation. Nor have sufficient numbers of supply ships been strengthened to take advantage of certain ice conditions even after the ice has been broken through by icebreakers. It is estimated that large and more powerful icebreakers, backed up by stronger resupply ships, could extend the shipping season for weeks and even months. If the government is sincere in its desire for development in the North, its lack of emphasis on building up a larger Canadian icebreaking fleet reveals a policy lacuna.

Furthermore, the day of extensive commercial shipping through the Arctic waters may be closer than the government recognizes. The American need for Alaskan oil is giving a fresh impetus to technological developments intended to overcome some of the difficulties of Arctic shipping — the structural requirements of tankers, the necessary navigational aids, the terminal facilities that large tankers would require, and the safeguards against environmental damage. Recent assessments by American shipping experts foresee the use of the Northwest Passage as an essential link in the transport of Alaskan crude oil to the United States east coast by the late 1980s.[28] They have maintained that a large fleet of nuclear-powered Arctic icebreaking tankers, each with a capacity of 240,000 tons, will be moving two million barrels of oil a day through the Northwest Passage by 1989 and four billion by 1995. Clearly, should the United States embark on such an extensive shipping program, the Canadian jurisdictional position would be weakened if American icebreakers were required to open the Passage for these tankers. While a vastly increased Canadian icebreaker fleet is not an immediate requirement, this is obviously a situation that the government should follow closely. Given the long time needed to build icebreakers, it would be desirable to have construction plans in readiness.[29]

There seems little danger, however, of foreign icebreakers challenging Canadian sovereignty. In the unlikely event that a United States icebreaker were to sail into Canadian waters without government approval, in a way that could be considered a challenge to sovereignty, it would provoke a major incident. Its progress could easily be followed by aircraft, and if for any reason military action had to be taken, aircraft would again be the most effective means. But in fact political and diplomatic instruments would be the main weapons in such a situation.

Of incidental interest in a study of Canadian policies in the Arctic since 1970 is the question how these policies have been formulated, and how much co-ordination exists between the responsible departments and agencies. During 1969-70 policy advice was formulated by an *ad hoc* group, whose principal participants were Ivan Head of the Prime Minister's Office and members of the External Affairs legal division, assisted on occasions by A. E. Gotlieb, the former legal adviser of External Affairs. In late 1969 an Interdepartmental Committee on the Law of the Sea — a reconstitution of the earlier Interdepartmental Committee on Territorial Waters — was formed to prepare Canada's position for the impending Conference on the Law of the Sea. Represented on the Committee are the Departments of External Affairs, Energy, Mines and Resources, Environment, Indian and Northern Affairs, Justice, National Defence, Industry, Trade and Commerce, the Canadian International Development Agency, the Privy Council Office, the Ministry of Transport, and the Ministry of Science and Technology. The Committee is chaired by the legal adviser of the Department of External Affairs, and a member of that department has been designated as law-of-the-sea co-ordinator, indicating that the central role, as one would expect, lies with External Affairs. Working groups under the Interdepartmental Committee on the Law of the Sea are formed to work on particular issues, with varying representation depending on the problem under discussion. These groups report to the Committee and the report then goes to the Minister of External Affairs; that Department naturally plays a central role in formulating the approaches to be made and carrying them out. At the Caracas and Geneva sessions of the Law-of-the-Sea Conference the official Canadian delegation was headed by the External Affairs expert on the subject (the former legal adviser). A recent analysis of Canadian policy formulation for law-of-the-sea questions concludes that:

Canadian law of the sea interests do not all point in the same direction but it has been the civil servants in the legal bureau of the Department of External Affairs — not the competition of interest groups — that have balanced the several considerations. These officials have maintained a cohesive coastal state policy that has in turn enhanced the ability of the Canadian delegation to play an important leadership role in the international negotiations.[30]

It is open to question how much interdepartmental committees such as the Interdepartmental Committee on the Law of the Sea actually co-ordinate policy. Their main function is to exchange information and to identify differences of approach between government departments. Shifting personnel between departments helps in the process of information exchange. Thus two officials of the legal bureau of the Department of External Affairs were transferred to the Department of the Environment, one to help prepare the departmental position for the Stockholm Conference on the Environment, the other to work on fisheries questions in preparation for the Law-of-the-Sea Conference. But on all major questions differences are submitted to a Cabinet Committee or to the full Cabinet for resolution, or on less important issues the reconciliation may be attempted bilaterally between the two ministers involved. In fact the evolution of the Cabinet Committee system owes much to the desire of ministers to make decisions themselves regarding the available policy choices on any issue rather than have a reconciliation effected at the bureaucratic level.

Responsibility for formulating and executing policy in domestic affairs is assumed by the department concerned, and the Department of External Affairs would not be involved. The only grounds for intervention by the Department of External Affairs would be if it was felt that a proposed policy might undermine Canada's position in respect to claims to sovereignty in the Arctic. Where there is an overlapping of jurisdiction, for example pipeline construction in the Arctic, interdepartmental committees may be set up, such as the Advisory Committee on Northern Development and the Task Force on Northern Oil Development. The Advisory Committee on Northern Development involves every department and some agencies operating in the North. The full committee, chaired by the deputy minister of Indian and Northern Affairs and normally involving the deputy ministers of the other departments, meets seldom, usually only on tough problems in major areas of interest. However, as with the Interdepartmental Committee on the Law of the Sea, there are specialized sub-committees or working groups concerned with particular issues such as transportation, employment of native peoples, or science and technology. Only those departments with relevant interests would be present at meetings of these working groups. There are also two co-ordinating sub-committees chaired by the two Commissioners for the Yukon and the Northwest Territories.

Similarly the Task Force on Northern Oil Development has five subcommittees interested in pipelines, environmental and social impact, economic impact, transportation, and markets for oil and gas. As with the Interdepartmental Committee on the Law of the Sea, the primary function of these committees is to exchange information and to clarify differences of interest or intention where these may exist, so that policy submissions to the Cabinet Committee can clearly identify policy choices and their implications.

Another time-honoured technique for consultation that should be mentioned is informal bilateral contacts between the responsible officials of the departments directly involved. Programs for development in the Arctic often involve serious conflicts of interest and objective. The fragile ecology of the region does not easily withstand or recover from the physical damage that is associated with resource development. The rights of native peoples to share in the potential economic benefits, along with concerns about the social effects of development, can be cause for delay and caution. Inevitably policies designed to promote these various objectives are often in serious conflict. The various interdepartmental committees and informal consultations can identify these differences, but the final choices normally have to be made in Cabinet.

A further dimension of consultation that is normally an important part of policy formation in Canada, namely consultation with provincial governments, has little importance for Arctic policy. The Northwest Territories and the Yukon are dependent territories and the federal government's jurisdiction is absolute in this whole region. Thus while the members of the Interdepartmental Committee on the Law of the Sea did consult provincial authorities across Canada concerning the Canadian position to be taken at the Law-of-the-Sea Conference,[31] the interest of the provinces was focused almost entirely on the adjacent temperate waters.

Since 1969 and 1970 Canadian policy formation has received much less public attention and there have been no comparably dramatic assertions of sovereignty and jurisdiction. There has, however, been an enormous range of domestic activities that, taken together, have substantially increased Canada's potential for claiming effective occupation of the land and waters of the Arctic.

The results of the Law-of-the-Sea Conference could be decisive one way or another for international recognition of Canada's claims to sovereignty, and it has been widely recognized that the Canadian delegation has worked vigorously and effectively in representing Canadian interests. The third Law-of-the-Sea Conference may not, however, define whether the Northwest Passage is to be regarded as internal Canadian waters. In that event the government must be in a position to respond to the needs of international shipping. This will require keeping the Arctic ship-construction programs under constant review and being prepared to embark quickly on an icebreaker-construction program if this should become necessary.

Some commentators think it is possible that other states would employ economic or military weapons to threaten Canadian sovereignty. Defences against such challenges cannot be mounted by promulgating regulations and establishing interdepartmental committees. Rather, they would have to be faced at the political level, and the principal defence in such circumstances must be the will and determination of the government and people. The government has demonstrated by its actions in recent years that any encroachment on a reasonable exercise of Canadian sovereignty and jurisdiction in the Arctic would be strongly resisted. As long as there is no weakening of this will, such challenges are unlikely to be offered.

NOTES

[1] House of Commons *Debates*, 15 May 1969, p. 8720.

[2] House of Commons, Standing Committee on Indian Affairs and Northern Development, *1st Report*, 16 December 1969, p. 7.

[3] House of Commons *Debates*, Hon. Mitchell Sharp, 16 April 1970, p. 5948.

[4] House of Commons, Standing Committee on External Affairs and National Defence (SCEAND), *Minutes of Proceedings and Evidence*, J. A. Beesley, 18 May 1973, p. 12:20.

[5] The government was prepared to argue its territorial-extension legislation before the International Court of Justice.

[6] SCEAND, *op. cit.*, 6 November 1973, p. 22:41.

[7] Toronto *Globe and Mail*, 15 August 1974.

[8] SCEAND, *op. cit.*, 6 November 1973, p. 22:44.

[9] *Ibid.*, J. A. Beesley, 15 November 1973, p. 23:11.

[10] J. A. Beesley, *Address to the 9th Regional Meeting of the American Society of International Law*, College of Law, Syracuse University, 8 April 1972, pp. 15-16.

[11] SCEAND, *op. cit.*, J. A. Beesley, 18 May 1973, p. 12:20.

[12] *Ibid.*, 23 November 1973, p. 23:10.

[13] Prime Minister's Office (PMO), *press release*, 20 May 1971.

[14] PMO, *press release*, 28 May 1971.

[15] SCEAND, *op. cit.*, J. A. Beesley, 18 May 1973, p. 12:19.

[16] *Ibid.*, p. 12:20.

[17] Government of Canada, *Defence in the 70s* (Ottawa, 1971), p. 10.

[18] *Ibid.*, p. 8.

[19]In 1971 Yellowknife had a headquarters staff of thirty-five; it rose to ninety in 1972 but declined to forty-seven in 1973.

[20]One minor exception was a small barge that had sunk in 1969.

[21]Richard Rohmer, *The Arctic Imperative* (Toronto, 1973), pp. 105, 171.

[22]*Canada Gazette*, part II, vol. 106, no. 16, Shipping Safety Control Zones Order, 2 August 1972, p. 4.

[23]R. M. Logan, *Canada, the United States and the Third Law of the Sea Conference*, Canadian-American Committee, C. D. Howe Research Institute (Montreal, Quebec) and National Planning Association (Washington, D.C.), pp. 57-60.

[24]Gordon W. Smith, 'Sovereignty in the North: The Canadian Aspect of an International Problem', in R. St. J. MacDonald, ed., *The Arctic Frontier* (Toronto, 1966), p. 249. Another ice island, T-1, was apparently sighted first by a U.S. Air Force plane.

[25]In this particular case, however, if the ice island were judged to be subject to a sovereignty claim, it would still be a question as to whose sovereignty. The floating ice island had been a U.S. naval research station for twenty years and might be thought of as a U.S. island, although Canada would doubtless claim jurisdiction on the grounds of pollution control when the island was floating in Canadian Arctic waters. The Ministry of Transport has already used its jurisdiction (under an International Civil Aviation Organization convention) to investigate an air crash on the island.

[26]Toronto *Globe and Mail*, 19 May 1971.

[27]Similarly the presence of Soviet submarines in a Norwegian fiord during 1974 has not been considered a challenge to Norwegian sovereignty of those waters.

[28]New York *Times*, 1 December 1974, 'Waters off Jersey will Become Terminus of North-West Passage'.

[29]While recent steps have been taken to approve design plans for new icebreakers, no construction contracts have been let as yet. However in November 1975 the Canadian government announced that Canada would build a heavy, 28,000-ton icebreaking cargo vessel for use in the Arctic.

[30]Ann L. Hollick, 'Canadian-American Relations: Law of the Sea', *International Organizations*, 28 (Autumn 1974), 776.

[31]SCEAND, *op. cit.*, 15 November 1973, p. 23:33.

C.C.G.S. *d'Iberville* in Jones' Sound, Eastern Arctic, in 1957.
Courtesy National Film Board

8 CANADIAN SOVEREIGNTY AND ARCTIC INTERNATIONAL RELATIONS
by Franklyn Griffiths

When Canadians think of the Canadian Arctic they tend to view it from the perspective of internal affairs. The area does however have a bearing on foreign affairs, principally because of the unwillingness of the United States to accept Canadian sovereignty over the waters of the Northwest Passage. The Canadian government, if not the Canadian people, is fully aware of this. It has been attempting to improve our position there through vigorous participation in multilateral discussions on the law of the sea, through cautious unilateral extensions of our jurisdiction on pollution prevention and other grounds, and through a basic commitment to Canadian-American bilateral negotiation as the essential framework within which progress has to be made. But in practice multilateralism and unilateralism in roughly equal proportions are both firmly subordinated to bilateralism in official policy. Some have argued the case for a reversal of Canadian policies so that unilateralism would take precedence over bilateralism. The question to be considered here is whether a greater emphasis on multilateralism is desirable and feasible as a means of strengthening our position vis-à-vis the United States in the Arctic. If so, what should be the balance between unilateralism, bilateralism, and multilateralism in Canadian actions? Comparatively little thought has been given to this issue, possibly because of the irresistible pull of bilateralism, perhaps because those who advocate greater unilateralism are not internationalists. The report that follows is therefore provisional in nature. It is intended to open the subject of Arctic multilateralism for further discussion and research.

There are two approaches to Arctic affairs—activism and gradualism. Gradualism is, broadly speaking, the policy of the Canadian government. Activism is the approach of those who would like to see a more dynamic defence of Canadian interests. The paper will first present the two conflicting points of view, and then consider the question of whether a greater degree of multilateralism in Canadian policies is desirable in the first place. Attention will then be given to various aspects of the international situation affecting the practicality of Canadian multilateral initiatives and their place in the ensemble of Canadian activity related to the Arctic.

THE ACTIVIST APPROACH

A statement of the activist approach could well begin with the assertion that Canada presently lacks the political will and the physical means to achieve its objectives in the Arctic. The Canadian government seeks effective occupation, control (including pollution prevention), and recognition of its sovereignty over the territorial land mass, the Arctic archipelago, the waters between the islands, a twelve-mile territorial sea, and the continental margin and adjacent waters extending 200 miles and in places much further from Canadian shores. Barring the issue of the 200-mile plus 'economic zone', most Canadians believe that sovereignty already exists over everything to the northernmost tip of the northernmost island, if not right to the North Pole. The maps we have all been seeing since childhood have told us so. The fact is however that Canadian sovereignty over the waters of the Arctic archipelago, and over the Northwest Passage in particular, is not accepted internationally. Nor has sovereignty been explicitly proclaimed by Canadian governments, which have instead been making a point of telling other powers that they have a right to disagree with us on this matter. Even the limited claim to jurisdiction made in the Arctic Waters Pollution Prevention Act of 1970 is contested. So also is our extension in 1970 of Canadian territorial waters to twelve miles as it applies to the gateways or choke points of the Northwest Passage. Nor does Canada have the wherewithal to enforce its sovereignty in the event another state chose to brush Canadian authority aside in pursuit of its own interests. Even now, when the challenge to Canadian sovereignty in the Arctic has dramatically increased under the pressure of the search for new sources of energy and innovations in transporting oil and gas, Ottawa shows little sign of having the imagination and willpower required to bring the situation back into line with the beliefs of a largely unsuspecting Canadian people.

Among the states that stand in the way of Canadian sovereignty and pollution-prevention measures in the Arctic, the United States is the principal offender. If Washington had its way, the Canadian Arctic would consist of our continental land mass, the Arctic islands, a limited territorial sea bordering this land, and some form of offshore economic zone. Substantial bodies of water between the Arctic islands would be high seas and thus open to virtually unrestricted navigation. The Northwest Passage would be declared an international strait through which the warships, commercial vessels, and aircraft of the United States and other powers would be permitted not merely innocent but free passage. The Arctic Waters Pollution Prevention Act would be withdrawn, and ships passing through the Northwest Passage would conform to international pollution standards, but only if they chose to enforce them themselves. In addition a good deal of what Canada currently claims as its Arctic seabed would be open to resource exploitation by American-based multinational corporations without benefit of substantial regulation. Were these views to prevail, the Canadian Arctic archipelago would be cut in two by an international strait, the risks of pollution would be greatly increased, and the United States would gain access to large expanses of Canadian seabed. Add to this the capital and the advanced resource technology that the United States has to offer and that the Canadian government has been seeking for northern development, and the Arctic is in real danger of becoming North American without ever having been effectively Canadian.

In the fifties and early sixties, when the economic significance of the Arctic was considerably less than it is today, Ottawa lacked the nerve to draw straight baselines around the outermost islands, to declare the waters therein internal Canadian waters, and to project our territorial-waters and seabed claims outwards from the baseline. Instead it was hoped that with the passage of time we would be able to control the passage of foreign vessels by virtue of a sovereignty increasingly recognized by the international community. This recognition would be obtained by means of co-operation with the United States, by prudent unilateral moves, by patient efforts to elaborate a more favourable international law of the sea, by continued references to our commitment to the defence of a sovereignty that has never been fully declared, and by the deployment of inadequate surveillance and enforcement capabilities that we trust will not soon be put to the test. At the same time, the issue has not been fully and frankly explained to the Canadian people by their ministers in Ottawa, who have instead sought in public to smooth over our differences with the United States, while trusting to the workings of quiet diplomacy and the law-of-the-sea negotiations to moderate American pretensions.

Our difficulties arise basically from the fact that the Arctic has been firmly placed in the procrustean bed of bilateral relations with the United States, and becomes merely one of the many sets of issues simultaneously under discussion with Washington. As such it repeatedly falls victim to trade-offs and compromises as the government of the day seeks to maximize Canadian benefits in what are short-sightedly viewed as more urgent and practical matters under negotiation with the Americans. In view as well of the federal government's failure to acquire a superior fleet of icebreakers in order (1) to regulate future operations of American tankers strengthened against ice, (2) to offset the new American icebreakers that will give superior mobility in the Arctic to the United States, and (3) to reduce American opportunities to exploit our vulnerability in the Arctic for resource-bargaining purposes, it can only be concluded that Ottawa is determined to surrender our sovereignty piecemeal in a process of national self-immolation.

It may be recalled that Procrustes was a robber who placed his victims in a bed that was always too long or too short, and then either stretched the occupant to fit or cut him down to size. By placing the Arctic in the framework of total Canadian-American relations, we have already assisted the United States in cutting the feet from under our position. The extension of Canadian territorial waters to twelve miles and the pollution-prevention legislation of 1970 are cases in point. In both acts Ottawa retreated from the assertion of Canadian sovereignty to the position that we were extending our jurisdiction. It was hoped that the United States would accept these relatively modest claims and acknowledge Canadian authority over the Northwest Passage. But Washington chose to deny the validity of both acts. The result was that we suffered a net loss of sovereignty and by our own actions reinforced the American contention that our jurisdiction is less than complete. For if the waters within the archipelago were Canadian in the first place, why did we need to enlarge our claims to twelve miles for the territorial sea and 100 miles for pollution control? Hoping to avoid a confrontation that would damage our position on seemingly more important issues, and yet seeking a way of limiting American freedom of action in the Canadian Arctic, Ottawa compromised Canadian sovereignty to no avail. Having laid the Arctic down in the bed of Canadian-American relations, we find that the bed still does not fit.

Next we may reasonably expect a new American challenge in the form of the new U.S. icebreakers and possibly other vessels as well passing through the Northwest Passage without notifying and receiving permission from the Canadian government, in disregard of Canadian laws and regulations. We would look on powerless to act. In this the United States would literally be moving to decapitate the Canadian Arctic by dividing the archipelago into two sections separated by an international strait that would allow free transit to foreign ships; such a situation would greatly increase the risk of major pollution. Alternatively Washington might only have to signal that it was preparing to have a vessel sail through the Northwest Passage, and Ottawa would scramble to avert a confrontation by buying the Americans off. In either case the United States might then be expected to retreat from its position on the Northwest Passage in return for continental-energy arrangements and provisions for joint military operations in the Arctic. The ensuing agreements would be presented to the Canadian public as a masterful defence of Arctic sovereignty and a boon to the Canadian economy. In reality, we would have saved the head but cut the legs off above the knee. Then we would try the bed for size once again.

We simply have to be much more active in the defence of Arctic sovereignty. The Canadian government must move right away to acquire the superior icebreaking fleet that is required to enforce sovereignty, pollution-prevention regulations, and other legislation we might wish to enact. While it would be impractical to divorce the Arctic completely from the total range of issues being negotiated formally and tacitly with Washington, we should take a stand and avoid any further move that might compromise sovereignty. For example we could well insist that the United States first accept our essential Arctic claims as a precondition for further negotiation on resource-sharing agreements compatible with Canadian resource requirements. Instead of misleading the Canadian people with disingenuous statements that we are co-operating successfully with the United States when the Americans are actually succeeding in encroaching on our jurisdiction, the federal government must openly explain the gravity of the situation we face. In so doing it would tap a vast reservoir of public opinion that unquestionably supports the concept of a Canadian Arctic, and would, by the same token, support a more vigorous and forthright effort to make the Arctic authentically Canadian. A public presentation of the real issues would also demonstrate to Washington that it was dealing with a government determined to insist on its rights. If it came to it, we should be prepared to draw straight baselines to enclose the waters of the Arctic archipelago. Again, an informed public opinion would be an essential prerequisite for such a move, a move that would hardly be comprehended if announced without prior explanation.

All of this will undoubtedly have an unsettling and even a disruptive effect on Canadian-American relations. But the alternative is a continuing silent surrender of sovereignty and a further loss of control over our own destiny. Of all the issues in Canadian-American relations, the Arctic offers the best prospect of public support for a firm Canadian stand. It is the optimum issue on which to begin really reversing the tide of dependence on the United States.

GRADUALISM

A presentation of the gradualist outlook begins with the assertion that the situation on balance has been evolving in our favour. The Americans, in inclining towards the Alaska pipeline, have for the time being reduced the likelihood of using the Northwest Passage to transport oil to the eastern

United States. At present pipelines down the Mackenzie and possibly one day from the Arctic islands along Hudson Bay seem the most likely alternative routes for such natural-gas and oil supplies as Canada might make available to the United States. Ultra-large cargo submarines remain futuristic transportation solutions in view of the capital costs and the technical and environmental problems involved, and aircraft and dirigibles capable of carrying oil and gas seem even more unlikely. Illicit offshore drilling in areas of the seabed claimed by Canada is also improbable, for companies must have secure title to their finds given the great cost of drilling operations. On the other hand, Mexico has recently announced a large oil discovery, and this could well be followed by other discoveries, including natural gas, that could lessen American energy interests in the Arctic. As for the use of the Northwest Passage for international trade, this route is relatively unattractive for shipping manufactured goods whose transportation costs are but a small part of their total unit cost; and insurance costs for goods shipped by this route would be quite formidable.

The Canadian Arctic is therefore not going to experience a significant increase in foreign maritime traffic for some time to come. Such increases that do occur will concern primarily the shipping of Canadian resources to foreign and Canadian ports, and will thus be readily subject to Canadian authority and regulations. In the meantime the Arctic Waters Pollution Prevention Act exerts a beneficial effect on actual and potential shippers, who must now plan to meet Canadian requirements in deploying and developing vessels for use in our Arctic waters. Furthermore, the greater the *de facto* foreign compliance with the 1970 legislation, the stronger its status in international law, and the larger the international recognition of Canadian sovereignty.

If direct challenges to Canadian authority are not likely to arise soon from American and other resource-transportation interests, it also happens that the law-of-the-sea negotiations have been moving in a direction favourable to Canadian claims. The forthcoming session or sessions of the Law-of-the-Sea Conference could of course fail, bringing on a rush to unilateralism that would be extremely unfortunate in view of Canada's interests in wide international agreement relating to our position in the Arctic. Nevertheless as of November 1974 the chances of failure are perhaps only 30 per cent. What this means is that we may just manage a short end-run around the Americans in the coming year.

To be specific, the outlook is not unpromising for international acceptance of a new archipelagic-waters agreement that would allow us to draw straight baselines and settle our position except for the problem of innocent passage. Although our situation is an exposed one in that some of our inter-island baselines would be more than 100 miles in length, the good land-to-water ratio in the Canadian archipelago makes our claim more defensible than those of Indonesia, the Philippines, and Fiji, whose islands are quite dispersed. Thus, while Britain and the United States are opposed to more than a sixty-mile gap in archipelagic baselines, a compromise formula may be worked out to our benefit. In this event our only remaining problem would be right of transit through the Northwest Passage and whether we could be successful in having this treated as a special case. Since the United States and other maritime powers are demanding unimpeded passage through international straits, and are reluctant to begin making exceptions, Canada may experience some difficulty in making the case that the Northwest Passage is not an international strait since it has not been used for international navigation, and that its waters should be regarded as internal waters within the Canadian archipelago. Instead a compromise may be necessary: in return for international recognition of our jurisdiction in this instance, we could allow innocent passage commensurate with foreign naval and shipping interests and Canada's right to guard against pollution and other threats to its security. The fact that the Northwest Passage has figured very little in right-of-transit discussion at Caracas, other waterways being of much greater concern to the major maritime powers, does offer some hope for a special solution in this instance. As for the 200-mile economic zone, it seems destined to remain whether or not the Law-of-the-Sea Conference succeeds. The wide international support that has developed for this concept should permit effective Canadian control over its seabed resources, offshore fisheries, the risk of pollution, and the conduct of scientific research — even though control by a coastal state of the seabed to the outer edge of the continental margin may have to be qualified by the taxation rights of an international seabed authority. In sum, the international legal environment is increasingly favourable to Canadian sovereignty and environmental regulation in the Arctic. While it can hardly be expected to solve all our problems, it does permit guarded optimism.

So also does a considered view of the nature of American objections to Canadian Arctic claims. These arise more from the global interests of the United States in naval mobility and freedom of commerce than from an acquisitive interest in the Canadian Arctic as such. Washington opposes the Arctic Waters Pollution Prevention Act primarily because of the restrictive effect that international acceptance of the principle embodied in the Act — interference with the right of innocent passage — would have on freedom of passage elsewhere in the world. It resists exclusive Canadian jurisdiction over the Northwest Passage for the same reason. Anything else would lower the capacity of the United States to make political use of its naval power in peacetime, and would greatly increase the cost and difficulty of shipping when different coastal states insist on different regulations for ships. That the United States is not thinking primarily of the Northwest Passage is also indicated by the fact that the effect of its proposals would be to give Soviet warships free transit through the Canadian Arctic—an outcome that would hardly be greeted enthusiastically by the U.S. Navy. Again there is reason to hope that an agreement on special status for the Northwest Passage can be worked out with Washington. The Americans may of course seek to utilize the issue of Arctic jurisdiction as a means of improving their bargaining position in resource-sharing negotiations. But this should not cause us to conclude that the real object of United States actions is the denial of Canadian sovereignty and the creation of a North American Arctic. Our differences with the United States arise primarily from American interests and commitments elsewhere in the world, and not from any American desire to appropriate the Arctic for its own purposes.

All this suggests a need to avoid over-reacting to American policies where the Canadian Arctic is concerned. The situation is not ripe for confrontation, and if it came to one we would inevitably be the losers. While the Arctic is a vital issue for Canadians, it is a secondary issue in Canadian-American relations. If properly managed it should remain so. In these circumstances Canada would be making a great mistake if it raised the Arctic to the top of its agenda with the United States and emphasized unilateral as opposed to bilateral solutions to our problems there.

Unilateralism has its place, of course, and the Arctic Waters Pollution Prevention Act and the extension of the territorial sea to twelve miles serve to illustrate what can be accomplished for Canadian sovereignty by a measured use of this approach. These acts certainly did not represent a surrender of Canadian sovereignty. According to international law, sovereignty is not weakened either by failing to assert it constantly, nor by neglecting to enforce it in every way, nor by asserting and enforcing it in a limited manner. The official declarations accompanying the legislation of 1970 were precise in saying that it represented only a partial assertion of Canadian rights and was not a denial of the more extensive jurisdiction we claim. To state otherwise is to provide comfort to our opponents. It is to miss the point that the graduated unilateralism of 1970 effectively promoted Canadian sovereignty and a more favourable international law without qualifying our authority over the waters of the Arctic archipelago.

Similarly, it is beside the point to suggest that the Canadian government has disguised the gravity of our differences with the United States. Leaving aside the question of the character of American intentions, we should realize that the legal and political situation is sufficiently complex to make it difficult for Ottawa to open a public discussion of the problem without running the risk of lending at least some support to the American legal position. Some Canadians might also be tempted to exploit the issue for partisan political advantage. And Washington could well gain from the ensuing division in Canadian opinion. Moreover, if a Canadian government itself drew attention to the existence of differences with the United States over the status of the waters of the Northwest Passage and related issues, a substantial segment of the Canadian public would undoubtedly respond by demanding that something be done immediately. Something would indeed have to be done, and this to the detriment of good relations with the United States and at a time when we were making fairly good progress precisely without making the Arctic a central issue. The logic of the situation is thus one that prevents full official disclosure unless it were a prelude to going all the way and drawing straight baselines that would still have to be enforced. To argue that Ottawa has improperly withheld information from the Canadian people is to slight the reporting that has appeared in the Canadian media since 1969, to display ignorance of the economic and political realities, and to miss the prospects for a gradual approach to the real problem of obtaining American and international recognition of our sovereignty in the Arctic.

Suppose, on the other hand, that the worst came to the worst and the United States unexpectedly chose to defy Canada openly. There would be little we could do about it. If they sent a tanker strengthened against ice through the Northwest Passage without a by-your-leave, there would be no way of stopping them. Would we fire on a loaded supertanker, ram it, or place one of our icebreakers in the way so that it would be rammed and thus stop the transit? The first two moves could be seen as acts of war, and all three would entail the risk of major pollution, something we are trying to prevent. In practice we could only protest, withhold co-operation, and seek to mobilize other states on our behalf. Protest would be largely ineffectual. The Canadian economy would be jeopardized by deteriorating bilateral relations. And the United States could be expected to react with great severity if we invited in the other superpower—the only state that could effectively redress the balance if it were indeed willing to become involved. Success resides not in the commitment to pursue a confrontation through to the bitter end, but in avoiding a confrontation in the first place.

It follows that requests for a dramatic increase in Arctic surveillance and enforcement capabilities are inappropriate. New and more powerful icebreakers, for example, would be expensive to obtain and would not offer a commensurate improvement in Canada's ability to deal with shipping using the Northwest Passage without Canadian permission. The existing icebreaker force is capable of dealing with the present scale of shipping emergencies, and does not yet need to be augmented in view of the relatively low volume of Arctic commercial traffic that can be foreseen. More generally, the assertion of exclusive maritime jurisdiction throughout the Canadian Arctic would present substantial new military tasks that would be very costly to perform. In particular we would have to be able to monitor and prevent passage of Soviet and American nuclear submarines. Again it is prudent to avoid making unilateral changes in the status quo by asserting explicit claims of comprehensive sovereignty over the Arctic waters that would be costly and virtually impossible to enforce. Such claims would not in any case gain us anything that we don't already have since our sovereignty is already 100 per cent complete on the ground that these are historic Canadian waters.

TRYING HARDER

Both activism and gradualism are to a degree composite viewpoints that have not until now been fully and publicly stated. Within both schools of thought shadings of opinion are to be observed, with the result that a more discriminating analysis could well yield three or even four major tendencies in the Canadian approach to questions of Arctic sovereignty. This applies particularly to the gradualist school—an official viewpoint that in reality is doubtless less monolithic than that presented here. The two orientations that have been described do nevertheless capture some of the essential differences over methods, means, and timing that presently exist among Canadians concerned with Arctic affairs. While all unite in defence of sovereignty, the differences of approach are so substantial that the activist view suggests gradualists are leading us to piecemeal liquidation, whereas the gradualist assessment entails the opinion that activism risks a sudden and pointless deterioration of our position. How then should we conceive of the situation?

If asked to choose between the two approaches, I would say that the activist case is the stronger. The gradualist view is persuasive on many matters of detail, including the character of American intentions and the difficulty of enforcing exclusive Canadian jurisdiction. But Arctic sovereignty should not be handled as a secondary issue low on the agenda of items under discussion with the United States. After all it is the physical integrity of Canada that is in question. This is surely a priority matter for a self-respecting people. It should not merely be viewed but also treated as such.

Quite apart from the muted sense of purpose that characterizes the gradualist approach, there is its belief that gradualism actually works, that the situation is in fact evolving in a direction that favours Canadian interests. This is questionable. While the United States may not now be moving to develop a tanker route through the Northwest Passage, the necessary surface and submarine technology is under development. While the explicit positions of the American government on Arctic law of the sea are primarily a reflection of the global preoccupations of the U.S.

Navy, the operations of the S.S. *Manhattan* were evidently financed by the Navy, which therefore would not be acting out of character in supporting a new test of Canadian sovereignty. At the same time the gradualist view makes light of the extent to which a leisurely Canadian approach to the problem of Arctic sovereignty gives the large multinational corporations interested in Arctic minerals, particularly the integrated oil companies, a capacity to influence the direction of northern development in Canada. Their investments and activities intensify Canadian economic dependence on the United States, reduce Ottawa's freedom of action in the assertion of Canadian political objectives, and thus run counter to progress in the defence of Arctic sovereignty that might be made by other gradual means. As for the Law-of-the-Sea Conference, we have made considerable progress but it could still be touch and go. Realignment or failure to agree on any major issue at the Conference may be expected to affect other issues under consideration, including archipelagos, pollution controls, and straits. In effect, time could be working against us, not for us, as the gradualist outlook suggests. At a minimum, we may be marking time when we should be making more rapid and substantial progress.

It is also by no means certain that the limited unilateralism of 1970 (the Arctic Waters Pollution Prevention Act and the extension of Canadian territorial waters to twelve miles) represented progress in the elaboration of sovereignty. In general the gradualist reading of international law is correct: limited assertions of jurisdiction do not subvert a larger claim to sovereignty. In this particular case, however, the principle may not apply, for it requires that a clear claim to sovereignty be made in the first place. I am told that official Canadian claims have unfortunately been exceedingly imprecise over the years. It is not certain what Arctic waters Canadian officials were claiming when they referred to 'Canadian waters' in the region. No one in authority seems to have said 'all the waters within the Canadian Arctic archipelago', although this doubtless was the intention. When a comprehensive claim to sovereignty is not made explicit, and when others may legitimately infer that the claim being made is less than complete, a limited extension of jurisdiction may well serve to limit sovereignty. The matter may be clarified by legal scholars, but it is not likely to be settled by the highest authority, the International Court of Justice. Canada waived the Court's jurisdiction in the pollution-control legislation of 1970, thereby supporting the inference that Canadian sovereignty within the archipelago was insufficient to withstand a test in court. What this means is that in international law the gradualist policy of recent years may ultimately be shown to have compromised sovereignty. Again the situation has not thus far been developing as favourably as the gradualist outlook would suggest.

It is also the case that gradualism places a high value on negotiation and the consent of others, particularly where the United States is concerned. It requires international stability and a decent respect for Canadian interests on the part of the American government. But this is an era of unusual instability. A new Middle-East conflict, an oil embargo, and a sharpening of Soviet-American relations for these and other reasons; a deepening recession, if not a depression, in the United States and other Western countries; a faltering, if not a collapse, of the international monetary system; a failure of the Law-of-the-Sea Conference; a breakthrough by internal American interests pressing for the unilateral assertion of United States maritime claims—these and other destabilizing developments are all within the realm of possibility. Any one of them could cause the United States to reorient its domestic as well as foreign policies in a direction that emphasized greater unilateralism and self-help. Two or more such developments could radically transform the context in which Canadian sovereignty in the Arctic is pursued. Although American responses to a significant deterioration of the situation at home and abroad are difficult to predict, they could well entail a considerably more resolute attempt to secure long-term energy sources and to achieve the necessary freedom of movement for United States vessels. Canada might experience greatly increased pressure to meet American economic requirements both for resources and resource exploration, and for maritime mobility. In particular the threat of unilateral transits of the Northwest Passage by American vessels could be used to great effect in bargaining over continental-energy arrangements. If the United States chose to play rough on the Arctic issue in looking to its own interests, the Canadian government would be faced with a choice between prompt concessions or concessions after a bout of defiance for which the Canadian people would be ill prepared. The result would almost certainly be a great step forward to a North American Arctic as part of an integrated North American economy. Whether or not the United States government had this as a specific objective at the time, this could well be the consequence of a marked deterioration in the international and domestic economic environment confronting American policy-makers. The foregoing is of course quite speculative as well as pessimistic. But pessimism is not entirely out of place at the present. It suggests that Canada should be moving more rapidly to settle the problem of Arctic sovereignty, and to reduce the opportunity the question of sovereignty presents to Washington in a Canadian-American crisis that would arise essentially from causes external to the Canadian-American relationship.

The gradualist approach is not producing adequate results under present circumstances and could suddenly be revealed as quite inappropriate in a changed international environment. If the Law-of-the-Sea Conference fails to yield major gains for Canada, and if we are spared a deterioration in the international setting during the coming months, a new line of policy should seriously be considered. Since Canada may not after all have oil and natural-gas surpluses for export to the United States, it may not make sense to tie discussion of oil- and gas-exploration arrangements with Washington and the oil multinationals to prior American recognition of Canadian sovereignty over the waters of the Arctic archipelago. Instead, Ottawa should concentrate on long-overdue measures to make Canada more authentically an Arctic power. The limited Canadian scientific research effort in the Arctic should be greatly expanded. Aerial surveillance should be intensified, and the requisite aircraft acquired as a matter of urgency. Above all, procrastination on the icebreaker question should end and a superior Arctic icebreaker capability should be acquired as rapidly as possible. At the same time studies should be undertaken to determine the feasibility of boarding and otherwise dealing with foreign vessels engaged in an unauthorized transit of Canadian Arctic waters. These and other actions would help to demonstrate that Canada was determined to ensure effective occupation and control of the Arctic archipelago. Very substantial expenditures would be involved, and this would necessitate vigorous public support. To this end, and in order to show that the Canadian government had strong backing, politicians, the media, and others concerned should move in on the Arctic-sovereignty issue and begin to alert the public to Canada's new requirements. Since American officials will ordinarily prefer to gain their resource and maritime-mobility objectives without provoking an open clash, increased Canadian readiness to defend the national interest should also help to reinforce American restraint under present circumstances. Indeed American awareness of the heightened importance of Arctic sovereignty to Canadians could cause them to reassess the importance of their interests in the Northwest Passage relative to other issues under discussion with Canada. In this event Ottawa could seek American recognition of Canadian sovereignty by proposing an agreement on co-operation in the use of icebreakers in Canadian and American Arctic waters. This proposal might well be presented in the context of a larger Canadian-American Arctic negotiation including delimitation of the Yukon-Alaskan offshore boundary, continental-defence arrangements associated with the development of new warning systems, and joint environmental research projects.

Barring a qualitative transformation of the international situation and a marked increase in American demands on Canada, Washington could still continue to withhold co-operation and recognition of Canadian sovereignty even after Ottawa had become committed to a policy of increased activism. What then? Parliament could take the next step of passing legislation drawing straight baselines, with the support of informed Canadian opinion. Although effective enforcement would be difficult against surface vessels and virtually impossible against submarines, Washington might prefer not to put its counter-claims to the test by a flagrant transit of the Northwest Passage that would do great harm to Canadian-

American relations without the assurance of offsetting benefits for the United States. Instead the risk might be one of measured economic retaliation. Canadian readiness to accept this risk would depend again on the level of public awareness and the importance Canadians attached to the integrity of their country. Should this storm be weathered, Canadian Arctic-sovereignty claims would have been fully articulated and Canada would be able to continue its efforts to establish unquestionable occupation and control.

Alternatively, in the event of a dramatic reversal of American fortunes, Washington's response to increased Canadian activism might be to assert its interests and perceived rights by a variety of moves that could include unilateral transits of the Northwest Passage or the threat to make them even before Canada had drawn straight baselines. Canada would then have to be prepared to accept an open confrontation and the full consequences of its economic dependence on the United States. But, to repeat, if a confrontation occurred, it would be essentially for reasons beyond Canadian control. Though a policy of increased Canadian activism would doubtless make it easier for some in the United States to justify their own unilateralist preferences, American actions would be primarily a response to economic and political developments outside the Canadian-American relationship proper. The gradualist reluctance to become involved in a confrontation must be shared by all who seek a more effective affirmation of Canadian sovereignty in the Arctic. But there can be no saying that Canadian activism would in itself be a prime cause in provoking the United States into a confrontation. If confrontation comes, Canada had better already be committed to an Arctic policy of activism with full public support. If it does not occur, greater activism still offers an improved prospect of realizing the Canadian national interest in the Arctic.

Thus far the discussion has been cast in terms of dealing directly with the United States to produce a more rapid confirmation of Arctic sovereignty. But whether Canada largely co-operates with or is in conflict with the United States, it tends to be at a disadvantage in view of the unequal power relationship. In addition to a more active and self-reliant defence of sovereignty in bilateral relations, the Canadian government could explore the possibility of bringing other states into play in support of its position. One of the comparatively bright spots in the current picture is the progress that has been made in the multilateral negotiations over the law of the sea. It seems appropriate to seek out other modes of multilateral co-operation capable of reducing our vulnerability to American pressure. In particular, it is fitting to consider whether the other three states with territory and waters north of the Arctic Circle — the Soviet Union, Norway, and Denmark — might profitably be introduced into the picture.

THE PROSPECTS FOR MULTILATERALISM

In principle there are two basic alternatives open to Canada where Arctic multilateralism is concerned. Neither is entirely hypothetical, for as will be seen we have had experience with both. The first alternative is to try to draw in the Soviet Union, thereby making the defence of Arctic sovereignty a three-power exercise involving Canada, the United States, and the U.S.S.R. The second is to promote regional co-operation among all five Arctic powers as a means of constraining the United States and reducing conflict more generally in the area. Other alternatives—a small-power Arctic political grouping (Canada, Denmark, Norway), or a four-power western grouping (the latter three plus the United States)—do not seem very promising: the former would produce little for Canada, and the latter would probably create a new arena for American influence on Canada. Nor is a combination possible involving Canada, Denmark, Norway, and the Soviet Union, owing to the continuing East-West conflict and special differences between Norway and the Soviet Union. We will return in passing to these sub-regional alternatives for Canadian multilateral diplomacy. In the following passages, however, I plan to focus on the two main options, first mentioning some political manoeuvering that has occurred in recent years, and then looking at the main conflicts in Arctic international relations to see what might actually be accomplished if Canada chose to pursue either or both of its two principal choices.

The option of drawing on Soviet support in the defence of Arctic sovereignty was reportedly offered to Ottawa by the Soviet Union in 1967. At that time Moscow apparently suggested that in return for Soviet recognition and support of Canadian straight baselines, Ottawa would allow Soviet icebreakers the right of transit through the Canadian archipelago. This Soviet offer was evidently rejected by the Canadian government together with an accompanying Soviet request to bring ore ships and icebreakers to take ore out of Coppermine. One Ottawa official who is in a position to know said in an interview with me that he never ever heard of a Soviet proposal to support Canadian straight baselines, and virtually denied that it had been made. However another official who is in a better position to know reported the Soviet offer to one of my colleagues. It also happens that the Soviet Politburo member Dmitri Polyansky visited Canada in August 1967. I am inclined to believe that a Soviet proposal was indeed made, and that the idea of direct Soviet involvement in the Canadian-American conflict over the Northwest Passage would not be entirely novel to Moscow should Canada wish to raise the matter.

Whether or not Canada resolves to seek Soviet diplomatic support, it is worth noting that Canadian and Soviet policies in the Arctic have already converged to a substantial degree. American opposition not-withstanding, both Canada and the Soviet Union have established twelve-mile territorial seas. Both have unilaterally enacted pollution-prevention measures for the Arctic, and though the Soviet legislation applies to territorial waters only, it has the same effect as the Canadian act in that it includes key narrows in the Northern Sea Route. Both states also seek exclusive jurisdiction over their respective Arctic waterways. In public, Moscow's position on Canadian Arctic sovereignty has been one of benign silence. In private, Soviet representatives reportedly tend to say they are with Canada. More generally, by acting unilaterally to assert their sovereignty over the waters of the Northern Sea Route (without however claiming sovereignty in so many words), the Soviets have helped to create an international context more favourable to Canadian claims. Thus, even though the report of the Soviet initiative of 1967 may not prove fully accurate as presented here, existing parallels in the legal and political positions of the two countries do in principle offer a basis for further co-ordination of policy.

As regards five-power Arctic co-operation, we find that Canada has had previous experience here as well. In 1970-2 Ottawa sought privately to promote a gathering of the Arctic states to reach agreement on the status of waterways, rights of passage, pollution controls, and other mat-ters. This initiative grew out of American efforts to restrain Canada from its 1970 pollution-prevention legislation by urging Ottawa first to try to convene a conference of the Arctic powers to resolve the major problems of the region by international agreement rather than by unilateral action. The Canadian government went ahead with the Arctic Waters Pollution Prevention Act and with the American proposal as well. In canvassing support for a conference, Ottawa evidently had little expectation of suc-cess, but thought there still might be an outside chance of agreement on a combination of international rules that together would have preserved the essence of Canadian sovereignty. The western powers went along, but the Soviet Union finally torpedoed the whole idea. Conceivably this was because of the jealousy with which Moscow has traditionally guarded its own Arctic jurisdiction against foreign intrusion. Although the Soviet Union might under certain circumstances be ready to participate in the delimitation of Canadian Arctic jurisdiction, it is evidently very reluctant to allow others a say in what occurs in its own sector of the region. The implication of this whole episode is that comprehensive five-power Arctic co-operation is not an alternative that Canada can profitably expect to pursue in the near future.

The outlook is, however, slightly more promising where limited, spe-cial-purpose five-power co-operation is concerned. Late in 1973 Canada joined with the other regional states in a negotiation in Oslo that led early the next year to a treaty on the conservation of polar bears. The impetus for this conference came from the Soviet Union, which may have perceived an opportunity to capitalize on the momentum generated by the Canadian activity of 1970-2. In Oslo the biologists involved, including the Soviets, reportedly reached a rapid consensus on what needed to be done, whereas the diplomats evidently took a good deal of time to arrive at a mutually acceptable document. As might be expected, the treaty is consistent with the maintenance of national sovereignty in that it approaches polar-bear conservation as a matter of co-ordinated national activity. In addition to prohibiting the taking of bears (with minor exceptions), it obliges the contracting parties to co-ordinate their separate research programs, to exchange information on management procedures, and to consult with one another with the object of giving further protection to polar bears. More generally, the treaty recognizes the principle that the Arctic states have a special responsibility for protecting the flora and fauna of the region. If an exceedingly limited but nevertheless productive agreement of this kind has recently been obtained, it seems reasonable to expect that additional five-power environmental and conservation measures might also be realized.

There may thus be an opening for Canada to propose an Arctic conference with a modest agenda including co-operation and exchange of information on one of a variety of topics such as conservation, weather research, and marine pollution control. Co-operation in Arctic meteorological research may prove the more promising. If there is one environmental issue the Soviets are likely to take very seriously, it is the weather. The fate of the annual harvest and hence the success of the entire Soviet economic planning process depend heavily upon the unpredictable and sometimes catastrophic behaviour of this variable. The Soviets themselves call the Arctic the world's 'weather kitchen'. To speak to Moscow about Arctic meteorological co-operation may therefore be to evoke particularly sympathetic vibrations within the Soviet establishment that would enhance the prospect for this as opposed to other regional environmental measures.

If successful, an initiative of this kind could provide support for the objectives of Canadian sovereignty. Assume for example that the project included voyages by meteorological vessels with national or multinational scientific staff, and that these voyages included passage through the waters of Arctic coastal states. In this situation the coastal state would be expected to give a by-your-leave, and in so doing it would be exercising its sovereignty. The operation of such vessels within the Canadian Arctic archipelago would thus strengthen regional-state recognition of Canadian sovereignty. The United States might accordingly be inclined to resist a proposal for co-operation in Arctic meteorological research. But this would be to place Washington in an awkward position in view of the practical merits of such a proposal. As it is, the United States and the

Soviet Union have already been considering co-operation in Arctic weather modification even to the point of discussing the damming of the Bering Strait.

Special-purpose regional multilateralism of this kind would doubtless yield only small sovereignty gains to begin with. Nevertheless it deserves serious consideration on ecological as well as political grounds. The Arctic Waters Pollution Prevention Act was very largely a fig leaf for the maple leaf: it was primarily a means of defending sovereignty, and was not followed up by the sizeable increase in scientific research and other activity that would have demonstrated an enduring ecological interest in the Arctic as well as the pressing need to act politically in 1970. A more active commitment to limited regional co-operation on conservation and environmental affairs would allow Canada to make good its obligations as one of the five stewards of a region whose ecosystems cannot properly be treated in a segmented manner. In the longer term, it could open the way to more comprehensive collaboration and the larger benefits this promises for Canadian sovereignty goals, the requirements of the Arctic environment as such, and the reduction of interstate conflict.

The two major alternatives that have been suggested for a Canadian effort to secure greater external support for its Arctic sovereignty objectives do thus have a certain reality and are not merely a result of abstract reasoning. A brief look at the state of current and possible future relations among the Arctic powers — principally Norway, the Soviet Union, and the United States — may assist in further specifying what might in fact be accomplished by Canada on a multilateral basis.

The Soviet-American relationship, which dominates this as other regions, is one of limited collaboration between adversaries. Though the Strategic Arms Limitation Talks have not thus far markedly reduced the pace of the superpower arms race, arms-control agreements are viewed by substantial numbers in both countries as important stabilizing measures that reduce the danger of war and create a climate increasingly favourable to co-operation in economic, technological, and scientific affairs. While there are signs of increasing disaffection with *détente* in both states, and while both continue to seek unilateral advantage in local conflicts, Soviet and American actions have over the years become increasingly constrained by the need to avoid disrupting the process of direct bilateral co-operation. Despite inevitable ups and downs in the level of superpower tension in the future, the long-term outlook seems to be one of hesitantly expanding collaboration. In the short term, however, the possibility of a substantial deterioration in relations is quite real, owing to unusual instabilities in the international system.

At present the conflict in Soviet-American relations directly concerning the Arctic is expressed in political-legal as well as military terms. The United States rejects the unilateral assumption of exclusive jurisdiction by

Moscow in its sector of the region. In the mid-sixties the United States sought on two occasions to traverse the Northern Sea Route with ice-breakers, but was forced back by Moscow. Whether or not the new American icebreakers are employed to further United States legal and political objectives in the Soviet sphere of the Arctic, it seems reasonable to suppose that the Barents Sea will become an area of intensified military-strategic interest. A major portion of the Soviet nuclear ballistic missile fleet is based on the Kola Peninsula. The U.S.S.R. is acquiring submarine-launched missiles capable of reaching American targets from just off the Kola coast. Insofar as American thinking on deterrence accepts damage limitation in a nuclear war rather than mutual assured destruction, it will be in the interest of the U.S. Navy to be able to get at Soviet nuclear submarines in the waters off the western Soviet Arctic and Norwegian shores.

On the other hand there are indications of emerging Soviet-American co-operation in the Arctic. For example, if the vast Soviet-American natural-gas project were eventually to go through, American tankers carrying liquefied natural gas could be travelling to and from a port in the western Soviet Arctic even as military-strategic rivalry continued in the area. In addition there are the oil-exploration activities of the *Glomar Challenger*. Now a joint venture with substantial financial contributions and scientific participation from the Soviet Union as well as the United States and West Germany, this vessel was reported to have embarrassed the Norwegian government recently by its discovery of high-quality oil at two unauthorized drilling sites in the Norwegian Sea. Although military-political conflict prevails over economic and scientific co-operation in superpower relations in the Arctic, the pattern promises to be increasingly mixed as the two governments slowly weave a web of mutual dependence in this as in other areas.

The state of Soviet-American relations is obviously a key determinant of what can be done by Canada on a multilateral basis in the Arctic. Insofar as Moscow regards the development of Soviet-American co-operation as a priority matter, it will be reluctant to inject itself into the Canadian-American Arctic dispute in opposition to the United States. In this connection it should be noted that the Soviet proposal to Canada in 1967 was made at a time when Soviet-American co-operation was at a low ebb. Although superpower relations have recently become somewhat more abrasive, the Soviet stake in collaborating with the United States is still considerably greater at present than it was in 1967. This suggests that despite the similarity of Soviet and Canadian Arctic policies and the reported Soviet proposal of 1967, Canada may not after all be able to secure Soviet support in drawing straight baselines around its Arctic archipelago unless a freeze or momentary reversal in the process of East-West co-operation occurs.

In addition to Canadian-American and Soviet-American conflicts in the Arctic, there is a third major dispute, this time between the Soviet Union and Norway. One of the principal issues here is the delimitation of the offshore boundary and seabed rights out from the Norwegian-Soviet frontier to the area of the Spitsbergen archipelago. Among other things, the Soviets seek control over substantial areas of the seabed claimed by Norway. In this they are evidently guided not merely by a desire for access to the oil that may lie there, but also by a need to limit western economic and naval activity in an area of vital strategic significance to the U.S.S.R. As of November 1974 Norway has been engaged in bilateral Arctic negotiations with the Soviet Union; interestingly enough, it also rejected an American invitation to become a member of the International Energy Coordinating Group—an association of oil-consuming nations that is a special project of the American Secretary of State. If talks with the Soviet Union fail, Norway could reveal an interest in joining Canada in a western grouping of Arctic powers directed against the Soviet Union. On the other hand, since Canada's differences are primarily with the United States, a Soviet-Norwegian agreement, by reducing the Norwegian propensity to lean towards the United States, could favour greater co-ordination of Canadian-Norwegian positions.

Faced with a proposal to formalize a four-power western subgrouping of Arctic states, Canada might ask for American recognition of its Arctic sovereignty claims as the price of entry. A positive American response seems improbable, for Washington could achieve many of the objectives of such a group through bilateral consultations that would obviate the need for compromise on the Northwest Passage. Should the United States be willing to compromise, however, Canada's legal and political problems in the Arctic could be very largely solved, and Ottawa would have little reason to withhold participation.

Suppose however that the Norwegians and Danes sought a three-power grouping with Canada. This would not markedly improve our position vis-à-vis the United States, and would have the probable disadvantage of appearing to Moscow as an American-inspired combination directed against Soviet interests. The western powers should not succumb to an excessive concern for the avoidance of moves that annoy the Soviets. In this instance, however, Canada's ability to draw on Soviet support in a future contingency would be reduced in return for but slight present gain. There thus seems to be little to recommend a small-power Arctic grouping. Canada should nevertheless lose no opportunity further to improve its relations with Norway, which next to the Soviet Union is the major potential supporter of Canadian Arctic sovereignty requirements.

Returning to Canada's two major alternatives—of relying directly on the U.S.S.R. for support of straight-baselines legislation or of promoting five-power environmental co-operation in meteorological or other matters

—we see that the former is inhibited by Soviet-American collaboration, whereas even the limited sovereignty-producing measures envisaged by the latter would have to surmount conflict among the regional states.

There are obvious additional difficulties with the Soviet alternative. For one thing, informed Canadians at present feel more strongly about Solzhenitsyn's *Gulag Archipelago* than they do about Canada's Arctic archipelago. A rapprochement with the U.S.S.R. on the Arctic issue in opposition to the United States would at present be unthinkable for a substantial proportion of the population, and could conceivably remain so for many even if it meant letting the Northwest Passage go. Also there is the question of the Soviet interest in such a project: it could be used as a means of applying pressure on the United States, and might be dropped once American compliance had been obtained on other issues under discussion between Moscow and Washington. More important still is the probable retaliation of the United States following the announcement of a Canadian-Soviet arrangement on straight baselines and rights of passage for Soviet vessels in the Canadian archipelago.

The inevitable conclusion is that in practice neither of the two alternatives is capable of providing Canada with a rapid improvement in the outlook for Arctic sovereignty. Appealing to the Soviet Union is too much too soon. Five-power environmental co-operation is too little too late. A combination of the two alternatives may however yield worthwhile gains at a worthwhile pace.

The alternative of seeking direct Soviet assistance is best viewed as a response available to Canada if a major confrontation with the United States that involves the Northwest Passage should occur. Since a Canadian-American confrontation would arise primarily from a reassessment of United States needs in a changed internal and international setting that could include a worsening of Soviet-American relations, Moscow might be more favourably disposed towards intervention than seems to be the case at present. The existence or imminence of confrontation would also be required to justify both the threat Canada would pose to American interests by inviting Soviet intervention, and also the breach with past Canadian actions that turning towards the U.S.S.R. would involve. Nevertheless the United States should be made aware that if forced to do so Canada might very well seek Soviet support for straight baselines in the event that unauthorized American transits of the Northwest Passage seemed imminent. Similarly the Canadian public should be made aware now of the full range of contingencies that might have to be considered in the case of a confrontation concerning the Arctic. To convince Washington of Canada's earnestness and also to probe Soviet intentions, unofficial and official Canadian-Soviet consultations on a range of issues concerning potential Arctic co-operation should be initiated as part of the early phases of an activist policy. Thus, while Canada would not expect to take up the Soviet option except in the case of a confrontation, it would not delay either in preparing for such an eventuality or in employing these preparations to communicate the seriousness of its purpose to the United States.

As for the alternative of five-power co-operation on environmental and particularly meteorological affairs, this could be acted upon right away. Though it would not offer great gains for Canadian sovereignty, even modest regional agreements on atmospheric research, pollution controls, and the preservation of species should be pursued with imagination and vigour for purely ecological as well as political reasons. At the same time the preliminaries and formal negotiations involved would provide an appropriate context for bilateral as well as multilateral discussions among the Arctic powers. In particular, if the United States were willing to support regional environmental co-operation, Canada could openly discuss matters of mutual concern with the U.S.S.R. without provoking excessive alarm in Washington. Thus five-power environmental multilateralism could be pursued for sovereignty as well as ecological purposes, and as a precondition for more ambitious Arctic co-operation. It could also provide a framework in which Canada could more easily begin to explore Soviet intentions and their bearing on Canadian Arctic-sovereignty requirements.

In sum, by combining the Soviet and five-power environmental alternatives Canada stands to maximize the limited opportunities offered by the international environment to obtain confirmation of its sovereignty in the Arctic. Though the Soviet and five-power environmental alternatives taken separately do not meet Canada's present needs, in combination they provide a relatively flexible means of reducing its dependence on the United States.

AGENDA

To conclude very briefly, this paper has recommended increased activism in the defence of Arctic sovereignty. Where the current gradualist policies subordinate unilateralism and multilateralism to stability in bilateral Canadian-American relations, it seems desirable and practical instead to reverse the unilateral-bilateral proportion. The preservation of good relations with the United States should be a subordinate consideration in a new policy line emphasizing self-reliance and intensified Arctic multilateralism. What this might mean in practice is indicated by the following agenda.

1. Allow several months to see whether the law-of-the-sea negotiations succeed. Pursue the possibility of an omnibus agreement that provides the widest possible international recognition of Canadian sovereignty in the waters of the Arctic archipelago. Simultaneously discuss with Washington

a special arrangement on the status of the Northwest Passage as a Canadian waterway open to American vessels conforming to reasonable Canadian pollution-control and security requirements. Do not accept American proposals for free transit in return for economic concessions or concessions on alternate sea-law issues.

2. Embark in 1976 on self-reliance programs, including icebreaker development, expanded scientific research activity, aerial surveillance, and public information. Seek a five-power Arctic conference on meteorological or other appropriate environmental issues. Initiate conversations in this context with the Soviet Union on preliminary items of Arctic co-operation. Seek a comprehensive bilateral negotiation on the Arctic with the United States, including new continental-defence arrangements and co-operation in the use of icebreakers.

3. Draw straight baselines without reference to the Soviet Union but with public backing adequate to withstand limited American retaliation short of confrontation. Continue the endeavour to establish effective occupation and control. Widen discussions with the U.S.S.R. to consider conditions for *post facto* Soviet support of straight baselines.

4. Draw straight baselines with immediate Soviet support, in the context of a major Canadian-American confrontation.

It is to be hoped that a sense of proportion would prevail in Washington well before it came to item 4. Canada must nevertheless be ready to confront the possibility of the Soviet alternative if it is to induce the United States to display greater respect for Canadian rights. Again it is the physical integrity of the Canadian nation that is in question. If gradualist policies have not thus far succeeded in convincing the United States of the importance of Arctic sovereignty to Canada, a commitment to activism may bring the message home.

9 MARINE SCIENCE, TECHNOLOGY, AND THE ARCTIC: SOME QUESTIONS AND GUIDELINES FOR THE FEDERAL GOVERNMENT

by John W. Langford

... [T]here is not now, nor is it conceivable that there will ever be, from any source, challenges to Canadian sovereignty on the mainland, in the islands, in the minerals lying in the continental shelf below the Arctic waters, or in our territorial seas. This ... is the result of quiet, consistent policies on the part of all Canadian governments.... These policies will reflect Canada's proper interest not only in the preservation of the ecological balance ..., but as well in the economic development of the north, the security of Canada, and in our stature and reputation in the world community ... [1]

(Pierre Elliott Trudeau, 24 October 1969)

INTRODUCTION

The legal and political issues associated with the question of Arctic sovereignty and economic development have become part of the conversational repertoire of many well-informed Canadians since the discovery of oil and gas in the North, the voyages of the S.S. *Manhattan*, the passage of the Arctic Waters Pollution Prevention Act, and amendments to the Territorial Sea and Fishing Zones Act. However the actual and potential impact of new scientific knowledge and modern technology on the long-run development of the Canadian Arctic has largely remained the subject of articles in technical journals and conferences of engineers.[2] Neither the media nor the Ottawa political/bureaucratic arena have shown any sustained interest in this question. Two results of this isolation and indifference have been a low level of initiative and participation by Canadian industry and the federal government in the establishment of an integrated Canadian Arctic research and development policy, and the acceptance of a philosophy for assessing the development and application of new technologies to the North that largely ignores the criteria related to the vital issues of Canada's sovereignty over the high Arctic and

Canadian involvement in its economic development. This paper will attempt to outline, first, the degree to which the search for a better understanding of the Arctic environment and the perfection of new machines and techniques might significantly affect Canada's 'effective occupation' and long-run resource-development capabilities, particularly in the area of marine transportation, and second, the degree to which Canada has access to and command of this new knowledge and technology. In the course of this narrative it should become evident that on the whole Arctic marine science and technology has received support in this country only when it promises to lead to *immediate* economic returns.[3] The absence of national goals such as Arctic sovereignty and long-run economic development from prevailing federal processes for the funding and assessment of science and technology has had two results. First, future marine-transportation and support systems in the high Arctic are geared almost exclusively to short-run resource-extraction projects and are operated largely by other maritime nations. Second, Canadian marine-oriented research and development in the high Arctic has been unthinkingly linked to foreign efforts in the field—with Canada continuing to play a disturbingly minor role.

No one would claim that it is possible at this point in time to make an airtight case for significant government expenditures on an Arctic marine-transportation and support system on the basis of a *proven* long-run economic demand for such a system. However there is substantial evidence to support the likelihood that eastern Arctic mineral deposits of lead-zinc, iron and coal, and Arctic-islands reserves of natural gas will by 1985 loom large as resources vital to the self-sufficiency and balanced growth of the Canadian economy. One thing is absolutely certain, neither the federal government nor Canadian industry will be in a position to create the substantial marine-transportation and support system that may be required unless some significant continuing commitments are made in the near future to research and development across a broad front and to the implementation of specific construction projects.

Although Prime Minister Trudeau may be correct in stressing the unlikelihood of a direct challenge to Canada's Arctic sovereignty in the future, the nature and degree of Canada's effective occupation of the high Arctic (even if it exceeds the minimum standards set by international law) will always be related to the federal government's ability to foster the development and application of advanced marine technologies. As Lydia Dotto, the science writer for the Toronto *Globe and Mail*, so succinctly put it in reference to Canada's ability to operate above and below Arctic waters, '...when it comes to asserting national claims in international circles, it is generally a good idea to be able to put your technology and manpower where your mouth is.'[4] This is particularly significant in view of the federal government's seeming reliance on a limited functional approach to Arctic sovereignty as embodied in the Arctic Waters Pollution Prevention Act.[5] The ability to enforce the provisions of this legislation and any other expression of functional or unlimited authority in the high Arctic will depend to a large extent on scientific and technological leadership with respect to the polar marine environment and transportation. Not only has the Cabinet been somewhat ambivalent about its sovereignty claims in the high Arctic, but it has done little since 1970 to ensure Canada's capacity to operate effectively in the passages and seas surrounding the Arctic islands. The public was told in 1973 that the Cabinet had approved an 'oceans policy' calling for Canada to achieve 'world recognized excellence in operating on and below ice-covered waters' within five years, but the policy was never widely publicized and there have been few significant policy and program changes within the federal departments concerned to carry out the government's commitments in this area.[6] The Prime Minister's assurances in 1969 that Canada's Arctic sovereignty will not be challenged because of the 'quiet, consistent policies' of past and present governments does not provide much comfort in 1975 when one examines the federal government's unco-ordinated and miserly approach to Arctic research.

In the last ten years, although marine transportation in the Arctic has been shifting increasingly from the resupply of local communities and the servicing of joint Canadian-American military facilities to the establishment of a transportation infrastructure to support rational economic development, the federal government shows few signs of being conscious of this shift.

POLAR ICEBREAKER TECHNOLOGY: A STORY OF GOVERNMENT DELAY AND UNCERTAINTY

While it is always important to stimulate technological advances and assess their application to national goals, it is particularly so when examining the rapidly evolving transportation system within the Canadian Arctic.[7] It seems possible that technology could literally work miracles here over the next few decades. While the student of Arctic transportation is faced with myriads of new and revised engineering wizardries in all modes, polar-icebreaker technology is a particular area in which controversial advances are being made by several Arctic or Arctic-oriented nations while the federal government continues to procrastinate in developing a coherent policy and program.

In fact, the era of polar-class icebreakers is almost upon us as a result of the interest provoked by the highly publicized progress of the S.S. *Manhattan* through the Northwest Passage during the summer of 1969. The American firm, Lockheed Shipbuilding and Construction Co., should have the first of a brace of polar icebreakers ready for delivery to the U.S. Coast Guard by the fall of 1975. It has been suggested that these particular vessels may not be the final word in polar-class icebreakers because their weight (12,000 tons) is not balanced in relation to their horsepower (60,000 or more shaft horsepower); nevertheless they do represent a distinct American commitment to technological superiority in marine transportation under conditions remarkably similar to those found in the Canadian high Arctic.[8] Other nations have shown an impressive level of commitment. Finland's Wartsila shipyard has designed a 140,-000-shp., 50,000-ton, polar icebreaker for year-round operations.[9] In addition to the 39,000-shp. *Lenin*, a 16,000-ton nuclear-powered polar icebreaker operating with mixed success since 1960, the Soviet Union has in service a more powerful gas-turbine-powered vessel, and is presently outfitting for commission in 1975 a second nuclear-powered icebreaker of 25,000 tons and 36,000 shp. designed to assist in keeping its western Arctic passage open year-round. Moreover it has been reported that the Soviet Union is soon to begin building a nuclear-powered 70,000-shp. vessel that would be the world's largest icebreaker.[10]

By comparison, only in mid-1974 did the Treasury Board authorize the Ministry of Transport to begin funding the design (including an examination of nuclear-propulsion systems) by German and Milne Ltd in Montreal of a class-7 Canadian icebreaker (80,000-100,000 shp. and 20,000 tons) suitable for polar-ice operation during eight months of the year.[11] The commitment of funds ($500,000 in 1975-6) is only for the design stage, which is expected to last four years. If the government decides to build the vessel in 1977-8 it will be at least 1982 before it is ready for the Coast Guard.[12] The Ministry has also commissioned German and Milne Ltd to begin a feasibility study of a 200,000-shp. class-10 icebreaker of 30,000 tons displacement, which could not possibly be commissioned before 1985. The conclusion to be drawn from these hesitant and noncommittal steps is that neither the Ministry of Transport nor the Cabinet is yet convinced of the need to commit substantial funds to the development of advanced polar-class Canadian icebreakers despite the arguments of Arctic shipping experts and the evidence that other nations are investing heavily in this area.

During the 1974 federal election campaign the government further complicated the decision-making process concerning polar-class icebreakers by maintaining that if elected a Liberal government would support the design and manufacture of polar-cargo vessels that would combine the role of polar-class icebreakers and cargo ships.[13] Such vessels, it was maintained, would be the first manifestation of a government policy to reserve Arctic commercial shipping for a new Canadian merchant marine and would also lessen the urgency for a decision on the icebreaker-building program. The latter thesis is only defensible if the icebreaking

OBO (oil, bulk, ore carrier) contemplated is in excess of 150,000 dead-weight tons and therefore capable of providing all its own icebreaking capacity throughout at least an eight-month season. Moreover, logical technological trade-offs between large icebreaking OBOS and traditional polar-class icebreakers would only be relevant to an icebreaker in the class-10 range. Canadian shipping consultants such as Captain Thomas C. Pullen, former commander of the icebreaker H.M.S.C. *Labrador*, have consistently maintained that icebreakers in the class-7 range are essential to Canada for a wide variety of tasks from surveying to the monitoring of communications and activities of other vessels in Arctic waters.[14] The government's thesis is also implicitly questioned in a comprehensive study, 'Arctic Resources by Sea', completed for the Ministry of Transport by Northern Associates (Holdings) Ltd (Montreal) in late 1973. This study argues that government polar icebreakers of 'appropriate capability' would be a critical component of any commercial shipping system in the Arctic.[15] The role of the icebreaker would be to render assistance to commercial vessels in an emergency, escort less ice-capable vessels, perform hydrographic and environmental services, monitor and control pollution, take part in search and rescue operations, and provide logistic support of all kinds.[16] There is no indication in the Northern Associates report that the development of commercial icebreaking vessels for the high Arctic precludes the need for polar-class icebreakers even when the commercial vessels in question are extremely large. It seems reasonable to conclude that although the roles contemplated for a class-10 icebreaker might eventually be usurped by large OBOS, by improved air-cushion vehicles, or even by rotary ice-cutting vehicles for instance, the case for proceeding quickly with the construction of at least one class-7 icebreaker is quite powerful.[17]

The most curious aspect of the government's attempt — both during and after the 1974 election — to relate the class-7 icebreaker decision to the newly announced initiatives regarding the development of a commercial icebreaking vessel is that the commercial vessel contemplated would be completely inadequate in trade-off terms. While the Minister of Transport indicated during the campaign that the government would fund the development and building of a prototype cargo vessel, little was said about the size or power contemplated. In fact, Federal Commerce and Navigation Co. in Montreal had already done much of the design work through a grant from the Program for the Advancement of Industrial Technology on a 28,000-toon icebreaking ocean-bottom seismometer (class two) to operate during a 20-week season in the eastern Arctic. While the 1975-6 estimates set aside $1,675,000 for work on an icebreaking cargo vessel, the Ministry of Transport made no firm commitment to support the construction of this vessel or to participate with the marine industry in the operation of a prototype until June 1975. No more has been said about the design and construction of a more ambitious ice-breaking cargo vessel. This represents another rather serious delay on the part of the government in view of the fact that no private Canadian shipbuilding company or consortium can be expected to sustain the development and application of new marine technology for the Arctic without government financial assistance in the form of shared ownership of prototype vessels or a substantial building subsidy.

The situation is particularly exacerbated by the obvious effort being directed towards the development of this new technology in other countries. The S.S. *Manhattan*, although ostensibly a Humble Oil project, was supported financially by the U.S. Navy.[18] The mixed results of the *Manhattan* experiments, the inadeqacies of the U.S. *Wind*-class icebreakers under Arctic conditions, and the decision to opt for a pipeline to carry Alaskan oil south to Valdez from the North Slope of Alaska have led the U.S. to place more immediate emphasis on the development of icebreakers than on icebreaking cargo vessels. However, as a result of the S.S. *Manhattan* voyages, the U.S. government has access to a vast amount of unique data on the problems confronting icebreaking cargo vessels in the high Arctic, which provides a solid foundation for an expanding research and development program by the federal Department of Commerce's Maritime Administration.[19] As a recent study puts it, '[o]riented towards both Great Lakes and Arctic regions the objectives of this program are to evolve a range of analytical and technological capabilities to both assess and provide for marine transportation services and port facilities in these frigid environments.'[20] These services and facilities in the Arctic will have as their major objective the transportation of natural resources (largely oil and liquefied natural gas) to U.S. east-coast ports and other world markets. With an alarming candour the study outlines a twenty-four-year scenario in which, after the 'legal and political considerations' are ironed out, and the U.S. and Canada agree 'to share equally in the control and allocation' of the estimated 220-320 billion barrels of crude oil available in the Arctic, 'up to 62 new Arctic icebreaking tankers, designed specifically for the Northwest Passage, could be needed' for year-round operations by the year 2000 to service U.S. east-coast needs.[21] The paper also concludes that:

[a]dditionally, there will be a need for greatly expanded U.S. Coast Guard icebreaker capability to provide support to this new fleet. In addition to icebreaking, this support would include search and rescue, environmental surveillance, ice reconnaissance, maintenance of navigational aids, and other safety-related functions.[22]

After describing the twenty-four-year scenario, the study proceeds to outline some of the research and development programs of the U.S.

Maritime Administration and the time it will take to develop Arctic crude carriers. The design stage of the latter will last until 1981 when construction will begin on two prototypes [and suitable terminals]; depending on how well they perform and on further design work, construction of the fleet of oil carriers would begin in 1987, and the vessels would begin to operate commercially in 1989. The present Maritime Administration program is not focused exclusively on carrying oil from the western Arctic. It includes significant expenditures on liquefied-natural-gas production and tanker-delivery systems for use in the Arctic islands, as well as studies in co-operation with the U.S. Coast Guard of several innovative methods of icebreaking and various propulsion systems.[23] Both the data arising from the *Manhattan* voyages and the information that the *Polar Star* is expected to begin providing in 1975 will be critical elements in the Maritime Administration's continuing oil-carrier design work. In addition the Administration is funding a design study of an oil-transportation system using large submarine tankers; preliminary designs for such a system featuring nuclear-powered submarines were first produced by General Dynamics Corporation in 1971.[24] On the basis of the numerous successful journeys of U.S. Navy nuclear submarines under the polar pack, and the knowledge gained from the operation of the Submarine Research Facility in San Diego, the U.S. government is far ahead of other Arctic-oriented nations in the development of polar submarines.

The German government has been working with German shipbuilders (most notably A. G. Weser) for over two years on studies of icebreaking cargo vessels. The Germans are designing special ships to transport mineral resources (such as lead-zinc and iron ore from Baffin Island), oil, and liquefied natural gas to Germany.[25] One design, already on the drawing board, is for a 70,000-dwt bulk carrier and another for a 250,000-dwt oil tanker. Weser is also doing considerable basic research and development on shipbuilding materials, hydrodynamic gearing, welding techniques, and electrical machinery to complement its Arctic-vessel design work, and to facilitate the step from the drawing board to the shipyard.[26] All this effort is being made with a close eye on the pollution regulations resulting from the Arctic Waters Pollution Prevention Act, and in consultation with the marine-inspection authorities within the Canadian Ministry of Transport. An equally advanced (but smaller scale) Arctic cargo-vessel technology is being developed in Finland, a country faced with a complete barrier of coastal ice during the winter months. To date the Finns have developed a fleet of bulk carriers and oil tankers, stengthened against ice, the newest being a 6,000-dwt product tanker with a special hull form, double-skin construction, and an air-bubbling system.[27]

The Administrator of the Ministry of Transport's Arctic Transportation Agency made the following statement in 1973 with reference to this new marine technology for the Arctic.

. . . [I]f the marine mode is to play an important role, as seems very likely, I am confident that in conjunction with industry-shipping, ship-building, and resource developments — the Ministry will have its homework done to apply to the need when it arises. Whether the initial step is a quantum leap — directly into a cargo icebreaker suitable for year-round use in the High Arctic or whether it is a more conservative approach to extending the shipping season in less severe ice zones, remains to be seen, and will probably depend on the extent of innovation involved as well as the commitments forthcoming from the industries concerned.[28]

It is difficult to share this official's confidence in the Ministry of Transport's (or Canada's) ability to lead in the development of polar-class icebreakers or icebreaking cargo vessels over the next decade. The above statement is couched in the language of 'response' not 'leadership'. The government has shown great reluctance in doing its 'homework' in this area and, as a result, Canada is in danger of falling behind other nations in the development of a broadly based marine technology for the high Arctic. On several occasions since the fall 1972 there have been news stories and expressions of anxiety in the Canadian press and the House of Commons about exploratory talks between the Canadian and West German governments concerning the possibility of joint co-operation in developing icebreaking cargo vessels.[29] In view of the considerable German advances on these vessels and the substantial involvement of the Germans in resources exploitation in the eastern Arctic, there are solid grounds for believing that this would not be a partnership of equals. There is also considerable evidence to support the contention that both the United States and the Soviet Union will be in a position to begin commercial shipments of oil, gas, and minerals through high-Arctic waters from resource-development projects in the near future. The link here between resource exploitation and sovereignty is a close one. The prospect of fleets of foreign cargo vessels plying the Northwest Passage and the waterways of the eastern Arctic years before Canada's modest and incipient efforts in Arctic-vessel development bear fruit does little to enhance one's expectations concerning our 'effective occupation' of the high Arctic and our ability to control and share in its economic development.

MARINE SUPPORT SYSTEMS

A nation's ability to traverse the Arctic seas and passages for whatever purpose depends as much on its mastery of the science and technology of Arctic marine-support systems as it does on its advances in vessel technology.[30] One American spokesman put the problem of marine-support systems this way in 1969 prior to the S.S. *Manhattan* voyages:

> While a respectable body of knowledge has been accumulated on sea and ice dynamics, this information, in the context of the total problem, is only a scratch on the surface. So difficult are operating conditions that existing icebreakers can operate only seasonally in this environment. Although sketchy traffic lines have been founded from previous transits, the hydrographic information necessary to commit regular shipping to the Northwest Passage does not exist; and there is almost a total lack of aids to navigation throughout the area.
>
> Terminal problems in the Arctic are equally difficult. There are no deep-water ports and the coast is generally shallow. During much of the year the polar pack is grounded along the coast. The resultant dredging action of the ice makes the use of underwater piping to an offshore loading facility hazardous. Some type of year-round loading facility that is suitable for use in this climate needs to be invented.[31]

The federal government and several private Canadian concerns have made some highly visible scientific and technological advances in marine-support systems over the last four or five years. However the integration of the private and public sectors is poor, and *in toto* Canada has made only small and uncertain strides towards achieving the goal set for it by the Ministry of State for Science and Technology in 1973—that of developing an internationally recognized skill in operating above and below ice-covered waters within five years.[32]

On the 'science' side, research into marine-support systems is presently focused largely on the study of the various kinds of ice and waterways within and adjacent to the Canadian Arctic.[33] Much of this work is carried on with the co-operation or under the aegis of the Department of Energy, Mines and Resources' Polar Continental Shelf Project, a multi-year study designed to bring order and co-ordinated action to the whole problem of surveying the Arctic archipelago and the territorial and continental-shelf waters of the high Arctic.[34] Since 1957 the Meteorological Branch of the Department of Transport (now part of the Atmospheric Environment Service of the Department of the Environment) has been responsible for the development and operation of an ice program in Canada. This program involves both the collection of information about the formation, movement, and dissipation of ice, and the processing and communication of this information and forecasts based on it through 'Ice Central' in Ottawa. About 60 per cent of this activity is devoted to Arctic Canada and is based on a wide range of sources including aerial reconnaissance, satellite date, and U.S. Navy reports. Increasingly the collection of ice data is becoming a task for satellites, and the Canada Centre for Remote Sensing (an agency of the Department of Energy, Mines and

Resources) is playing a major role in experiments concerning the benefits for Arctic shipping of data produced by the Earth Resources Technology Satellite (ERTS).[35] ERTS and the NOAA-2 meteorological satellite, on which the Canada Centre for Remote Sensing is dependent for a good deal of its data, are both U.S. government satellites. Moreover, although the Centre is a federal government agency, most of its work in this particular area has apparently been supported not by government funds but by oil- and re-source-survey companies; and the experimental data has been used largely to assist them by providing ice information to their survey ships.

More universally available tools such as low-light television systems, infra-red scanners, and side-looking radar also provide access to ice data for what is in Canada largely an 'applied' ice research designed to pro-vide up-to-date information and predictions on ice conditions in Arctic waters. To date this work has proceeded at a rather slow pace due to the erratic flow of raw data from the various reporting sources. The advent of remote sensing based on satellites promises to improve the flow of certain kinds of ice data, but it is by no means certain that Canada will maintain access to the output of American satellites. Unfortunately the Department of Communications, which is responsible through its Communications Research Centre for Canada's satellite development, is directing most of its Arctic-related efforts towards the improvement of Canada's north-south broadcast and general communications facilities through the Com-munications Technology Satellite that will be launched in late 1975 and the development of third-generation broadcast satellites to replace the ANIK series after 1978. While the Ministry of State for Science and Tech-nology has shown some concern about the issue of Canada's access to foreign satellite data and launch facilities, the Department of Communi-cations seems to have given no attention to this issue and has only just begun to show interest in the possibility of developing a Canadian remote-sensing satellite with microwave instruments capable of studying Arctic ice cover. One senior Department of Communications official indi-cated to me in September 1974 that sovereignty had never been consid-ered as a criterion for a remote-sensing program or policy decisions within the Department despite the lipservice paid to it in Department of Communications reports.[36]

In addition to the production of ice atlases, day-to-day readings, and forecasts, a comprehensive ice-science program includes intensive efforts to understand many issues related to the physical properties of ice. The main focus of this facet of sea-ice research is the joint U.S.-Canadian Arctic Ice Dynamics Joint Experiment, a multi-year study of how ice formations such as pressure ridges, keels, and pingoes (which present extreme dangers for shipping) came into existence and develop.[37] Canada has always lagged behind the U.S. in this area. Just as the federal government began its Polar Continental Shelf Project in response to

American activities in the Arctic Ocean, Canadian involvement in the Arctic Ice Dynamics Joint Experiment was belated and, according to J. Tuzo Wilson of the University of Toronto, is substantially less than that of the U.S. — except in the provision of logistic support — largely owing to poor management and communications by federal bureaucrats.[38] Wilson concludes:

> Thus, in a nominally equal enterprise, Canada was in its not uncommon role of being a 'hewer of wood and drawer of water' and most Canadian university scientists were not sufficiently aware of the opportunity to have made any effort to participate.[39]

Canadian scientists, largely at McGill University, have also made significant advances in the laboratory study of ice dynamics,[40] but the spillover of this research to areas such as vessel design has been negligible because neither the federal government nor any other Canadian research institution has developed sophisticated Arctic-ice-simulation facilities in this country.[41] The design of ice-transiting vessels depends to an inordinate degree in Canada on access to ice-model basins because neither the government nor the shipbuilding industry has access as yet to data from comparable full-scale vessels currently operating in the high Arctic. At present ice-simulation facilities are available in the United States, the Soviet Union, the United Kingdom, West Germany, and Finland.[42]

Not only is access to ice and meteorological data of high quality likely to become a problem because of U.S. domination of remote-sensing techniques and the projected dependency on nuclear submarines to study high-Arctic ice,[43] but the need for efficient data processing is rapidly outstripping the capacities of the federal government for forecasting, communications, and ice-atlas development. It would appear that the Atmospheric Environment Service is moving unnecessarily slowly to meet the processing problem through the development and application of advanced computer technology. Much could be learned from the Russians in this respect as they seem to have developed an extremely sophisticated data collection, forecasting, and communications system for their Arctic sea lanes.[44] A more flexible and less expensive satellite-communications system is required to feed ice and weather information to ships in the high Arctic, but the Communications Technology Satellite experimental program contains no projects directly focusing on the development of reliable ship-to-shore communications for use in Arctic waters.[45] However recent developments on the international scene and within the Ministry of Transport, the Department of National Defence, and the Department of Communications give cause for cautious optimism concerning improvements in this area. Agreement appears to be near on the establishment (with Canadian participation) of an international consortium to build and launch a global satellite for marine communications before 1980. The Ministry of Transport is also preparing to test the usefulness for Arctic ship-to-shore communications of an on-board satellite terminal and stabilized-antenna platform developed in the United States by the Scientific Atlanta Co. to be used with two geo-stationary American maritime satellites (MARISAT) to be launched in July 1975 (at the time of writing). MARISAT is basically a 'gap-filler' for the American navy, however, and may have limited coverage and usefulness in the high Arctic. The Ministry is presently planning to upgrade its ship-to-shore communications in the eastern Arctic through the installation of three special repeater-transmitter-receiver units hooked to ANIK. While these planned facilities will fill holes in the network of communications and navigation aids covering the approaches to Churchill and Arctic Bay, they do not answer the need for a Canadian capacity for direct satellite communications of ice and navigation data to ships operating throughout the high Arctic. The Department of National Defence has some plans for a satellite system to be used for Arctic search-and-rescue. The Department of Communications also has an ultra-high-frequency communications system—involving three satellites and portable and ship-board terminals—in the project-design stage. What is uncertain is how these proposals will fare when they reach Treasury Board.

The federal government's support for gathering hydrographic and bathymetric data in the high Arctic has been equally ambivalent. The government has been involved since 1959 in a program to collect data of this nature for the entire polar continental shelf. However while large-scale survey work has been done on existing Arctic harbours and in areas where resource exploitation is imminent, there are few large-scale charts available for the Northwest Passage and the Beaufort Sea.[46] Except for some soundings done from helicopters, hovercraft, and coastal-survey vessels, the bathymetric and hydrographic work done each season in the high Arctic by the Department of the Environment depends, ironically enough, on the routes travelled by the Ministry of Transport's Coast Guard icebreakers. Because of the limited capabilities of the existing fleet and its heavy involvement during the summer shipping season in Arctic resupply missions, the Canadian Hydrographic Service of the Department of the Environment can do little more than scratch the surface of the survey problem. It is estimated that considerably less than 10 per cent of the polar continental shelf has been adequately charted since the program began in 1959.[47] Moreover almost nothing has been done to develop new techniques or equipment to increase the productivity of the limited resources devoted to this work, despite the fact that hydrographic experts within the Department of the Environment feel that the National Research Council could make useful technological advances in this area with a modicum of effort.[48]

Rounding off the spectrum of scientific knowledge and technological innovation required to develop sophisticated marine-transportation systems for the Canadian high Arctic are three interrelated areas in which the federal government's involvement should be substantial but is, in fact, extremely limited. First, why is the federal government doing so little about the study of marine pollution under Arctic conditions? A complete understanding of the complex and highly destructive relationship between oil, ice, and water is necessary for the development of technology to prevent and control pollution under the Arctic Waters Pollution Prevention Act and to clean up the inevitable spills. However the federal government has supported little useful work in this field and will undoubtedly be faced with major decisions concerning the exploitation and transportation of oil and gas from areas such as the Beaufort Sea before suitable empirical data on pollution hazards and control-and-recovery techniques are available.[49] A similar complaint can be made about the federal government's support for the research and development effort required to design terminals and harbours in the Arctic. The government has taken some useful initiatives, including a comprehensive study of the prospects for creating an oil port for supertankers up to 325,000 dwt on Herschel Island in the Beaufort Sea,[50] and involvement in the development of the dock at Strathcona Sound for the Nanisivik mine project. However there are more difficult questions that the government has largely ignored, including the problem of ice scouring of underwater pipelines required to connect to offshore terminals and to carry oil and natural gas south from the Arctic islands to possible tanker terminals. Some work on the scouring phenomena is being done at Memorial University. Another issue is the technology required to construct submarine terminals under the ice; as part of its research and conceptual design on submarine tankers, the U.S. Maritime Administration is funding some work in this area,[51] but the Canadian government has not encouraged the development of Canadian expertise in the creation of under-surface loading and unloading systems. Finally there is the issue of the development in Canada of submersible vehicles and diving skills for the Arctic where they may well become crucial components of ice-study programs (including scouring), pollution detection and control techniques, ship repair, underwater search and rescue, and research on terminals for vessels. This is an area where Canadian industry, educational institutions, and private organizations are making unique progress in the design, construction, and operation of small manned submarines, underwater habitats, and deep-diving equipment.[52] Except for the Defence and Civil Institute of Environmental Medicine (part of the Defence Research Board) no federal government agency is actively involved in Arctic underwater technology and skill development, and it remains an aspect of the Arctic marine-support system to which the federal government has given little consideration beyond the occasional provision of logistics and transportation facilities.[53]

FEDERAL GOVERNMENT EFFORTS: TOO MANY
UNCO-ORDINATED FINGERS IN A SMALL PIE

The preceding sections should make it reasonably clear that the public and private sectors in Canada have not devoted sufficient resources to the accumulation of knowledge and the development and application of new technologies to service national goals in the Canadian Arctic. In addition, little or no concerted effort has been directed by the federal government to the question of the relevance of such national goals as Arctic sovereignty to the program of Arctic marine science to be pursued and the choices to be made between the various hardware and techniques presently being developed. These difficulties are part of the federal government's inability to make much progress in the development of a national science policy (or policies) and to develop an organization for supporting and assessing scientific and technological development in Canada.[54] Despite the highly advertised efforts of the Trudeau government since 1968 to put together a national science policy and a bureaucratic structure to administer it, the result in most cases has been a story of increased bureaucratic infighting, poor communications within the bureaucratic structures and between the bureaucracy and industry, and an inability to be specific about the priorities for research and development and the government's intended role in assessing and supporting them.[55]

The whole area of Arctic marine-transportation research and development is illustrative of these many pitfalls. It is certainly not the case that the federal government has done nothing in this field. Several departments and agencies have spent millions of dollars on specific programs and projects and have built up large planning and research staffs. The most active agencies have been the Ministry of Transport, the Department of the Environment, the Department of Energy, Mines and Resources, the Department of Communications, the Department of Indian and Northern Affairs, and the Defence Research Board of the Department of National Defence. There has also been some involvement by the Department of Public Works, the Department of Industry, Trade and Commerce, and the National Research Council of Canada.[56] A cursory glance at the organization of Arctic marine-transportation research and development activities within the Ministry of Transport should give the reader a microcosmic sense of the bureaucratic fragmentation of effort in this area. The Transport portfolio contains at least four agencies that are involved in developing either policies or programs for Arctic research or technology. The Marine Administration, including the Coast Guard, has the responsibility for developing programs for all marine activities in the Arctic as well as overall marine policy and planning. The Transportation Development Agency has as its major role the identification, stimulation, and support of major scientific and technological improvements in the transportation system in Canada, and thus plays a major part in the management and funding of Arctic transportation research and development projects. The central Policy, Planning and Major Projects Branch (as well as a further unit under a new Senior Assistant Deputy Minister) has the responsibility for recommending long-range goals and priorities for the entire Ministry, and therefore has a significant impact on the importance attached to marine transportation in the Arctic. In addition the Arctic Transportation Agency is responsible for developing and recommending Arctic transportation policies and for co-ordinating the program activities of the various administrations (including the Marine Administration), despite the fact that the Agency has no budgetary responsibility for the Arctic programs of these administrations.[57] The reorganization in 1970 of the Transport portfolio was designed – at least in part – to integrate all Arctic transportation planning and programming under the Agency's control, but its lack of responsibility, its isolation from the technological planning function, and its general lack of bureaucratic 'clout' have all contributed to reducing the effectiveness of the Agency's efforts. This kind of problem is not confined to the Ministry of Transport.

If the situation within a ministry appears to be unsatisfactory, the integration of Arctic research and development programs across all government departments is far worse. Before 1971 the co-ordination of Arctic science and technology (including transportation technology) was shared by the Science Council, two sub-committees of the Advisory Committee on Northern Development – the Sub-Committee on Science and Technology, and the Sub-Committee on Transportation – and, to a lesser extent, the Transport Committee of the interdepartmental Task Force on Northern Oil Development.[58] In addition the Canadian Committee on Oceanography, an association of senior officials from leading government departments and four Canadian universities involved in oceanography, has played an active role in co-ordinating a wide variety of marine-research activities. However through its Sub-Committee on Arctic Oceanography (previously known as the Working Group on Ice in Navigable Waters), the Committee has largely limited its interest in Arctic marine transportation to the narrow problems related to scientific ice studies.[59] Despite the existence of these co-ordinating structures, very little was accomplished in terms of the overall integration of *Arctic* marine science and technology, and projects and programs were begun and continued by various federal agencies without any reference to specific national goals. As a report in 1973 of the Advisory Committee comments:

In 1970 the Advisory Committee on Northern Development . . ., through its Sub-Committee on Science and Technology, carried out a review of federally sponsored and supported activities in the Canadian

Arctic and sub-Arctic. A major conclusion of the review was the need for guidelines and priorities for scientific activities that extend beyond departmental objectives, and were related to the national objectives and plans for northern Canada which were being developed at that time.[60]

Cabinet expected that the formation of the Ministry of State for Science and Technology in 1971 would go a long way towards solving this problem of integrating programs and national goals for all scientific and technological activity supported by the federal government. To date this Ministry has not been successful in developing a national 'science policy', and has been an almost unrelieved failure in developing goals and priorities for Arctic marine science and technology and integrating the programs of the various federal agencies (and the research and development efforts of the wider community).[61] It seems clear that the same kinds of problems that have plagued agencies (such as the Arctic Transportation Agency) at the departmental level have also hindered the Ministry, particularly in its efforts 'to contribute to the formulation of policies through the coordination of the programs of departments and agencies in areas where some rationalization or concerted action is required.'[62] An acid test of this failure is the fact that both sub-committees of the Advisory Committee on Northern Development (Science and Technology, and Transportation) continue to play an active—if largely unproductive—role some four years after the Ministry was established and, by all accounts, the Ministry does not play an overwhelming part in the deliberations of the sub-committees.[63] The plodding nature of the Advisory Committee's goal-setting and co-ordination and the marginal impact of the Ministry are confirmed by the fact that more than two years after a major Advisory Committee seminar on guidelines for scientific activities in northern Canada, the Sub-Committee on Science and Technology had not yet prepared a set of draft guidelines and the Ministry had taken no visible initiative in this area. The Ministry's lack of effectiveness means that other federal agencies—particularly the Department of Indian and Northern Affairs through which the Advisory Committee on Northern Development structure reports—continue their attempts to enlarge their 'piece of the action', thereby ensuring that widely supported objectives and policy proposals will be a very long time reaching the Cabinet Committee on Science and Technology for government approval. The slow pace in the particular area of Arctic marine transportation is further illustrated by the fact that a special Steering Committee on Marine Transportation, established by the Sub-Committee on Transportation in November 1973 and chaired by a representative of the Ministry of Transport's Arctic Transportation Agency, had met only once by January 1975 and had gone no further than establishing general terms of reference.[64]

It will thus come as no surprise to learn that the Ministry has done little to contribute to the mobilization and rationalization of research and development in Canadian industries and universities. Aucoin and French's indictment of the Ministry's efforts in relation to the entire scientific and technological community applies with equal force to the particular subject of Arctic marine transportation.

> ... [W]hile a significant number of contacts have been made by the Ministry, their *ad hoc* nature has meant that government-community relations have only been altered to the extent that community representatives must now interact with yet another government agency. For a community which has been, in large part, unsophisticated in its treatment of policy issues, this has simply added to its frustrations.[65]

While Ministry officials (and consulting firms employed by the Ministry) have examined and catalogued many of the initiatives in Arctic marine science and technology that have been taken by industry and the universities, little has been done to communicate government objectives to the companies and research units or to solicit views on what useful role the federal government can play in organizing and funding research and development on a national scale. Two results of this neglect are noteworthy. First, there is little communication between the various entities involved in Arctic marine-related research and development across the country. Second, Canada has few non-government research and teaching institutions able to concentrate suitable resources on Arctic marine problems.[66] The most notable institution of this kind, The Arctic Institute of North America, has received in recent years almost half its funds from the United States government, and less than a third from the Canadian government despite the fact that, as the Institute's 1973 Annual Report points out, 'the North understandably is of much greater significance for Canada than for the United States.'[67]

There are several ways in which this problem of stimulating and co-ordinating Arctic marine science and technology both within the federal government and throughout the wider community might be overcome.[68] One typically Canadian solution, proposed during the 1972 Mont Gabriel seminar on guidelines for scientific activities, was that the federal government immediately establish 'an independent but expert overall study, possibly even at the level of a Royal Commission, of Arctic transportation in all its phases'.[69] While such a study might provide policy direction and program assessment, it would entail unnecessary delay and would not provide long-term integration of programs. Other suggestions include the establishment by the Ministry of a specialized interdepartmental committee focusing on the development of a comprehensive program for achieving Canadian excellence in operations on and below ice-infested waters.[70] This committee, in the style of existing Advisory

Committee on Northern Development sub-committees, would discuss and co-ordinate all relevant departmental programs, especially those in the area of research and development. To improve communications the committee could release reports at various intervals to Canadian industry and universities and a permanent committee secretariat could provide the wider community with a focal point for relations with the federal government on Arctic marine research and development questions. The likely success of such a committee as the *primary* agent of departmental integration, however, is extremely doubtful because it would run the risk of falling into the same paralysis as the sub-committees of the Advisory Committee. Moreover, unlike the Advisory Committee, the committee would be operating under the aegis of a Ministry that at present lacks significant statutory and cabinet authority.

An alternative 'new agency' solution comes from a school of thought that believes that urgent consideration should be given to the establishment of a single government department charged with providing all the federal maritime services from research and development to pollution control and search and rescue—but excluding maritime defence. Another approach is to create an Arctic transportation Co-ordination Agency, which would be charged with the integration and development of the entire northern transportation network. Such an agency might parallel the organization of the Northern Command in the Department of National Defence, taking on the co-ordination of transportation activities of other government departments and the provision of transportation services for non-government activities in the North. The latter agency would be a more powerful version of the present Ministry of Transport's Arctic Transportation Agency with responsibilities and authority extending beyond the boundaries of the Ministry of Transport. The most fundamental drawback to both these proposals is that they involve massive program shifts from existing departmental structures and significant legislative changes. This would mean delays in implementation and a lengthy period of 'disintegration' and disruption while the new structures took hold. Moreover solutions of this variety do not guarantee any improvements in the particular area of research and technological development.

Finally there are two more modest approaches that, while they do not assure improvements in research and development either, share the advantages of maintaining existing organizations and concentrating particularly on Arctic marine science and technology. The first would involve following the advice of Aucoin and French with respect to the Ministry of State for Science and Technology, and 'pruning the ministry's activities in order that its efforts could be more sharply focused on a few policy matters'.[71] Arctic marine science and technology could then be declared by Cabinet to be a specific area in need of policy and program development, 'thus legitimizing the interventionist role of the minister and the ministry of state in the context of the federal executive-bureaucratic system'.[72] In addition, the Sub-Committee on Science and Technology could be detached from the Advisory Committee on Northern Develop-ment and reconstituted as the interdepartmental Committee on Arctic Sci-ence and Technology under the guidance of the Ministry of State for Sci-ence and Technology, and its membership restricted to place initial em-phasis on marine issues.[73] Another complementary organizational innova-tion would be the creation of a Standing Advisory Body on Arctic Marine Science and Technology with representatives from government, industry, and universities, designed to improve communications on Arctic marine research and development between the government and the wider com-munity and to assist in establishing goals for all Arctic marine science and technology.[74]

The second (and final) approach is founded on the premise that most departments concerned with Arctic marine science and technology have lost confidence in the integrative and co-ordinative skills of the Ministry of State for Science and Technology and would not respond to the Ministry's leadership of a reconstituted interdepartmental committee. This problem might be circumvented by the adoption of the 'joint venture' approach modelled on the organization of the Polar Continental Shelf Project. The fostering of Arctic marine science and technology becomes the prime responsibility of a designated minister from an established line department. This minister is named the manager of the 'joint venture' and, with the assistance of three or four respected deputy ministers and a tough committee of assistant deputy ministers with budgetary powers, con-trols a common budget pool to which all the participating departments contribute. There is a growing consensus among critics of performance of the federal government in this area that a simple and 'brutal' approach of this nature is what is required to force the entire structure of the govern-ment to revamp its Arctic marine-transportation policies and programs quickly to assure Canada's Arctic sovereignty and optimal involvement in the economic development of the North.

SOME GUIDELINES FOR THE FEDERAL GOVERNMENT

If the federal government's long-run objectives include ensuring Canada's sovereignty in the Arctic through a policy of effective occupation, through the development in Canada of internationally recognized excellence in operations on and below ice-infested waters, and through strong Cana-dian involvement in and control of the economic development of the high Arctic, then what policies and programs should the government be pursu-ing in the area of marine science and technology? The following attempt to outline program areas of critical importance to Canada's future in the

Arctic obviously will suffer from a lack of timelessness as circumstances change, but it hopefully will serve as a useful talking point on an important issue.[75]

The most immediate need is a stepped-up level of support for and commitment to the polar class-7 icebreaker. Developments in the United States and the Soviet Union combined with the problem of the extremely long lead times required to procure vessels that are technologically innovative mean that the need for this commitment is urgent. A crash program for the polar class-7 vessel would result in a faster flow of technological data on large icebreaker design and would visibly increase the government's capacity to provide icebreaker services in the high Arctic over a longer operating season. The icebreaker-building program should be complemented by a program of support for the design and development of a nuclear-propulsion system capable of providing the enormous shaft-horsepower requirements of heavy polar-class vessels.[76]

To ensure that the development of icebreakers is closely related to a viable Canadian capacity to engage in commercial traffic in the high Arctic, the government should continue to give high priority to the construction of an icebreaking bulk-cargo vessel of 28,000 dwt designed by Federal Commerce and Navigation Co. If this vessel were completed quickly, it would enable the government, the shipping industry, and the ore smelting industries in Canada to participate directly in the shipment of metals from Baffin Island, and it would serve as a prototype for further commercial vessels. The government should also begin to support design work on a much larger (at least 150,000 dwt) icebreaking oil tanker, and, at the same time, give some attention to the research issues associated with the development of semi-submersible and submarine oil-carrying vessels.

The government should begin or increase expenditures for technological development of several aspects of marine-supporting systems. The Ministry of Transport and the Department of Communications should be allowed to co-operate beyond the discussion and preliminary design stage in the construction of a low-cost ultra-high-frequency communication satellite that would satisfy the urgent need for a flexible communications and telemetry system in the North, and would provide the capacity to transmit weather and ice information directly to vessels in the high Arctic.[77] In addition to ice and weather information, the Arctic mariner requires practical navigation aids. A program of support is required to provide from existing technology a package of equipment (which may include improved guidance/control systems, collision-avoidance radar, image-intensified television, infra-red scanners, data buoys, and seabed course-tracking systems) that will allow the mariner to feel as secure navigating through darkness, white-outs, 'growlers' and 'bergy bits' as he would in more open southern waters. This package, and the installation of highly accurate navigation and positioning networks in critical parts of the high Arctic, should incidentally have a salutary effect on the potentially prohibitive level of marine insurance rates for extended commercial vessel operations in the North.[78]

Another major area of concern is the design of terminals and harbours for icebreaking cargo vessels and the submarine tankers of the future. A joint government-industry program in this area would have to be based on studies of the effect of large ice masses on prototype storage and terminal structures (including submarine terminals in depths up to 300 feet) and a comprehensive analysis of the problem of ice-scouring of the underwater pipelines that would be required in the construction of off-shore oil or liquid-natural-gas terminals in the Beaufort Sea and western archipelago. In the eastern archipelago and Baffin Bay, where deep-water harbours can be built, systems would have to be developed to keep ice from piling up and rendering the harbours impassable.

All the above will require a knowledge of sophisticated man-underwater technology. While this technology is quite advanced in Canada, there is a role for the federal government in assessing and integrating the various interdisciplinary activities. The government can also play a substantial role in funding the development of more complex manned and unmanned submersible vehicles and diving systems designed to investigate the impact of ice on underwater structures and to take part in underwater search and rescue operations.

On what I have loosely termed the 'science' side of Arctic marine transportation research and development, there is an equally important role for the federal government in collecting fundamental knowledge concerning the Arctic marine environment and assisting in establishing institutions to carry on basic research and train people for future work in the high Arctic. In support of its efforts to make navigation safe, the federal government must increase the scope of the Department of the Environment's hydrographic and bathymetric charting program. For the most part this would involve freeing Ministry of Transport icebreakers to spend a longer survey season on the main Arctic shipping routes; however, owing to the shortage of suitable icebreakers, more emphasis will have to be placed on developing microwave remote-sensing systems for conducting at least preliminary surveys of the major routes.[79] More substantial federal funding is also needed for an immediate program of ice studies, principally in the Parry Channel and selected routes to it from the Queen Elizabeth Islands and Amundsen Gulf.[80] While a good deal of this necessary ice data could be collected through surface observations, airborne radar, and satellite remote-sensing equipment, some experts argue that only submarines could provide the necessary under-ice profiles required for commercial shipping. Unfortunately Canada has no assured long-run access to data either from submarines or satellites and the federal government is consequently faced with substantial costs in order to develop the mechanisms for obtaining a satisfactory knowledge of the ice-mantle in the high Arctic—the Department of National Defence would have to acquire nuclear submarines for surveillance, and the Department of Communications' satellite program would have to change its objectives.[81] Whatever approach to ice studies is adopted (and the decision has to be made quickly), it must be complemented by the funding of a sophisticated ice-test facility capable of simulating difficult ice conditions including ridges, keels, and pressure fields. This test tank should probably be designed and built by 1978 by the Marine Dynamics and Ship Laboratory of the National Research Council, and it must have the capacity to test fixed installations (such as marine terminals) as well as vessel designs.

Another major component of the marine-support system in the high Arctic is ecosystem research and pollution control. This is an area directly related to the regulations laid down under the Arctic Waters Pollution Prevention Act, and Canada's capacity to control marine pollution is a direct measure of its ability to occupy the high Arctic effectively. To come to grips with this problem the Department of the Environment and the Ministry of Transport must be given the capacity to co-operate in a massive five-year program of research and technological development in the following areas:

(1) basic research on the way Arctic ocean systems function and the effect of pollutants on the biology and the behaviour of organisms in the oceans;

(2) a detailed analysis of the relationship between oil and ice under extreme temperature conditions;

(3) the integration and development (where necessary) of equipment and techniques for detecting and containing oil under permanent ice cover and in ice-infested marine waters. This would entail the development of a joint industry/government contingency plan for controlling pollution designed to operate year-round throughout the high Arctic.[82]

Finally the federal government must support polar education and research, without which government, industry, and the educational institutions will be incapable of carrying out the long-run research and development tasks involved in maintaining Canada's sovereignty and economic interests in the waters and islands of the Arctic archipelago. The needs in this area are obvious. It is impossible to study naval architecture and marine engineering in Canada to a graduate-degree level; therefore the government should support the development of suitable faculties within existing universities, ensuring that a good deal of emphasis is placed on the problems associated with developing polar-class vessels. A similar effort should be made to support the development of research and teaching facilities in polar oceanographical studies, and to encourage the continued development of practical skills and research in the area of man-

TABLE 2
EXPENDITURE ESTIMATE
HIGH-ARCTIC MARINE TRANSPORTATION
SCIENCE AND TECHNOLOGY PROGRAMS
1975-80

Items	Status	Cost*
Ships		(in $ millions)
Class-7 icebreaker	design and build by 1980	125-200
Class-10 icebreaker/ alternatives	research, conceptual design and decision	2
Icebreaking OBO (50,000 dwt)	design and build by 1980	35-50
Icebreaking OBO (150-200,000 dwt)	design	5-10
Semi-submersible and submersible cargo vessels	research and design	2-5
Nuclear-propulsion system	research and design	5-10
Marine Support Technology		
Communications-satellite system	design, build, and launch by 1980	70
Navigation & positioning networks	integrate and build by 1980	10-15
Arctic harbours/terminals	research and design	2-3
Submersibles and man-underwater systems	rationalization and funding	2-4
Marine Science and Education		
Hydrography and bathymetry		n.a.
Ice studies		n.a.
Pollution studies/control		10-12
Research and education structures		10-15

*These low/high figures are very rough estimates based on available data. The five-year program would probably not entail expenditures in excess of $500 million, an average annual expenditure of $100 million to achieve the objectives outlined in this paper.

underwater systems. In line with the demands of the Arctic Waters Pollution Prevention Act and the likely expansion of Arctic shipping, the federal government must expand its traditional role in the area of marine education to include facilities particularly for the training of ice navigators. The final recommendation flows from the fact of Canada's lamentably low level of participation in field research in the high Arctic (e.g. the annual Arctic Ice Dynamics Joint Expedition). The federal government must take steps to ensure that both the funds and the support facilities are made available to a wide variety of Canadian researchers to take part in annual or year-round research efforts in the Arctic.

All the above programs would do little over the next five years if they were not founded on a clear federal-government policy favouring the participation of Canadian firms in the development of Arctic shipping and marine-support systems.[83] A policy of this nature, combined with more substantial subsidies to shipbuilders, would do much to ensure a positive response by industry and the universities to invest in equipment and research development. The Cabinet must also be prepared to turn aside the virulent criticisms that the above programs would raise within the federal bureaucracy, particularly within the Treasury Board Secretariat and the Department of Finance. Both these central agencies, subscribing to the mechanics but not the spirit of cost-benefit analysis, will undoubtedly remain true to form and insist that unless *immediate* economic gains can be realized, expenditures of the above proportions on science and technology for the Arctic are unwarranted. One Department of Finance official, in a recent discussion, asked me what would be wrong with a situation where U.S. and German icebreaking cargo vessels were the exclusive users of high Arctic waterways. Clearly programs designed to ensure Canada's long-run leadership in marine science and technology in the Arctic would be expensive. Perhaps they might even necessitate cutbacks in other federal government programs. Nevertheless they are essential if Canada is to continue to exercise sovereignty over the high Arctic and to ensure its strong participation in the long-run economic development of the area. Where issues of this nature are at stake, the Cabinet cannot allow itself to be held hostage by the arguments of Treasury Board and the Department of Finance for short-run 'economic efficiency'.

NOTES

[1] House of Commons *Debates*, 24 October 1969, pp. 39-40.

[2] Modern technology is more than new or proposed hardware. As Jacques Ellul has pointed out, the phenomenon of modern technology is in effect, 'the totality of methods rationally arrived at and having absolute efficiency (for a given stage of development) in every field of

human activity'. See J. Ellul, *The Technological Society* (New York, 1964), p. xxv. The distinction between science (the search for empirical knowledge) and technology (specific techniques or machinery) is classically considered to be an important one in that the latter is said to be developed within a particular setting (e.g. a society or nation) only on the basis of institutional stimulation and encouragement of the former. While this distinction is useful, it should be noted that the line between science and technology is a blurred one, and as often as not science progresses on the basis of technological change rather than *vice versa* (i.e. advances in the study of the characteristics of the Arctic-ice mantle depend on improvements in remote-sensing technology). Obviously, due to their interaction, you cannot have one without the other.

[3]The federal government's preoccupation with the relationship between transportation research and development and short-run economic development in the high Arctic is adequately illustrated in Science Council of Canada, *Canada, Science and the Oceans*, Report no. 10 (Ottawa, 1970); R. W. Stewart and L. M. Dickie, *Ad Mare: Canada Looks to the Sea. A Study on Marine Science and Technology*, Science Council of Canada, Special Study no. 16 (Ottawa, 1971); Canada, Advisory Committee on Northern Development (ACND), *Science and the North: A Seminar on Guidelines for Scientific Activities in Northern Canada* (Ottawa, 1973); and ACND, *1972 Government Activities in the North* (Ottawa, 1972). The general impression that federal-government agencies are largely interested in Arctic scientific and technological research only where the results will lead quickly to resource exploitation is borne out by interviews with officials associated with various sub-committees of the government's Advisory Committee on Northern Development. This preoccupation, in view of the multinational character of Canada's resource-exploitation industry, has contributed to the acceptance of an international research and development effort in the Canadian high Arctic.

[4]Toronto *Globe and Mail*, 23 May 1974.

[5]See E. J. Dosman, 'The Northern Sovereignty Crisis, 1968-70', pp. 34-57.

[6]'New oceans policy aims at stimulating offshore industry', Toronto *Globe and Mail*, 13 July 1973; see also Capital Communications Ltd, *Ottawa R & D Report*, 8 (1974), 4. An increase in the Canadian capacity to provide technologically advanced transportation services in ice-infested or ice-covered waters was seen to be a particularly important part of this new thrust.

[7]See T. D. Heaver, 'National Objectives and Transportation Planning', *Transportation Research Forum Proceedings*, 14 (1973), 149-59; J. W. Langford, 'Technological Innovation and Canadian Transportation', *Transport Canada (September-October 1974)*, 6-10.

[8]See H. E. Fallon, 'The New Coast Guard Icebreaker Class: Its Design and Its Future', in B. F. Slocum, ed., *Arctic Logistics Support Technology* (Washington, The Arctic Institute of North America, 1972), pp. 42-50; and 'Gas Turbines to Provide Maximum Power for New U.S. Coast Guard Icebreakers', *The Motor Ship* (January 1974), 497-8.

[9]See R. Rohmer, *The Arctic Imperative* (Toronto, 1973), chapter 15.

[10]*Transportation Development News* (December 1973), 19-20; and (January-February 1975), 36.

[11]The class number approximates the ice depth (in feet) that the vessel is capable of penetrating. This classification system is part of the regulations proclaimed under the Arctic Waters Pollution Prevention Act, Sections 11 and 12.

[12]It is estimated that the total cost of the icebreaker now being designed would be considerably in excess of $100 million. See 'Government plans enlarged order for ships', Toronto *Globe and Mail*, 20 June 1974.

[13]See 'Liberals wants icebreakers to carry cargo', Toronto *Globe and Mail*, 20 June 1974.

[14]See, for instance, Captain T. C. Pullen, 'Surface Marine Shipping', *Proceedings, Fifth National Northern Development Conference*, 4-6 November 1970, p. 116; and 'Larger ice-breakers are "key to Arctic"', Montreal *Star*, 30 March 1974.

[15]Arctic Resources by Sea—Executive Summary', prepared for the Ministry of Transport by Northern Associates (Holdings) Ltd, November 1973, p. 11.

[16]*Ibid.*

[17]The preceding argument owes much to advice from Captain Pullen and Mr Tom Peirce. See also 'Innovative drill rig's ice-cutting mechanism may be adaptable for ships', Toronto *Globe and Mail*, 8 November 1974.

[18]See E. J. Dosman, 'The Northern Sovereignty Crisis, 1968-70', pp. 34-57.

[19]See 'The Great Arctic Ice Gamble', *Surveyor* (August 1969), and Pullen, 'Surface Marine Shipping', *op. cit.*, pp. 114-15.

[20]G. H. Levine, R. P. Voelker, and P. B. Mentz, 'Advances in the Development of Commercial Ice-Transiting Ships', advance copy of paper to be presented to the Annual Meeting of the Society of Naval Architects and Marine Engineers, New York, 14-16 November 1974, p. 1. Lest there be any doubt concerning the definition of 'Arctic', the authors of this paper refer specifically on the same page to the Arctic Ocean, Baffin Bay, and the Beaufort, Bering, and Barents Seas as the focus for a 'new frontier' in marine transportation. The insensitivity of this paper to the existence of a boundary line between the United States and Canada is quite remarkable, particularly since one of the authors is an employee of the U.S. Maritime Administration.

[21]*Ibid.*, pp. 2-4.

[22]*Ibid.*, p. 4.

[23]P. B. Mentz, 'The Maritime Administration's Commercial Ice Transiting Marine Transportation Systems Program', Society of Naval Architects and Marine Engineers, Great Lakes and Great Rivers Section, 25 January 1973.

[24]See *Traffic World* (15 July 1974); O. C. S. Robertson, 'Transport by Submarine in Arctic Waters', *North*, 13 (1966), 5; and J. L. Helm, 'Freighter Submarine Tankers', *Proceedings, Fifth National Northern Development Conference*, 4-6 November 1970, pp. 118-28. Canadian Arctic Gas Pipeline Ltd examined transportation by submarine in its recent study and estimated that 45 oil-carrying submarines of the dimensions described by General Dynamics would be required to compete with a pipeline. See Canadian Arctic Gas Pipeline Ltd, 'Alternative Corridors and Systems of Transportation', Section 14e, Part 2.9, 1974, p. 63; cf. U.S. Department of the Interior, *Final Environmental Impact Statement, Proposed Trans-Alaska Pipeline*, vol. 5: *Alternatives to the Proposed Action* (Washington, 1972), p. 78.

[25]Metalgesellschaft A. G. of Germany and Billiton B. V. of Holland have a 22.5 per cent equity interest in Nanisivik Mines Ltd on Baffin Island. The entire output of this lead-zinc mine is to be exported for the foreseeable future as there is apparently neither market nor smelter capacity for these metals in Canada. See Department of Indian and Northern Affairs, 'Nanisivik: Canada's First Arctic Mine', *Communique* (18 June 1974).

[26]See 'Bremen shipyard believes it can open Northwest Passage', *Financial Post*, 28 September 1974.

[27]*Shipping World and Shipbuilder* (April 1974). The Finnish Wartsila shipyard has also done design work on submarine tankers; see B. M. Johansson, 'Oy Wartsila Ab, Polar Shipbuilders', *Polar Record*, 16 (1972), 29.

[28]M. G. Hagglund, 'Northern Transportation—The Developing Federal Role', in *Transportation Research Forum Proceedings*, 14 (1973), 101.

[29]See, for instance, 'Exploratory talks', Halifax *Chronicle-Herald*, 19 March 1974.

[30]It may be that art must be joined with science and technology in Arctic navigation, for the successful ice pilot is one who in guiding a ship in Arctic waters employs intuitive powers beyond mere knowledge of the environment and the available technology. See O. C. S. Robertson, 'Sea Transportation in the Arctic: A Response', in B. F. Sater, *Arctic and Middle North Transportation* (Montreal, 1969), pp. 133-5.

[31]W. F. Cass, 'Sea Transportation in the Arctic', in Sater, *op. cit.*, p. 130.

[32]Toronto *Globe and Mail*, 13 July 1973.

[33]See G. H. Legg, 'Ice and Transport in Arctic Canada', Slocum, *op. cit.*, pp. 160-72.

[34]See ACND, *1972 Government Activities in the North*, pp. 43-9.

[35]'"Quick look" system could make Arctic shipping safer, less costly', Toronto *Globe and Mail*, 13 February 1974; 'All-weather satellite could aid Arctic shipping, study says', Toronto *Globe and Mail*, 6 January 1975.

[36]See, for example, the section on the Department in ACND, *1972 Government and Activities in the North*, p. 26.

[37]*Ibid.*, pp. 43-9. At a less comprehensive level, the German firm A. G. Weser, in addition to its involvement in ice-breaking cargo-vessel design, is co-operating with Brock University, Steltner Development and Manufacturing Inc. (St Catharines), and the Arctic Institute of North America in ice and vessel-routing studies in the eastern Arctic. See *Financial Post*, 28 September 1974.

[38]J. Tuzo Wilson, 'International Research: Discussion Paper', in ACND, *Science and the North*, p. 250.

[39]*Ibid.*

[40]See, for instance, Ice Research Project, McGill University, *Annual Report 1972*.

[41]ARCTEC Inc., an American firm operating in Canada, and the Ocean Engineering Centre at the University of British Columbia should shortly be providing limited ice-simulation facilities in Canada. See 'Arctic without the ice', Montreal *Star*, 28 March 1974.

[42]Levine, Voelker, and Mentz, *op. cit.*, pp. 5-6.

[43]The need for nuclear submarines is outlined in 'Arctic Resources By Sea', p. 15.

[44]See Peter Ward, 'Costly Cutbacks in Arctic', Toronto *Globe and Mail*, 2 December 1974.

[45]See Canada, Department of Communications, *News Release*, 6 November 1974.

[46]F. K. Hare, 'National Environment—Discussion Paper', in ACND, *Science and the North*, p. 82; cf. 'Arctic Resources by Sea', Part II, Section B, pp. 1-7.

[47]Personal interview, September 1974; see also F. K. Hare, 'National Environment; Discussion Paper', in ACND, *Science and the North*, p. 82.

[48]Personal communication, 1974. The technological advances that have been made are in the areas of special equipment for sounding through ice and for collecting oceanographic information over the ice break-up period. See ACND, *1972 Government Activities in the North*, p. 69.

[49]For an example of the short shrift being given to 'oil and ice' studies note the priority attached to them in relation to drilling schedules in the continuing exploration of the Beaufort Sea. See Canada, Department of Indian and Northern Affairs, *Dialogue North: Offshore Edition*, no. 3, 1974, p. 10; the whole problem of the pollution of the Arctic marine environment by various kinds of oil is given only an occasional reference in the 1973 ACND volume on guidelines for future scientific activity in the North, ACND, *Science and the North*.

[50]Canada, Department of Public Works, 'Herschel Island, Feasibility of a Marine Terminal', 1971.

51Canada, Transportation Development Agency, *Transport Development News* (August-September 1974), 25.

52Firms such as Can-Dive Ltd and International Hydrodynamics Co. Ltd, and research and education institutions including Memorial University, Seneca College, and the MacInnis Foundation have been most involved.

53Unfortunately, despite the 'oceans policy' statement, the federal government is not even making a particular effort to keep the control of this technology in Canadian hands. International Hydrodynamics Co. Ltd was recently purchased by P & O Interships (U.K.).

54A more detailed account of the attempt to develop a science policy for Canada can be found in G. B. Doern, *Science and Politics in Canada* (Montreal, 1972); and The Senate of Canada, *A Science Policy for Canada*, vols 1-3 (Ottawa, 1970, 1972, and 1973).

55See P. Aucoin and R. French, 'The Ministry of State for Science and Technology', *Canadian Public Administration*, 17 (Fall 1974), 461-81.

56ACND, *1972 Government Activities in the North.*

57For further information on the organization of the Ministry and its policy-making process see J. W. Langford, *The Reorganization of the Federal Transport Portfolio: The Application of a Ministry System* (Montreal, forthcoming 1975).

58*Reviews of National Science Policy, Canada* (Paris, 1969), contains further information on the organization of science-policy structures in the late 1960s. More detailed accounts of the operations of the Advisory Committee on Northern Development and the Task Force on Northern Oil Development are found in E. J. Dosman, *The National Interest: Ottawa and the North, 1968-74* (Toronto, 1975).

59See Stewart and Dickie, *op. cit.*, chapter 6; and Science Council of Canada, *Canada, Science and the Oceans, op. cit.*, pp. 22-5. The federal government also has on its organizational charts an Arctic Advisory Council, which was created to bring industry and government representatives together, but which never operated in this capacity and is now apparently dormant.

60ACND, *Science and the North*, p. 6.

61For a more detailed critique see Aucoin and French, *op. cit.*, pp. 466-76.

62*Ibid.*, p. 472.

63It is interesting to note that the Ministry of State for Science and Technology representative is not the chairman of either ACND sub-committee. The Sub-Committee on Science and Technology is chaired by the National Research Council representative and includes twenty-eight members from seventeen federal agencies and the two territorial governments. The Sub-Committee on Transportation is chaired by the Ministry of Transport representative and has thirty members from sixteen federal agencies and the North West Territories. The Transport Committee of the Task Force on Northern Oil Development concentrated a good deal of its attention on the transmission of North-Slope oil by pipeline and since 1972 does not appear to have played a significant integrative role in the Arctic Island and Beaufort Sea oil-transportation problems.

64One member of the Sub-Committee on Transportation estimated that since 1970 only 10 per cent of the Sub-Committee's meeting time had been devoted to high-Arctic marine transportation and related topics. Personal communication, December 1974.

65Aucoin and French, *op. cit.*, p. 474.

66For a 1971 survey of Canadian centres for marine science and technology see Stewart and Dickie, *op. cit.*, pp. 140-7.

67The Arctic Institute of Northern America, *Annual Report, 1973* (Montreal, 1974), p. 7.

68For comprehensive but somewhat dated recommendations concerning the restructuring of the entire marine science and technology policy-making network (including the formation of a Canadian Ocean Development Corporation) see Science Council of Canada, *Canada, Science and the Oceans*, pp. 22-5. This recommended structure does not focus on Arctic marine transportation; in fact in 1970 the Science Council was suggesting that the control of the ice-cover on the Gulf of St Lawrence and the management of the Strait of Georgia would be the most appropriate major projects for the new structure to tackle.

[69] ACND, *Science and the North*, p. 25.

[70] This suggestion (and the two others that follow) were made by working groups of experts brought together in February and March 1974 by MOSST to discuss various issues associated with Canada Research and Development Program in Arctic marine transportation. A similar recommendation is contained in 'The Need for Substantially Improved Canadian Sea and Arctic Surveillance, and the Determination of a Location for the Establishment of a New Joint Civilian/Defence, Combined Sea/Air Base in the High Arctic,' a brief prepared by the Naval Officers' Association of Canada, 27 May 1974, p. 33.

[71] Aucoin and French, *op. cit.*, p. 479.

[72] *Ibid.*

[73] The government may already be moving to create a new interdepartmental committee along these general lines, perhaps partly in response to pressures exerted by the Naval Officers' Association of Canada in their recent brief. See 'The Need for Substantially Improved Canadian Sea and Arctic Surveillance', p. 33.

[74] One commentator suggests that committees of this sort should be more independent of government and permanent in nature (along the lines of the Royal Society in Britain or the National Academy of Sciences in the United States) if they are to play a useful role in advising the government on objectives and priorities in research and development. See Wilson, 'International Research: Discussion Paper', ACND, *Science and the North*, pp. 254-6.

[75] The following discussion draws extensively on the unpublished preliminary recommendations of two seminars (Arctic Operator's Seminar and Arctic Waters Support Services Seminar) held in February and March 1974 by Philip A. Lapp Ltd for the Ministry of State for Science and Technology.

[76] 'Arctic Resources by Sea', p. 7. Further research will indicate whether or not the CANDU heavy-water design might be adapted for use as a nuclear-propulsion system for marine vessels. This system is potentially safer than those based on enriched uranium and may allow Canada to avoid the radiation-leakage problems experienced by the system used in the Soviet Union's icebreaker *Lenin*.

[77] In addition to the satellite system the government may have to place a system of low-cost microwave relay stations in the high Arctic.

[78] See 'Arctic Resources by Sea', p. 12. Utlimately the federal government will have to develop a traffic-control system comparable to present air-traffic control systems for all high Arctic shipping.

[79] 'Arctic Resources by Sea', p. 16. Surveying through the ice is generally not considered satisfactory for shipping since the use of this method prior to the *Manhattan* voyage failed to suggest the existence of 'pingoes' in the Northwest Passage.

[80] 'Arctic Resources by Sea', pp. 15-16.

[81] See Peter Ward, 'Costly cutback in the Arctic', Toronto *Globe and Mail*, 2 December 1974. A similar suggestion concerning the hire or purchase of nuclear submarines for the Department of National Defence is contained in a recent brief to the government. See 'The Need for Substantially Improved Canadian Sea and Arctic Surveillance', pp. 35-6.

[82] Canada, Science Council, *Scientific Activities in Fisheries and Wildlife Resources*, Special Study no. 15, June 1974, pp. 170-2.

[83]The Minister of Transport suggested a policy along these lines (which would presumably apply to Canadian flag vessels involved in foreign trade originating in the Arctic) during the 1974 election campaign but no definitive statement of policy has been made. See 'Liberals want icebreakers to carry cargo', Toronto *Globe and Mail*, 20 June 1974. The government has already declared a policy of reserving coastal shipping (including the Arctic) for Canadian flag vessels where suitable and sufficient ships are available; see Canada, Ministry of Transport, *News*, no. 57, 23 May 1974.

10 THE STAKES IN NORTHERN SOVEREIGNTY
by E. J. Dosman

The sovereignty crisis of 1968-70 confronted Ottawa with difficult choices. One option was to consider the Canadian Arctic archipelago as a single unit and draw straight baselines around the outermost edges to delimit a single strip of territorial sea surrounding the entire archipelago. Canadian Arctic waters in that case would have been enclosed as internal waters; other maritime zones such as contiguous zones and the high seas would have ceased to exist within them. One observer lamented that this approach was not followed at the time.

> It is submitted that, in the light of the Canadian administrative and other activities in the area, the absence of any concrete claim of opposition by any other state—*pace the situation that has now arisen*, sufficient time has endured for Canadian sovereignty over the entire Canadian Arctic as far as the Pole, and embracing land, islands, sea and packed ice to have become a fact in law. Had any question arisen, say, five years before the Manhattan effort, it is little doubt that the world at large would have recognized Canada's historic title to the whole area.[1]

Mr Dobell and Professor Dosman have traced the chief reasons why a decision was taken not to enclose Arctic waters at that time. First, Ottawa planners felt that no basis for extending so far-reaching a claim was foolproof: the various possibilities—historic waters; effective occupation; the sector theory; the archipelagic principle for the drawing of straight baselines around the island system—all could be challenged by other states as inapplicable or insufficiently founded. Second, and the more important, the U.S. was determined to prevent Canada enclosing the waters of the Canadian Arctic archipelago as internal waters.

The government of Pierre Elliott Trudeau expected U.S. retaliation should Canada declare sovereignty; it was worried, in fact, about the U.S. response to any Canadian initiative. As a compromise a functional approach—extending limited jurisdiction for specific, defensive, and non-acquisitive purposes but not making a claim to sovereignty—was adopted with the Arctic Waters Pollution Prevention Act of April 1970. Officially the government denied the existence of a U.S. challenge and further denied that the Canadian position in northern waters had been weakened. The effect of choosing a functional approach, however, was a significant disparity between government statements to the effect that Canadian northern waters were 'internal waters' and the facts of maritime jurisdiction in the high Arctic.

In view of this potentially dangerous situation, one objective of law-of-the-sea experts in the Department of External Affairs and related departments has been to close this gap by using all available international forums—such bodies as the International Maritime Consultative Organization, but particularly the third Law-of-the-Sea Conference. Indeed the Canadian delegation at the Law-of-the-Sea Conference has vigorously asserted extensive jurisdictional claims. As Professor Byers has pointed out in his essay, the North is only one area of the law of the sea that concerns the Canadian delegation, but it is apparent that the issue of northern sovereignty accounts in part for the delegation's acquisitive posture, somewhat out of touch with the Pearsonian tradition in Canadian foreign policies.[2] According to Mr Dobell, who gives the Canadian government high marks for safeguarding Canadian jurisdiction in northern waters, the elaboration of new international legal principles since 1970, as well as the increasing international legitimacy for coastal-state action in contiguous waters, has strengthened the Canadian position. As a result, if the third Law-of-the-Sea Conference should fail to produce an agreement, baseline legislation could more easily be employed to enclose Arctic waters. In such an eventuality, after five years of a concerted Canadian attempt to achieve multilateral agreement, Canadian unilateral action might be better understood internationally. Further, if Canada then claimed Arctic waters as historic waters its position would be stronger.

While Mr Dobell is optimistic that a gradualist approach is succeeding, other authors in the volume are less certain. Professor Griffiths in particular debated the relative merits of a gradualist as opposed to a more activist approach in which unilateral as well as multilateral approaches would be orchestrated to assure northern sovereignty. The activist-versus-gradualist controversy centres on different assumptions regarding the stakes in the North, the outlook for Canadian-American relations as they relate to the North, and Canadian capabilities for enforcing Canadian jurisdiction in the high Arctic.

THE STAKES IN NORTHERN SOVEREIGNTY

In the final resort the priority given to a foreign-policy issue depends on the stakes involved. The successful defence and international recognition of Canadian sovereignty over northern waters would yield three advantages for Canada.

(a) PUBLIC OPINION

Public and parliamentary reaction to the voyages of the S.S. *Manhattan* in 1969 and 1970 indicated beyond doubt that Canadians view the issue of northern sovereignty with considerable emotion. While legal opinion may disagree on the validity of a historic-waters approach to the Arctic, there is little doubt that the Canadian public overwhelmingly endorses it and perceives northern sovereignty as a legitimate Canadian territorial objective. Canadians probably believe that it has generally been achieved and recognized. The Trudeau government, by glossing over the U.S. challenge in the North 1968-70, must take a major responsibility for this dangerous misperception.

Quite apart from the resources or strategic value of the North, then, the issue of northern sovereignty is a potent political issue. No Canadian government can afford to retreat from that objective; for the same reason Ottawa is vulnerable to another challenge, given the current ambiguity of the law of the sea as it relates to the Arctic. According to Maxwell Cohen,

> Apart from the general question of Canada-United States economic and cultural relations and their meaning for the future of Canadian decision-making autonomy and identity, perhaps no other subject has so polarized the idea of the national interest or the continuing debate over Canada's Arctic claims and plans for its future.[3]

(b) PROTECTION OF A UNIQUE ENVIRONMENT

As well as wanting to control the resources of the Arctic by exerting sovereignty, enlightened opinion in Canada is concerned that the slow, cumbersome, and ambiguous development of the law of the sea cannot protect the Canadian Arctic. That increased navigation and economic development will occur is certain. As Professor Griffiths pointed out, unanticipated events such as a new Mideast war could dramatically increase traffic in the Northwest Passage—for example the United States would find it necessary to transport oil in tankers from the Alaskan North Slope. While the Arctic Waters Pollution Prevention Act 1970 was primarily intended to assert sovereignty, it also accurately recognized the urgent need for action to control the environment.

There are other factors besides pollution control that indicate the need for Canada's complete and unimpeded authority to enact laws and regulations for the Canadian Arctic archipelago. The elimination of two zones in the area, the territorial sea and the high seas (albeit affected by the jurisdiction claimed in the Arctic Waters Pollution Prevention Act 1970), would simplify liability procedures for ship disasters, as these currently have differing applications in the two zones, and would remove the remaining legal obstacles to an integrated national approach to economic development in the high Arctic. It would be clear which laws would apply in all areas of the Canadian Arctic archipelago. While of course foreign states might challenge a Canadian claim, a formal assertion of sovereignty would clear away doubts in Canadian circles about the sincerity of government statements. The high Arctic taken as a unit might then begin to receive the attention it deserves.

This is not to say that much could not be done within a framework of the functional approach; Canada has no interest in closing the area to foreign activity. The advantage of sovereignty as opposed to a more limited jurisdiction is that it facilitates the kind of holistic planning that will be essential to ensure that the native people, the environment, and Canada as a whole will benefit from the opening of the North. All the Arctic nations and the international community would benefit by enlightened Canadian leadership.

(c) SECURITY

The notion that the high Arctic is a strategic zone for great-power rivalry is well established. Both Professor Gellner and Professor Hockin underlined U.S. and U.S.S.R. security interests in northern waters, particularly in air and naval defence. Professor Gellner argued that the Arctic forms North America's defence barrier, or *glacis*, and that Canada must expect U.S. interest in the maintenance of appropriate defence establishments. Canada must also expect U.S. insistence on naval mobility through the Northwest Passage for both surface and submarine vessels.

The argument that Canada's defence interests are now distinct from Washington's definition of U.S. security has become compelling. As allies the two countries will continue to share defence objectives; but in two respects Canada would benefit from enclosing the Canadian Arctic archipelago as a security zone. First, the resources of the high Arctic, while as yet only partially established, will almost certainly be of increasing importance to Canada's future security and welfare. While sovereignty over the area alone does not ensure their careful development for Canadian markets, it would be one step towards a rational integration of Arctic resources into the Canadian economy.

As long as the ambiguity in the status of northern waters remains, the potential for bilateral trade-offs, as illustrated by Professor Dosman in his examination of the 1968-70 sovereignty crisis, is very considerable. Washington knows, after the 1968-70 crisis, how sensitive both Ottawa and Canadian public opinion are to a sudden pinching of the nerve of northern sovereignty. An optimistic assessment of this situation would be that the U.S. now knows Canada cannot be pushed around and so the U.S. will hesitate to revive its challenge; more probably, depending on the capabilities of Canada and the United States respectively in northern waters, northern sovereignty gives Washington considerable leverage over bilateral relations. While the apocalyptic scenario of Rohmer's *Ultimatum* is not to be taken seriously, it is simply good sense to take appropriate measures to safeguard strategic resources.

Second, the international situation has changed tremendously since 1945 and the cold-war period. Canadian-American differences have undermined the so-called special relationship between the two countries. Canada meanwhile has now grown into a major power. Given its interest in the Arctic, the U.S. will not hesitate to challenge Canada; Canada will have no excuse if it does not develop sufficient capabilities to meet that threat.

The three elements—public opinion, the protection and development of a unique region, and Canadian security—together form a cogent rationale for northern sovereignty. However the extent to which this claim can be maintained against the challenges depends on adequate enforcement capabilities.

THE QUESTION OF CAPABILITIES

If northern sovereignty is a core objective of Canadian policy, and if Ottawa has fought hard and well at the multilateral level, particularly at the third Law-of-the-Sea Conference, the scant concern for capabilities to retain control of the Arctic is alarming. The contributors to this volume are in agreement on this point, although some express more concern than others. Profesor Langford has painstakingly documented the obstacles to an effective research and development program in the Arctic. In particular he has demonstrated that Canadian leadership in this area, especially in icebreaker technology and ice research, is being challenged. Professor Gellner as well suggests that the problem in northern defence lies less in the legal field than in the area of enforcement. In the three main areas of northern-defence planning—surveillance, reconnaissance, and control—outlays and equipment do not match requirements, particularly in the event of unanticipated developments similar to the 1968-70 crisis.

Professor Byers echoes these concerns from the broader perspective of issues related to the law of the sea. Indeed in assessing the current third Law-of-the-Sea Conference it is apparent that the composition of the Canadian delegation suggests a greater preoccupation with west- and east-coast than with northern issues. The implications of this change of emphasis from the 1968-72 period, when northern concerns were predominant, could be significant. There are few votes in the high Arctic.

Only very recently in spring 1975 have serious interdepartmental discussions resumed on the requirements for implementing northern sovereignty. Plans for a northern defence base have again surfaced. At the same time the demonstrated ability of a Polish schooner to penetrate Arctic waters undetected for 300 miles in August 1975 cannot but generate concern regarding Canadian capabilities north of 60.[4]

THE PRIMACY OF CANADIAN-AMERICAN RELATIONS

The foremost consideration in the northern-sovereignty issue is Canadian-American relations. Given the overwhelming importance of bilateral relations for this country, as well as the American stake in the Arctic, Ottawa has attempted to restore communication with Washington on the topic after the sovereignty crisis of 1968-70 cast a shadow over the personal relationship between Prime Minister Trudeau and President Nixon.

The authors in this volume agree that bilateral relations are now much improved; differences, particularly with respect to the Northwest Passage, remain, but a close working relationship has been re-established. This is all to the good: neither country, depending on its Arctic capabilities, will benefit from a repetition of the 1968-70 crisis. Whether a compromise on transit of U.S. naval and commercial vessels through Arctic waters and the Northwest Passage satisfactory to both parties can be achieved remains to be seen.

There are differences, however, regarding the weighting of bilateral, multilateral, and unilateral approaches in ensuring and safeguarding northern sovereignty. Scholarly and legal opinion, whether on the legitimacy of claims based on historical rights and effective occupation, or on the right of Canada to territorialize the gateways of the Northwest Passage or enclose Arctic waters, must be tested in the crucible of state rivalry and enforcement. It is important not to fail.

CONCLUSION

Canadian control of the Arctic, while a legitimate foreign-policy objective in itself, is only significant ultimately within a broader developmental framework. History and geography have given Canada a responsibility to direct the course of economic activity in the Canadian Arctic archipelago and the Northwest Passage. Canada therefore has an opportunity to shirk or to fulfil the international and national obligations imposed by this huge task.

The first step is to ensure control, for sovereignty alone provides the necessary legal tools to institute an acceptable management system for the Arctic. The second and more difficult step is the elaboration of a development program that meets social and environmental as well as economic objectives. Finally an increasingly resource-hungry world will want access to Arctic resources: international factors will have to be weighed against short- and long-term national requirements.

The authors in this volume are in agreement that Canada has a strong claim to sovereignty in the North and that the drift of development in the law of the sea since 1970 has strengthened the Canadian position. But the apparent inability of Ottawa to match its jurisdictional claims with enforcement capabilities in the North is necessarily causing concern. It suggests that Canada is not fully committed to its stated objectives; it invites another U.S. challenge.

The lack of interdepartmental co-ordination adequate to enforce northern sovereignty suggests difficulties in the second area—that of economic and social planning north of 60. Unfortunately the evidence documents considerable weakness. If this volume has accurately traced a lack of attention to research and development in the North, the current pattern of resource activity similarly reveals the absence of clear objectives.

In theory *Canada's North 1970-80*, a document tabled in 1972 by the Minister of Urban Affairs and Northern Development, sets out national priorities in the Arctic: social and environmental objectives are to be weighted more heavily than the extraction of resources. In practice an *ad hoc* approach to economic development and social programs has continued. The opening of new projects in the high Arctic, such as the Nanisivik lead-zinc development at Strathcona Sound, Baffin Island, has not been related to the broader pattern of Arctic growth. It is now urgent that the future role of northern resources in the Canadian economy as a whole is analysed. It is equally urgent that suitable administrative machinery is devised to facilitate interdepartmental co-ordination.

Finally, the international dimension of resource development in the Arctic must be assessed on a continuing basis as economic activity increases. If the contention of this volume is correct—that such activity will increase the strategic significance of the North and the Northwest Passage—Canada cannot afford to lag in Arctic research or defence. Nor can this country presume to hoard indefinitely the mineral wealth of the North in the event of international shortages. The key issue is the balancing of priorities—national and international, social and economic.

The Arctic is Canada's last frontier, cold and distant from the large cities of the South to be sure, but of immense importance to the future of the country. There is too much at stake to permit loss by drift and neglect.

NOTES

[1] L. C. Green, 'Canada and Arctic Sovereignty', *Canadian Bar Review*, 48, 1970, 760.

[2] See A. E. Gotlieb and C. M. Dalfen, 'National Jurisdiction and International Responsibility: New Canadian Approaches to International Law', First Annual Conference of the Canadian Council on International Law, 13 October 1972, for a most interesting discussion of Prime Minister Trudeau's use of international law as a policy instrument.

[3] Maxwell Cohen, 'The Arctic and the National Interest', *International Journal*, 26, (1970-1).

[4] Toronto *Star*, 30 August 1975.

A NOTE ON THE CONTRIBUTORS

P.A. Brennan is a doctoral candidate in Canadian government and politics and international relations at York University. Mr. Brennan is working on several other articles on Canadian defence policy.

R. B. Byers is Associate Professor of Political Science and Associate Dean of Arts, York University. His articles on Canadian foreign and defence policy have appeared in a number of scholarly journals and books.

P. C. Dobell is the director of the Parliamentary Centre for Foreign Affairs and Foreign Trade, Ottawa. He is the author of *Canada's Search for New Roles*, the forthcoming 1971-73 volume of *Canada in World Affairs*, and several articles on international affairs.

E. J. Dosman teaches in the Political Science Department at York University and is author of *Indians: The Urban Dilemma*, and *The National Interest: The Politics of Northern Development, 1968-75.*

J. Gellner teaches as a visiting professor in the Political Science Department of York University. He is the editor of the *Canadian Defence Quarterly,* a frequent contributor to the Toronto *Globe and Mail,* and the author of *The Czechs and Slovaks in Canada, Canada in NATO,* and *Bayonets in the Streets.*

J. L. Granatstein teaches Canadian history at York University. He is the author of books and articles on political history and foreign policy, including *Canada's War: The Politics of the Mackenzie King Government, 1939-1945* and *Canadian-American Relations in Wartime: From the Great War to the Cold War.*

F. J. C. Griffiths teaches in the Department of Political Economy at the University of Toronto and is Director of the Centre for Russian and East European Studies. He is co-author of *Khrushchev and the Arms Race* and author of various scholarly papers.

T. A. Hockin teaches in the Department of Political Science, York University. He is author of *Apex of Power: the Prime Minister, the Cabinet, and Political Leadership in Canada* and *Canadian Condominium.*

J. W. Langford teaches in the Department of Political Science, York University, and is author of the forthcoming book *The Reorganization of the Federal Transport Portfolio: The Application of a Ministry System,* and numerous articles on Canadian transportation policy.

INDEX

Activism, 140ff., 149, 153
Advisory Committee on Northern
  Development, 25, 36ff., 39, 41, 42, 135,
  177, 178ff.
Air reconnaissance, 104f.
Alaska, 11
Alaska Boundary Dispute, 16
Alaska Highway, 20, 21, 23, 27
Alaskan North Slope, 11, 30, 37, 38, 41,
  113f., 118, 168, 195
Alert, 91
Allen, Ralph, 27
Amundsen Gulf, 89, 183
Anglo-Norwegian Fisheries case, 5, 6
Archangel, 103f.
Archipelagos, 5, 6
Arctic, S.S., 19
Arctic Ice Dynamics Joint Experiment,
  172f., 186
Arctic Institute of America, 37, 179
Arctic Ocean, 76, 107, 122
Arctic Training Centre, 91
Arctic Waters Pollution Prevention Act, 2, 8,
  41, 52, 53, 61, 63ff., 72, 74, 75, 80, 93, 94,
  97, 121, 125f., 129, 130, 141ff., 155, 157,
  163, 165, 169, 175, 184, 186, 194, 195
Argus aircraft, 79, 91, 93, 127f.
Arrow, S. S., 51
Atkinson Point, 118
Atlantic Richfield, 38
Atmospheric Environment Service, 171,
  173

Baffin Bay, 76, 105, 106, 117, 183
Baffin Island, 14, 91, 96, 126, 169
Baffinland Iron, 96
Ballistic Missile Early Warning System, 88,
  102, 108, 112
Baltic Sea, 103
Banks Island, 10, 89, 117
Barents Sea, 103, 158
Barrow Strait, 10, 50, 64, 89, 97, 106, 122
Baselines: *see* Straight baselines
Beaufort Sea, 63, 89, 96, 98, 113, 117, 130,
  174, 175, 183
Beesley, J. A., 50, 52, 64, 72, 124, 125,
Bering Strait, 11, 104, 106, 113, 157
Bernier, Captain J. E., 10, 15, 16
Bilateralism, 140, 142, 151ff., 196
Bilder, Richard, 65f.
Black Sea, 103

British Columbia, 14
British Petroleum, 38
BUIC, 88

Canada Centre for Remote Sensing, 171f.
Canada Shipping Act, 129
Canadian Chamber of Shipping, 70
Canadian Coast Guard, 79, 94, 98, 174, 176
Canadian Committee on Oceanography, 177
Canadian Hydrographic Service, 174
Canadian International Development
  Agency, 134
Canadian Rangers, 93
Canol Project, 20, 21
Cape Dorset, 91
Chedabucto Bay, 51
Chesterfield Inlet, 91
Christie, Loring, 16, 19
Churchill, 91, 117, 129
Closing lines : *see* Straight baselines
Coast Guard: *see* Canadian Coast Guard;
  U.S. Coast Guard
Coastal states, 4, 6ff., 47, 52, 54, 68, 69, 70,
  74, 116, 124, 125, 132, 146, 156, 194
Cohen, Maxwell, 10, 28, 29, 195
Cominco, 96f.
Communications Research Centre, 172
Conference on the Human Environment,
  124
Contiguous zone, 8, 64, 73, 193
Continental margin, 9, 68, 69, 141, 146
Continental rise, 9, 68
Continental shelf, 2, 3, 9, 29, 30, 42, 44, 47,
  52, 62, 67, 71, 96, 129
Continental slope, 9, 68
Co-operative Commonwealth Federation,
  24
Cornwallis Island, 91

Davis Strait, 63, 89, 96, 104, 106
Dawson City, 91
Dempster Highway, 91
Denmark, 3, 10, 35, 61, 103, 126, 153ff.
Department of Communications, 172,
  173f., 176, 184
Department of Energy, Mines and
  Resources, 36, 134, 171, 176
Department of the Environment, 78, 94,
  134, 135, 171, 174, 176, 183, 184
Department of External Affairs, 36, 37, 38,
  40, 41, 43, 46ff., 53ff., 64, 123, 134, 135

203